MEDIA MARATHON

MEDIA MARATHON

A Twentieth-Century Memoir

ERIK BARNOUW

DUKE UNIVERSITY PRESS   *Durham and London 1996*

© 1996 Duke University Press
Printed in the United States of America on acid-free paper ∞
Typeset in Trump Mediaeval by Tseng Information Systems, Inc.
Library of Congress Cataloging-in-Publication Data
appear on the last printed page of this book.

FOR BETTY

CONTENTS

MEDIA MARATHON

PROLOGUE

My habitat was always media—theater, magazine, radio, pamphlet, advertising, vaudeville, film, classroom, book, song lyric, animated film, video. For decades I kept on the go between them, without a sense of direction. Again and again, I found the ground shifting under my feet, telling me it was time to move on. It worried me; I felt like a white-collar vagabond. Then, after World War II, *communications* became a buzzword and suddenly exploded around us in titles of books, courses, and schools. It was reassuring: my peripatetic life seemed to have meaning. I gathered I had been living in a communications revolution. This fascinated me; the phenomenon of old media giving birth to new media, and then being replaced by them, and the ghosts of old media rising up in new forms, gave a whole new context to my wanderings. And the media shifts seemed to be power shifts at the heart of modern history.

The following pages profile media people—some famous, others less than famous or even infamous—with whom I became associated during a life in the media world. Each played a significant role in the upheaval. Each had an impact on my itinerary. Presented chronologically, they may give a sense of the changes through which we have lived. My life will be seen as a thread winding in and out of the story.

Today students are urged to have a career goal and to plan steps toward it. Amid constant change, how can they? Some of the media with which I became involved did not exist when I began; others seemed to be dying. There was no plan in my journey.

Nevertheless I had a preparation for it. My childhood was full of unexpected twists and turns, all posing communication challenges. My first eleven years were spent in The Hague, Holland, where my father, Adriaan

Barnouw, was a high school teacher of Dutch history and literature. His interests ranged beyond this: he had studied fourteen languages, including seven dead ones, and had begun translating Chaucer's *Canterbury Tales* into Dutch verse in the original meters. He hoped some day to be a professor at Leiden, where he had earned his Ph.D., but Holland was richly supplied with Ph.D.s and he knew he might have to wait decades. On a research trip to England, staying at an Oxford boarding house, he met a Yorkshire lass studying and teaching at a music school. She had sung under Sir Arthur Sullivan at the Leeds Festival and was ambitious. Also a bit of a renegade, she had published short writings under the pseudonym Madge Linney (anagram for her name, Anne Midgley) because it was not proper for a young lady to flaunt herself in print. She and Adriaan began bicycle rides to points of interest and one day were caught in a downpour and came back soaked and exhilarated. He cleaned her bicycle for her, which fellow boarders considered significant. Not long afterwards, while boating, he proposed to her. After days of hesitation she accepted. Marrying a Hollander—and a schoolteacher at that—seemed to many a dubious step. "It is my duty to inform you, Miss Midgley," said an official before whom she had to appear, "that in marrying this foreigner you do so entirely at your own risk." She asked, "If I married an Englishman, wouldn't I be doing it at my own risk?" In July 1905 they were married and she took up the role of wife of a Dutch schoolteacher in The Hague, soon bearing him four children: Willem, born 1906; Elsa, 1907; Erik, 1908; and Victor, 1915. She became soloist in The Hague's Anglican church, arranged home musicales, and gave lessons in English and Shakespeare to supplement her husband's income and because she craved action. The family also took in students as paying guests, some of whom Father tutored. They included sons of people on business in the Dutch East Indies, particularly Sumatra's tobacco business, and also occasional foreign students, usually English or German. In 1914, just before the Great War (known later as World War I), we moved to a sixteen-room house that offered increased space for students.

The following years stirred our lives in fantastic and sometimes whimsical ways. In an open-air market Father bought, for about five dollars, a huge parchment-bound sketchbook half filled with vigorous drawings of mid-nineteenth-century sailing ships and seamen at work. Remaining pages were blank. The book bore the inscription "A. van Beest." No such artist seemed known to Dutch art authorities, but an old pamphlet mentioned that one Albertus van Beest, a painter known along the water-front, having gotten a young woman with child, had boarded a ship for America. Father, in a letter to the American magazine *The Nation*, asked if any reader knew what had become of this Albertus van Beest. This brought word that the artist had settled in the whaling port of New Bedford and there pursued his career. It also brought a letter from the editor of *The Nation*, Harold deWolff Fuller, asking if Father was the Adriaan Barnouw he had known at the University of Leiden years earlier and, if so, would he supply some words on how the war situation looked from Holland? German troops were overrunning Holland's neighbor, Belgium, and sweeping into France. Much of Europe was becoming embroiled, but Holland remained a neutral enclave and was turning into a journalistic "listening post." Our schoolteacher-father evolved into a journalist, listed on *The Nation*'s masthead as European correspondent.

Other dramatic changes descended on us. Belgian women fled across the border by thousands. We had room for several, so acquired two Belgian maids and a Belgian governess for the duration of the war. Our beautiful governess, Mlle Le Page, liked to tell of her two suitors back home, both named Gustaf. She called one "Gus" and the other "Staf" and could not decide between them. At one time a maid did not come down for days from her fourth-floor bedroom, and Mother went up to see what was wrong. The girl had had a baby, born dead. We children learned about it long afterwards. The baby did not receive a ritual burial.

Meanwhile a British cousin, old enough to be my uncle (Mother came from a large family), had become a British army captain and an early prisoner-of-war in Germany. In 1915, following diplomatic negotiations, a number of German prisoners from England were interned into one part of Holland, a similar number of English prisoners from Germany into another part. When we learned that our cousin George Clark was among arrivals at an improvised settlement near The Hague dubbed Timbertown, we asked through official channels whether he might come to live with us. The request was granted and George arrived, resplendent in British uniform. He settled down to study Dutch history. (He eventually became a noted scholar and provost of Oriel College, Oxford.) It seemed desirable that a British captain should have a "boots" to look after his needs, so a Cockney corporal from Timbertown was allowed to move into our house to serve George. He answered the doorbell in his uniform.

Our home became a modern Babel: we children were addressed in

Dutch, English, French, Flemish, Cockney English, and could jabber in kind. Father started taking Russian lessons. From his sanctum we sometimes heard his teacher intoning in a deep voice, "*Awchen harashaw!*"—which apparently meant "Very good!" The maids taught us to say "*À bas les boches!*"

At a theater I saw my first film, a documentary on the torching of a Dutch barracks—a blaze that lit up the sky throughout The Hague. I also saw my first musical revue, the wondrous *Timbertown Follies*, staged by British troops in the nearby encampment. Almost everything was rationed. On cold winter evenings a number of us huddled around one peat fire, making a rag rug from old clothing. Spread across our laps, it helped us keep warm and busy. The rug seemed magnificent to me. The evenings remain a vivid memory.

If our childhood was extraordinary, we were hardly aware of that. We knew no other. Pedaling to school on my bicycle each day, I passed the Peace Palace built by Andrew Carnegie for the settlement of international disputes, then a series of streets with names like Javastraat, Borneostraat, Sumatrastraat, Celebesstraat, Balistraat—reminders of Holland's overseas domains, dwarfing the homeland. In my atlas they were colored orange; England's were pink, Germany's blue.

Further capricious turns awaited us with startling suddenness. The end of the war brought a split in the staff of *The Nation:* policy toward the Russian Revolution was the main issue. Several editors under deWolff Fuller broke away and raised funds for a new magazine to be called *The Weekly Review,* to debut in 1919. They cabled Father: would he come to the United States to join them as European editor? Father was torn but considered it far too risky; Mother was determined that we should go. Father was given a year's leave from his school; if things did not work out, we could return.

Father's fears were well founded: *The Weekly Review* would survive scarcely a year. But meanwhile events rolled on. Twenty trunks of possessions were packed; the sixteen-room house was sold. As Father got ready for his New York voyage, Mother took us four children (ages thirteen, twelve, eleven, four) to England to visit various relatives for as long as they could stand the invasion. We were to bide our time awaiting word from Father.

In June 1919, on the eve of his sailing from Holland, a new element entered the picture. There was at Columbia University a Queen Wilhelmina lectureship, endowed before the war by the Dutch government so that at least one major American university would offer studies on Holland, its language and place in history. The chair's first occupant, Leonard van Noppen, had decided to retire; a Dutch search committee looked for a replacement. Its task was difficult: the stipend was equivalent to only half a U.S. professorship. It occurred to the prudent committee that this Barnouw, a seemingly versatile schoolteacher, might without risk be offered the post on a one-year trial. They would not have to pay his passage—he already had his ticket. No long-term commitment need be made. Just before his sailing the offer was made and accepted. Father would handle the job on a part-time basis. *The Weekly Review* had no objection. A year later, as the magazine foundered, Columbia University would upgrade the lectureship to a professorship, provided that Father would add to his duties a course on Chaucer. It seemed a miraculous, heaven-sent offer.

Mother and her brood (though she was more impresario than mother hen) arrived in New York on the *Mauritania*, September 26, 1919. That week Willem and I entered the Horace Mann School for Boys, owned at the time by Columbia University. With us on the boat came the twenty trunks. Each member of the family also brought diverse cultural baggage toward a new life.

JOHN MULHOLLAND

". . . magic casements opening on the foam
Of perilous seas . . ."
—John Keats

We appeared at Horace Mann School in our Holland Sunday best—jacket buttoned to the neck, Eton collar, bow tie, short pants—and discovered we were curios. Our classmates, dressed in knickers (a garment unknown to us), seemed to find us a cause for hilarity. Others came to gaze at us. We were constantly asked, "Are you the boy who put his finger in the dike?" We didn't know what they were talking about; why would anyone do that? That Saturday, at horrifying cost, Mother took us to a down-town department store to outfit us with American images, but we still seemed to be oddities, thanks to our Dutch-British pronunciations. "Say book," my classmates would ask, then guffaw when I said it.

Academically we were found well ahead of our age level so were jumped a grade even though we knew nothing about some subjects like American history. I was put with students at least a year older than I was. They often laughed at jokes I could not quite comprehend; among the sophisticates I often felt oafish. But in classwork we caught up and forged ahead, and in soccer we were prodigies; Will and I had played it since our infancy. I was goalguard; he played forward.

After a period in a rat-infested flat not far from Columbia University, our family acquired a fine (but smaller) university apartment overlooking the campus. Willem, Victor, and I shared a room that could just accom-modate three beds and two bureaus. Elsa had the "maid's room," entered through the kitchen. Life had to be rigidly organized. In the evening we all worked—Elsa in her "maid's room," I at my desk in the hall, Willem and father at tables in the living room. Mother had her chair and in these days generally stitched or darned. Evenings, after dinner, were for study. No talk.

John Mulholland was my teacher in manual training, and under his supervision I began to make my mother a teawagon. He was also a magician, as everyone in the class knew. He sometimes performed for the whole school, and his Christmas performances at the Columbia University Faculty Club were already a tradition. We all knew he was biding his time, setting aside funds until he was ready to make the plunge into full-time professional magic.

Still in his twenties, he was tall and gaunt with a prominent Adam's apple and a droll, languid manner. He had large, powerful hands. He was constantly practicing—palming things or parading a half-dollar across his knuckles. Half the manual training class took up prestidigitation as a hobby.

It turned out to be his last year of teaching, so the following year I dropped manual training and never finished the teawagon. Mulholland was on his way—booked not into vaudeville, where Houdini and Thurston were great names, but onto the lecture circuit, where he regaled audiences with the lore and social meaning of magic, all the while buttressing his points with bits of magic from everywhere, old and new. He became an eminent historian of magic. Before long he was secretary of the Society of American Magicians and editor of the celebrated magazine *The Sphinx.* He was also a collector—his library of books on magic was said to be one of the largest, second only to that of Houdini, whom Mulholland knew well. Houdini, who had grown wealthy, bought any treasures that came to his attention. Mulholland acquired his by ceaseless searching in out-of-the-way places.

He lived in the Columbia University area not far from us, so I sometimes ran into him. One day he offered me a job. His collection was getting out of hand, he said; he needed to have it catalogued. He was aware that I knew Dutch and had a fair knowledge of French and German. These languages and English were the most prominent in his collection, so I was well equipped for the task. I jumped at the idea. On Saturdays from then on, for at least a year, I spent part of the day at his place, typing out three-by-five-inch cards, book by book. I was fourteen. Older classmates had begun to go tea-dancing on Saturdays at the Villa Vallee in down-

The immigrants in their Holland Sunday best: Willem, Elsa, Erik, and Victor.

town New York, run by Rudy Vallee. I wasn't ready for that. Besides, my allowance was five dollars a month, of which at least two dollars went for subway trips (a nickel a ride) to and from the Horace Mann School at 246th Street, at the northern edge of the city.

Mulholland paid me by the card (ten cents a card, I think), so if I spent time browsing through the books, it was at my own expense. I became acquainted with an amazing world. I even peered into the "locked books" of Will Goldstone, taboo to nonmagicians—I had to examine them, to get the cataloguing done. And the key was there in the bookcase.

Sometimes Mulholland was on hand. He loved to talk about his books and where he had found them, and about one of his favorite hobbies, the exposing of mediums. His library had many books on spiritualism, books like *Eusapia Palladino and Her Phenomena*—a favorite title of mine. One day he included me in a supper party with three fellow magicians. Around midnight, over Welsh rarebit, they began to challenge each other with legerdemain. I was overwhelmed. I got home about 4 A.M. Mother was terrified.

Half a century later, when I had become a Columbia University professor supervising courses in film, radio, and television, I ran into John Mulholland on Broadway. He had almost given up performing; arthritis was getting into his hands. But he was very busy with his collection, for which the Players Club had offered a home, at least temporarily. I mentioned that in exploring early film history I had often run across names I had first met in his collection. It had made me wonder whether magicians had played a larger role in the genesis of the motion picture than had generally been realized. Should I get some graduate student to dig into that? Mulholland said instantly, "That's a great subject. Come down to my collection and I'll pull out at least twenty books that have a bearing on it. A wonderful subject."

I never found a graduate student interested in pursuing this, and John Mulholland died not long after that encounter. But a few years later I did visit the Players Club and found the books he must have had in mind. In the late 1970s, when I joined the Library of Congress to head a new Motion Picture, Broadcasting and Recorded Sound Division, I had a chance to explore the Houdini Collection, which had become a treasure of the library's Rare Book Division. Then I wrote *The Magician and the Cinema*, which simply poured out of me.

Mulholland had introduced me to a world of magic that had been virtually wiped out by the miracles of film. For over a century many European capitals had enjoyed magic theaters that were the mecca and high point of family vacation trips, playing the role that Radio City Music Hall and Disneyland and Disney World would play for later generations. These theaters offered dazzling illusions that often made use of mirrors and hidden magic lanterns. In the 1790s a Belgian performer, Étienne

Projections onto smoke: *Fantasmagorie* as pictured in Robertson's *Mémoires*, 1831. (Library of Congress)

Gaspard Robertson, had scored spectacular successes in Paris projecting weird supernatural figures onto smoke rising from braziers in a darkened room. The twisting smoke could give immobile images a strange, unearthly motion. Establishing his show in an abandoned abbey decorated with skulls, Robertson began to "summon" the ghosts of leaders who had died in the French Revolution—with such startling effect that authorities became alarmed; he was warned to be more prudent in his choice of spirits. Imitations of Robertson's *Fantasmagoria* became a worldwide theatrical phenomenon during the following century. At magic theaters magicians used the same technology to stage descents into hell, Joan of Arc succumbing to the flames, and scenes from the burning of London. Optical technology could also produce such illusions as trips to the moon and voyages to the bottom of the sea, and disappearances of all sorts— especially of women. The magic theater entrepreneurs, who generally disclaimed occult powers, were avid students of scientific developments and offered their audiences science fiction in action. They constantly made use of the latest scientific breakthroughs to amuse, instruct, persuade, and bamboozle their audiences. Magicians became the royalty of entertainment.

But when, in the 1890s, they began including in their shows the new marvel of "living pictures"—creations of Edison, Lumière, and other in-

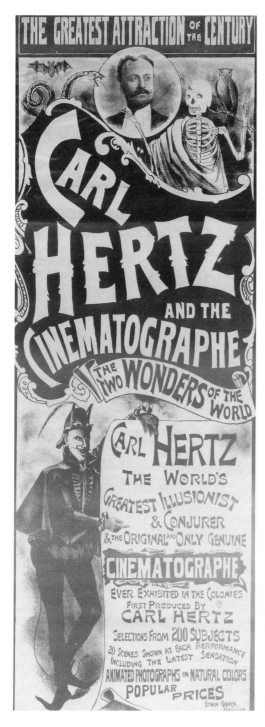

Australia's first film poster, 1896: Traveling magician promotes a new wonder—which will soon end his reign. (Library of Congress)

ventors of cinema—the magicians courted disaster. The film medium could do many of the magician's tricks, and soon took over the role of the magic theaters. In the 1890s leading magicians still roamed the theaters of five continents, with "living pictures" among their wonders. A few years later the same theaters booked films instead of magicians. To survive, a number of magicians turned filmmaker. Meanwhile, in many countries, countless people had first seen film as part of a magic show and accepted it as "magic."

My film students were often puzzled by this sequence. They asked, "Seeing a film, how could people possibly think of it as magic?" The answer is, "How could they not?" Those audiences knew that the newly crowned czar of Russia, or workers leaving a Lumière factory, had no business walking across a sheet hung in a Singapore theater. They knew at once it was professional trickery.

The question should rather be turned around: How is it that modern audiences watching a television news special feel they are watching reality—not a processed artifact? Is that perhaps a far more disturbing question, hanging over all television "reality"?

The magician seemed to have met a defeat, but it was not precisely that. He had, instead, evolved into a mammoth industry, in which the arts of amusing, instructing, persuading, and bamboozling could be pursued on a scale suitable to the twentieth century. The magician now went by many names: producer, director, editor, writer, special effects artist, animator, actor, p.r. man, advertiser, campaign manager—all engineers of human consciousness.

John Mulholland's magic collection—still remembered for the happy Saturdays it gave me—experienced transitions of its own. The Players Club, unable to maintain it or find a buyer, prepared to auction it piece by piece, but the collection was saved at the last moment by an anonymous angel who transported it to Hollywood and established it on Santa Monica Boulevard as the Mulholland Library of Conjuring and Allied Arts, with the fine magician Ricky Jay as curator. Unfortunately the angel, who was president of a savings and loan association, had indulged his passion for legerdemain by loaning himself funds from his institution's resources. He acquired the collection for a reported $850,000 and had big plans for it—which were aborted by the S&L scandals of 1989–90 and the prosecutions that followed. The collection became the property of the U.S. government and was again auctioned. This time it was bought by the magician David Copperfield, producer of magic spectaculars for the television era. He could outdo Houdini, who, in a show at New York's Hippodrome, had made an elephant disappear. Copperfield showed his television audience a sweeping view of New York Harbor with the Statue of Liberty at its center, then made the Statue of Liberty disappear. Millions "saw it happen."

THORNTON WILDER

"Art, that great undogmatized church . . ."
—Ellen Key

In 1925 I followed my brother Willem to Princeton; Elsa had gone to Mount Holyoke. We all had scholarships, for which our parents were duly grateful. I was also awarded the cheapest room on the Princeton campus—a garret room at the top of a venerable six-floor walk-up dormitory, Reunion Hall, since demolished. It assured me ample solitude for study. I sought to escape the solitude via work in the Theatre Intime, a student activity modeled after the French avant-garde theater. Theater became a compulsive interest. I also submitted verse to the Nassau Literary Magazine (the "Lit"), and played more soccer.

The second year brought a frenzy of anxiety about "getting into a good club." Princeton's eating clubs, well equipped with pool tables and card rooms, tended to be the center of social life during the last two years. Election to a club involved an intimidating ritual near the end of the second year. During a designated "bicker week," club delegations—all upperclassmen—visited likely candidates in their dormitory rooms to size them up and see if they would "fit in." The few delegations that struggled to the sixth floor of Reunion collapsed in exhaustion. The ensuing small talk—five or ten minutes of it—did not seem to open up vistas of compatibilty. I did receive a bid from one club and gladly accepted. It had several members from the Theatre Intime. It was not one of the "best clubs."

Through most of my first two years I felt "out of it." The sense of being a foreigner not certain of my place in the scheme of things kept coming back. Besides, at Princeton large groups from big prep schools—Andover, Exeter, Choate, Hill—set the norm. In classes they all seemed to know each other and talked across me—about weekend date arrangements *and upcoming football games. Had they no interest in the larger world? From the sense of being "out of it" I tried to develop a feeling of being "above it." I became scornful of Princeton's "complacence" and especially of "hundred-percent" Princetonians, who looked down on all "peculiar" classmates like those literati who went around without neckties, trying to look different. One weekend, in my garret room, my feelings took the form of a play. As I started to chart it, a three-act structure quickly emerged. I wrote it in three weekends.*

Open Collars was a campus smash hit, or at least a nine-days' wonder. Billed as a play of "student life at Kingston University," it was a satire, and I was sure it would make everyone furious at me. It didn't. The Theatre Intime awarded it first prize (twenty-five dollars) in its play contest and scheduled it for a week's run in the fall. I was asked to play the lead—Charley Burroughs, a starry-eyed rebel eventually expelled by the dean. Charley was caught in a conflict. His "hundred-percent" roommate despised the literati with whom Charley was consorting, especially an aesthete named Murdock, who was considered "all wet," a term that, in those days, served all derogatory needs. "He's so wet he ripples when the wind blows." The play was full of anti-aesthete sallies and of Murdock's more articulate ripostes against standard Kingstonians. The first-night audience—December 5, 1927—loved all the rhetoric. The Murdock role received a bravura performance from my classmate Bretaigne Windust, a student of French-English parentage with an English accent; he was in fact (I didn't tell him so) my prototype for the role. He also directed. (He would one day be the Broadway director of *Life With Father* and *Arsenic and Old Lace.*) Charley's roommate received a sterling performance from Myron McCormick (who would win Broadway celebrity with his GI role in *South Pacific*, in which he performed a belly roll evolved at Princeton). Another member of the cast, in the bit role of the loudmouth Reggie, was the freshman Joshua Logan (eventually a major force in the American theater, director and coauthor of *South Pacific* and a host of other successes). The set, designed by Norris Houghton (later cofounder of the Phoenix Theatre), depicted an archetypical Princeton room complete with leaded pane windows, Maxfield Parrish paintings, and signs stolen from railroad cars. The set always stirred an immediate wave of murmurs, seeming to welcome the audience the moment the curtain parted.

I could hardly believe the cascades of laughter that capped line after

Open Collars, 1927. Myron McCormick as ("100%") Steve, the author as Charley, and Bretaigne Windust as ("wet") Murdock.

line. Seats for the rest of the week were quickly sold. The *Daily Princetonian* carried a rave review and sent a student to my room to photograph me poring over a manuscript. The *New York Times* carried a photo in its December 11, 1927, rotogravure section. Princeton University Press decided to publish the play.* The *Princeton Alumni Weekly* carried a big story, with picture. A revival was scheduled for reunion week to enable alumni to see it. Samuel French applied for amateur rights; agents sent letters. Princeton's celebrated Dean Christian Gauss spoke words of praise; his only criticism was that "the hero, Charley Burroughs, otherwise Erik Barnouw" should not have been expelled.

The tenor of my life suddenly changed. People recognized me. I tried to dress the part and strode around confidently. I smoked a pipe. I was big-shotting. I was suddenly being invited to parties, including parties in faculty homes.

One such party was a particularly large affair. The place was packed.

---

* Erik Barnouw, *Open Collars: A Play of Undergraduate Life at Kingston University* (Princeton: Princeton University Press, 1928).

People stood around the smoke-filled room drinking punch and eating canapés, celery, and olives. I saw people I knew. Several said nice things about my play; I had learned to acknowledge these with suitable modesty. In the crush an earnest-looking gentleman came up to me and in a quiet voice said that if there was anything he could do to help, he would certainly be glad to. I thanked him. He added, "You know—introductions—finding an agent—things like that." He talked in short spurts and was hard to understand in the hubbub. I asked him what his name was. "I'm Thrntnwildr." It seemed to come out as a single word and I didn't grasp it. "What did you say it was?" "I'm Throntnwildr." Amid the noise, I suddenly realized that this was the man who had just won the Pulitzer Prize for *The Bridge of San Luis Rey*, the current best-seller. He was Thornton Wilder, a teacher at the nearby Lawrenceville School and now suddenly the big name in all book review sections. And I also realized he must be the guest of honor at this jam-packed affair; he was, in fact, the sole reason for it. I felt suddenly mortified, stammered a congratulation (I hadn't read his book), and was thankful when someone else came to claim his attention. Seeing a table loaded with copies of *The Bridge of San Luis Rey*, I bought a copy and later asked him to autograph it, which he did: "For Erik, with all best wishes and high hopes from his friend, Thornton Wilder."

I treasured it, but was not proud of my first encounter with him. I hoped that if there ever was a next one I would do better. The next came almost two decades later, during my radio-writing days. I had become an ardent admirer of Wilder's plays, seeing both *Our Town* and *Skin of Our Teeth* early in their Broadway runs. Both seemed sure to live as theater classics. So I was especially delighted when in 1946 the Theatre Guild, Broadway's most honored organization, asked me to prepare a radio adaptation of *Our Town* for its broadcast series *The Theatre Guild on the Air*, a new Theatre Guild venture sponsored by U.S. Steel. It was one of my first Theatre Guild commissions. I had a few weeks for the task.

I thought long and hard. Wilder had written *Our Town* to be performed with few props and no scenery. In this frugality, rejecting the sumptuous effects by which Broadway sometimes sought to challenge Hollywood, Wilder was in tune with the rising off-Broadway theater. *Our Town* was "theater of the mind," as was radio at its best. Radio may well have helped to nudge Wilder in this direction. He had also taken up the narrator, a presence in radio—as in the drama of earlier ages—but generally shunned by Broadway. For all these reasons *Our Town* seemed, at first glance, ideal for radio.

But I was troubled by the nature of the *Our Town* narrator. Called Stage Manager, he recognizes the presence of an audience in front of him and addresses it as such. The play script even calls for people in the audience to pop up and ask the Stage Manager questions about Grovers Corners, which he answers in stimulating detail.

There seemed no doubt that a vivid picture of Grovers Corners could be coaxed into being in the minds of radio listeners. But to interpose in this process a theater, a theater audience, a stage, and a stage manager seemed unhelpful—an encumbrance. I decided to change Wilder's narrator to something more at home in radio—a radio host. He could still be a bucolic character familiar with everything about Grovers Corners and could address the audience directly, but as a radio audience, not a theater audience. Now and then during the play this narrator could receive "phoned-in" questions from listeners, and could give answers such as those provided in the play. I had to take further liberties—the radio script had to be fifty-four minutes at most, so simplification was needed. But the transformation of the Stage Manager was the most drastic of my changes.

When I handed in my script at the Theatre Guild a week or so before the scheduled broadcast, I received news that set me back on my heels. Casting problems had taken some time but had finally been resolved. Thornton Wilder himself had agreed to play the Stage Manager. Everyone at the Theatre Guild was delighted with this casting; it was innovative, off-beat, attention-getting.

Wilder had not asked to see the adaptation in advance, either as author or performer. If he had, it would have been sent. Under present circumstances the normal procedure was for the entire cast to see the script for the first time when assembling for the informal first reading—on a Tuesday morning, five days before the Sunday night broadcast.

When the Theatre Guild staff and hierarchy had absorbed my script, some were clearly nervous. Some had always felt that a "classic" should be adapted with a special forbearance. That feeling had been reenforced by a recent set-to with George Bernard Shaw. Theatre Guild partner Lawrence Langner had traveled to England to confer with Shaw in the hope that at least one of his plays might be included in *Theatre Guild on the Air*. The Guild had, after all, staged a number of memorable Shaw productions on Broadway, including the 1923 world premiere of *Saint Joan.* Langner returned with the impression that Shaw had agreed that a few adjustments to meet the needs and opportunities of a new medium might be appropriate; the Theatre Guild soon afterwards sent a proposed adaptation. Shaw, still feisty in his nineties, apparently assumed otherwise. As related to me by Homer Fickett, director of *Theatre Guild on the Air,* Shaw replied with a postcard. Underlined for emphasis, he said simply that a Shaw presentation must be *"uncut* and *uncooked."* That ended the matter.*

The three Theatre Guild partners—Langner, Armina Marshall (Mrs. Langner), and Theresa Helburn—took turns supervising *Theatre Guild on the Air* programs. This time, perhaps in anxiety, all three turned up for the first reading. They greeted Wilder with all the honor due him, then stayed to watch.

The reading took place on the stage of the Vanderbilt Theater, as would the Sunday night broadcast. With Broadway in sharp decline and radio on the rise, the radio networks had taken over a number of midtown theaters. Invitation audiences had become an established phenomenon, useful in cementing business relationships: tickets were distributed through sponsors' advertising agencies, distributors, and dealers. This had become a recognized aspect of "merchandising."

We sat in an arc. Director Homer Fickett was on one side of Thornton Wilder, I on the other. Wilder seemed a much more confident figure than he had at our previous meeting. He greeted me as though he knew me, but I am not sure he remembered. Other members of the cast included Dorothy McGuire as Emily and James Dobson as George.

The procedure was casual. Actors were not expected to "perform" at this time. It was a matter of feeling one's way through the script, getting a sense of relationships and moods. Wilder showed no reaction to being something other than a Stage Manager. He made no comment throughout the first act; at the end of it would come a passage that I knew had caused concern at the Theatre Guild. The words belonged to the narrator. I had provided for him to say: "We're going to pause now for a moment. Going to have a 'commercial.' Know what I mean?"

Wilder read the line. The Theatre Guild group watched. Then he turned to me, smiling. "You know what we should have him say after the sec-

---

* The Shaw estate subsequently took a different view.

ond act? 'Now let's give the stations a chance to identify themselves.'" A murmur of appreciation came from the cast. I saw the partners exchange glances, and sensed a collective sigh of relief.

Wilder, unlike Shaw, was not inclined to think of his works as chiseled in stone. For Wilder, ideas and plays were capable of endless reincarnations, like the characters in his *Skin of Our Teeth*. *Our Town* had evolved from his experiments in *The Happy Journey to Trenton and Camden*. When *The Merchant of Yonkers* failed he revised it as *The Matchmaker*, then saw it triumph as *Hello Dolly!* Thanks to his exploratory spirit, I had weathered my second encounter with him. It had also clinched my association with the Theatre Guild, which was to last for fifteen years.

JOSHUA LOGAN

"We all live in a house on fire."
—*Tennessee Williams*

In the spring of 1928 — my junior year at Princeton — I was elected editor of the Nassau Literary Magazine *and about the same time was invited by the Princeton Triangle Club to write its musical for the following year. The combination was considered startling. The* Lit, *instrument of the literati, was no establishment organ; the Triangle Club was mainstream. Its annual musicals were a major Princeton tradition. Christmastime Triangle tours of major Eastern cities became everywhere the climax of the social season. Performances were preceded by big dinners and followed by formal balls in which the troupers (author included) got to meet the latest crop of debutantes and campus beauty queens. In New York the show occupied the Metropolitan Opera House and generally filled it. Everyone wanted to see the dancing chorus of burly Princeton men — athletes transformed into chorines. I had never aspired to involvement in the Triangle Club; it had never occurred to me. That had seemed part of a remote social scene. But now that I was invited, I wanted it. It would be another New World.*

I was to appear before a committee of seniors and juniors, all Triangle veterans, to present my plans. Dramatic locale and period would be central issues, with implications for the costumes of the dancing chorus as well as for plot, music, decor, and the spectacular scenic effects that had become a Triangle tradition. *Drake's Drum* (1923) had been famous for the surging seas behind its shipboard scenes. This was considered the greatest of all Triangle shows, the landmark to shoot at. Its hit song had been the haunting "Ships That Pass in the Night":

All the ships that pass in the night
To havens far and lands out of sight
Are like maidens we have known of yore
Who vanish, to be seen no more.
They bow, they smile, they fade in the darkness,
Harbingers so bright!
Sail on, we shall meet again
All those stately ships that pass us in the night.

I had seen few musicals. The father of a Horace Mann classmate had some involvement in the theater, and when audiences needed to be padded ("papered") my classmate became a distributor of free tickets. So I had seen musicals rather selectively, with the focus on flops.

Most of these had absurd, miraculous plots—which seemed an essential ingredient. I knew instantly what my plot must be. The hero would be the boy who put his finger in the dike, saving his nation and perhaps the world. The setting would be a Dutch village, a few brightly painted fishermen's houses nestled beneath a dike. The title would be *Zuider Zee.* There would be a huge storm. I could see people rushing in panic along the top of the dike and along the foot of it below, with huge waves seeming to splash up behind the dike. The idea seemed so perfect that I gave little thought to how to present it. My choice of this plot no doubt reflected a somewhat condescending attitude toward musicals of the time—at least, to those I'd seen.

The committee received me with the formality of a jury. They seemed to be saying, "Very well—state your case." So I explained my fascination with the boy who put his finger in the dike, having never heard the story until I came to the United States. It seemed to have everything a musical comedy would need: "romantic" plot, colorful setting, melodramatic climax, opportunity for comedy, scenic effects, and so on. Of course the boy would win the girl through his heroic deed.

Everyone looked very thoughtful. There was a long pause. Then one of them said, "I don't think it will work. Those hefty guys dancing look bad enough; in the big Dutch skirts they'll look ridiculous." Another said, "I agree." I started to protest but was taken aback by the furrowed brows before me. I sensed I had somehow misfired. The chairman of the group, my classmate Charlie Arnt—just elected Triangle president for the coming year—was proud of his Dutch descent and had seemed to respond to what

I was proposing. But perhaps he did not want to seem chauvinistic. Anyway, after a few more comments and serious pondering, Arnt said, "I'm sorry, Erik. That doesn't seem to do it." He assured me they did want me as author. Perhaps I should think about it some more and come back the following week with a new proposal.

I left fuming. As I walked across the campus I got even angrier. I felt they had acted like stupid bureaucrats. I was torn between fighting for my idea and throwing the whole thing up. Then I ran across Joshua Logan, the freshman who had appeared in *Open Collars* as Reggie, the boisterous friend of the hero's roommate, Steve. I had seen a good deal of him during *Open Collars* and we had become friends. I explained my exasperation. As we talked, he walked along with me to my room. There he began pacing up and down, expounding.

Josh could talk with amazing intensity. Telling a story, explaining a problem, arguing an issue, he would show such concentration that his friends had developed a game: they handed him things. In the midst of his harangue someone would hand him an ashtray or other object, which he would automatically accept, holding it until he had finished his point. Then he would look momentarily puzzled as to why he was holding an ashtray and put it down. On one occasion, trying to rush off for a train but also to finish a story, he was handed a bridge lamp. According to several witnesses, he held it for at least a minute. Ending his tale, he finally became aware of the bridge lamp in his hand, put it down with a show of annoyance, and rushed off. Josh showed this kind of intensity as he paced the room, expounding on *Zuider Zee*.

"It's a great idea. There should be two Americans in it, college guys, tourists. It gives a chance for a lot of comedy. They find the villagers a puzzle, the villagers find them a puzzle. Good satire both ways. Of course one of the Americans gets hot pants for the beautiful village girl, and she falls for him, but the local boy wins her back with his heroism. Now just before the storm . . ."

He plunged on, but I finally interrupted. "Josh, I'm supposed to go back next week and present a new idea. Why not come with me? I'll introduce you, and explain that I've asked you to work with me on the show, and that you're going to tell them some of the things we have in mind. How about it?"

Logan has described this moment in his memoir: "My heart flew out the window, around Nassau Hall, then settled back in its rightful place.

I spoke as quietly as I could manage. 'Well, if you really want me to, Erik.'"* Not until months later did he tell me that his sole reason for coming to Princeton had been the hope of working, if possible, on a Princeton Triangle show.

Introducing a freshman into the Triangle's conclave of elders must have seemed odd behavior. This was considered the domain of the upperclassmen. And Josh, doffing his black skullcap as we entered, must have seemed out of place. When I introduced him to make our presentation, I thought he began a bit too obsequiously, holding his skullcap in his hand. But Josh, a burly figure, could be a presence. Straightening up, he soon had his audience spellbound, including me. The Dutch setting was ideal, he explained. With those big women's skirts, you wouldn't be conscious of the football legs, except during the kick dances—and then you suddenly would be, which would be just great. Then he explained about the two Americans, and even began to improvise. I began to see Josh as one of the Americans and was sure others had similar thoughts. During his long, bravura presentation, he seemed determined not to stop until it was clear everyone was with him. Then a vote didn't seem necessary. *Zuider Zee* was in. We left in a state of elation.

There was, of course, the problem of writing it. Here *Zuider Zee* began to intersect with another project, which was being organized by my French-British classmate, Bretaigne Windust. Catapulted into leadership of the Theatre Intime, "Windy" had been in touch with leaders of the Harvard Dramatic Society about a visionary plan, and he had struck pay dirt. The plan was a summer theater company for college talents, to serve as their showcase for the professional theater. Charles Leatherbee, president of the Harvard group, had at once proposed locating it in Falmouth, at the foot of Cape Cod, Massachusetts. As soon became clear, he had persuasive reasons. Windy had drawn me into the plan, and the two of us paid a visit to Harvard and then, along with Charlie Leatherbee and Kingsley Perry of Harvard, convened in Falmouth to consider details. These fell into place with astonishing speed.

Summer stock was still a new idea. Yearlong theatrical companies existed in a number of major cities, in many cases headed by actors who became celebrated as regional idols. Most such companies, lacking air

*Joshua Logan, *Josh: My Up and Down, In and Out Life* (New York: Delacorte, 1976), p. 23.

conditioning, recessed for a time during the summer. Companies operating *only* during the summer had recently sprung up in a few places,
including two on Cape Cod, at Provincetown and Dennis. Perhaps a tradition was in the making here. But we found in Falmouth other, perhaps
more persuasive assets.

Leatherbee's divorced parents had both remarried, and both couples
maintained elaborate establishments near Falmouth. Both seemed intent on supporting Charlie's theatrical ambitions and aiding the summer
plan. In this they even seemed to compete with each other. Charlie's
mother had married Jan Masaryk, who was the son of the president of
Czechoslovakia and who himself later became its foreign minister. He
was at this time its ambassador to Britain. The couple had their residence
in London but summered in a fine villa near Falmouth, overlooking the
ocean. Madame Masaryk, as she was now known, had become rather
grand, an avowed patroness of the arts. Her first husband, the businessman Robert Leatherbee, had for their honeymoon converted a World War
I submarine chaser into a luxury yacht, long unused and lying at anchor
in Falmouth harbor; he offered this yacht, the *Brae Burn,* as a home for
the men of the company. (Quarters would have to be rented elsewhere
for the women.) The Falmouth location was clinched when we visited
the Elizabeth Theater, sole movie house in the Falmouth area. The nine
hundred-seat theater generally did poorly on Mondays and Tuesdays but
well enough the rest of the week. It had a stage. We proposed taking over
the theater Mondays and Tuesdays for live drama, on a percentage basis—
an arrangement that was promptly accepted. We thus acquired a central
location while eliminating movie competition to our performances, and
we avoided building costs. Leatherbee, Windy, Perry, and I each put up
one hundred dollars for initial expenses. The University Players Guild
(we later dropped the "Guild" at the request of the Theatre Guild—a request that flattered us considerably) was founded on this four hundred
dollars of initial capital. We began discussing talents we knew about at
various women's colleges, especially Radcliffe, Smith, and Vassar.

As we visited the yacht, I explained the problem of my Triangle commitment. Josh Logan and I would have to write the show during the
summer. Might he be made a member of the company? Windy favored
the idea; he told Charlie Leatherbee that Logan might be useful in a few
comedy roles and could of course help with scenery, as would all the
actors. Charlie concurred. To assist our collaboration they even decided

to award us the captain's cabin (it had once served as bridal suite) so that we would have a place to work. It had a desk.

Windy and Charlie, who assumed coleadership of the venture, were both avid organizers. Their plan was to house and feed all members of the company but to pay no salaries. A Harvard student volunteered to do all cooking in the ship's galley and did so miraculously while also serving as prop man. In fine weather we all ate on deck; otherwise we crammed into the small messroom. Once a week we were all guests of the urbane Jan Masaryk and Madame Masaryk and stuffed ourselves with gourmet food. Princeton student Grenville Braman, the Theatre Intime's ablest electrician, volunteered to do our lighting and simply transported all needed equipment from Princeton. (He would return it in the fall.) We began running up bills at local hardware and grocery stores and no one questioned our credit.

However, a few days before our first performance Mr. Leatherbee's accountant, who had been asking questions, sounded warning signals and suggested we all stop rehearsing a day or so to sell season subscriptions and raise more capital. It seemed our funds had dwindled to little more than one hundred dollars. So we all fanned out across the countryside to save the day. The face-to-face contacts involved in this door-to-door salesmanship probably boosted attendance considerably. By the end of the summer we found we had a balance of twelve hundred dollars.

Our first show was *The Dover Road*, a whimsical A. A. Milne comedy that we knew would be easy because it had just been done successfully at Princeton, with Bretaigne and myself in leading roles. Again directed by him, it sold out both nights at Falmouth. But our first truly exhilarating success came with *The Torchbearers*, by George Kelly, in which Josh Logan triumphed in a marvelously droll performance as Mr. Hossefrosse. This show was also a landmark in that a young actor from the University of Minnesota, Henry Fonda—who was serving as an apprentice in the nearby Dennis company—was in the audience, and was so enthusiastic that he afterwards paid us a backstage visit and ended up deserting Dennis and joining us. Soon afterwards he contributed another major success as a befuddled boxer in *Is Zat So?*

All this time Josh and I found isolated moments for work on *Zuider Zee*. Too often this task produced middle-of-the-night outbursts of creativity. I discovered that Josh, once fully wound up, found it impossible

Zuider Zee co-author "Josh" Logan. (Library of Congress)

to sleep or even relax. At almost any time of the night, long after we had decided it was time for sleep, he would erupt (sometimes with a whoop of excitement) with a new and irrepressible idea for *Zuider Zee*—song title, dance routine, plot gimmick, scenic effect, or simply a snatch of dialogue. Sleep became a forgotten luxury. Years later I realized that this pattern foreshadowed the manic-depressive crises that Josh would face in his career. But such thoughts were not with us in 1928.

Somehow the show—book and lyrics—got written. Early in the fall semester it went into rehearsal, with Josh as one of the Americans. From this point on I had little to do with it, being busy with the *Lit* as well

Zuider Zee: Holland saved once again. (Princeton Triangle Club)

as a new play of mine accepted by the Theatre Intime (not a success) and a fine soccer season. (My exploits as goalguard won me an invitation to try out for the official U.S. soccer team that would play in the 1928 Olympics; being still a Dutch citizen, I had to decline. When my father completed his naturalization a few months later, I automatically became a citizen, but too late for Olympic soccer.)

During the fall I sometimes dropped in on Triangle rehearsals and found Josh almost totally in control. In fact, for the rest of his college career, he became "Mr. Triangle." So dominant was his role that three years after leaving Princeton he was invited back to direct the Triangle on a professional basis so that it could recapture the fertile, ebullient style of his undergraduate years. Thus he started on the road that would lead to such successes as *I Married an Angel* (1938), *Knickerbocker Holiday* (1938), *Stars in Your Eyes* (1939), *Charley's Aunt* (1940), *Annie Get Your Gun* (1946), *Mister Roberts* (1948), *South Pacific* (1949), *Picnic* (1953), *Fanny* (1954), and numerous other productions musical and nonmusical, live and filmed, many of which also bore his stamp as writer or producer, solely or collaboratively. In the course of these years the musical—the "integrated" American musical—evolved into an honored genre to which Logan constantly contributed.

After graduation I seldom saw him, as our paths diverged. One highly charged meeting occurred in 1940. I had been approached by an NBC performer, the veteran folksinger Ethel Park Richardson, about a project on which she hoped for my help. Born in the Tennessee mountains, she was passionately devoted to the music and folklore of the area. (Later, during the television quiz show boom, she would win one hundred thousand dollars on *The Big Surprise* for her knowledge of folk music.) Her love for the idioms and linguistic rhythms of the mountains gave a special quality to her broadcasts on the NBC series *Heartthrobs of the Hills*. She had begun translating scenes from *Romeo and Juliet* into the mountain language she loved. This idea seemed especially valid to her because of the feuding tradition of the area and because the language was considered by some scholars close to Elizabethan English, having been shielded from outside influences by mountainous terrain. I was at first skeptical about her plan, then surprised by the excitement with which I read her scenes. Cherished passages had somehow acquired new life while retaining their original aura. They were familiar but no longer ritualistic. Richardson was in despair on how to organize the material; she wanted my help on construction, and I gladly agreed to work with her. When we had completed a sizable portion of a proposed three-act play, *Verona Junction*, I sent it to Josh. His phoned response electrified us.

He wanted to meet with us at once. When we met he seemed consumed with excitement. It was "very moving," he kept saying. He was determined to produce it; he wanted us to finish it as rapidly as we could. Meanwhile he proposed to sign a contract, paying us an option. He explained that, since the resounding success of his latest hit, *Charley's Aunt*—starring Jose Ferrer, a Princetonian and Triangle Club alumnus—finance was not a problem. Backers were coming to him, anxious to invest in a Logan production—whatever he chose. Scripts were coming in too. But this one, *Verona Junction*, was one he must do. We were to meet him the following Monday at the office of his agent, Leland Hayward, for the signing of the contract.

When Ethel Park Richardson and I appeared at the Hayward office, Josh was not there. Our questions received evasive answers. We were told the project was off. We finally learned that Josh had been persuaded that he was seriously ill, and had voluntarily entered a mental hospital in White Plains for observation. Josh later described this period in his memoirs.

> All during the preparation of *Charley's Aunt* I was in that seemingly enchanted state—never sleeping, always working, going, always going. I kept making small polishing changes up to twenty minutes before the doors opened on the night of the premiere. The mental manic state which I did not realize I had was working wonders.

The success of *Charley's Aunt* intensified the manic elation. It became his "entree everywhere."

> My checks were accepted easily. I gave tickets out like handbills— to a shoe salesman, a stenographer. . . . Scripts came to me by the dozens. . . . I began investing in plays, which merely increased the script load and seekers of advice. I had a self-assurance that was incredible even to me, and I seemed able to convince anybody of anything. It was as though I were speaking someone else's lines. I'd say to a girl in a store, "You're coming to bed with me tonight at eight— here's my card." And she came. My wishes were granted almost too easily. Life was a fantasy of utter freedom. But that ecstatic fantasy life was to turn sinister soon, become a nightmare world from which I would flee in terror.

This began a year of unbelievable torment, hospitalizations, escapes, wanderings, and fears. The terror was increased by knowledge that when Josh was three his father, under circumstances long kept from Josh, had stabbed himself to death with a penknife. Josh experienced two manic crises, both resulting in hospitalizations and utter despair. He recovered from both but was haunted by fear of a return—until salvation came in the form of lithium. This was a salt extracted from white clay, which it was found could moderate the manic-depressive swings, with dosage determined by periodic blood tests. Lithium gave him "another life." Still manic-depressive, he was no longer in terror of the consequences. Instead he saw it as the key to a career of sweeping achievement.

> My mind is extraordinarily active, exhaustingly so to others, delightfully so to me. . . . To some, I seem a bit larger than life, perhaps, surely now and then overemphatic, and always inclined to laugh too

loud and too long. For inside me still flows manic blood which pumps a manic heart, making my dreams, ideas, jokes, stories, tumble all over each other. . . .*

Josh decided not to lock his illness "in Jane Eyre's tower," but talk about it freely. He did so in many television appearances as well as published interviews. In doing so, he removed the fear of stigma from many lives besides his. To many in the industry it seemed to enlarge his stature.

I never again discussed with him the *Romeo and Juliet* project. The play, under the title *A Lovin and a Feudin,* was staged by the Pasadena Community Playhouse in May 1941. Richardson drove West in her camper to see it—and was mortified. It seemed to her to have become a hillbilly cartoon, a spoof on her beloved mountain people, a collage of stereotypes. She felt heartsick and wanted to put the play away, out of sight. I too put it from my mind; war rumblings were turning thoughts and media in other directions. But the project may have had a faint echo later in Josh Logan's career. In 1950 he transplanted Chekhov's *The Cherry Orchard* to his native Louisiana to become *The Wisteria Trees* starring Helen Hayes and played in the lilting language he cherished from his childhood. Josh and I, while at Princeton, had made a trip to Broadway to see a very young Helen Hayes in *Coquette.* She wrung tears from us and we both fell in love with her. Josh's devotion had its consummation in *The Wisteria Trees.*

We had little contact for several decades. But in 1980 I visited him in his Manhattan suite on the East River to tell him officially that the Library of Congress was prepared to serve as permanent custodian of his accumulated letters, scripts, stills, posters, and other memorabilia, mirroring a half century of U.S. cultural history. He welcomed this with the familiar ebullience, the gusto that had won him, in 1927, a bit part in *Open Collars.* It was a fine reunion. The Logan Collection is now in the Library.

* Logan, *Josh,* pp. 152–155.

TONY WONS

"You can tell the ideals of a nation
by its advertisements."
—*Norman Douglas*

The world seemed to be waiting for the class of '29. Many of its members were headed for Wall Street, others for law careers. Many had places waiting for them in family businesses. In my case, the Princeton graduate school suggested a teaching fellowship, but I rejected that. I was sure academia was not for me. Three openings, all of which seemed fabulous, awaited me: (1) a Palmer Scholarship for a year's travel abroad (main stipulation: mingle with other cultures and stay at least a year); (2) an offer from Time, Inc. to join the writing staff of a magazine to be called Fortune, to debut in February 1930; (3) an offer from a prosperous theatrical stock company in Rochester, New York, run by George Cukor and George Kondolf, to serve as assistant stage manager and occasionally act. I dared not say no to any of these. The day after graduation I reported to Rochester's grand Temple Theater and for six weeks—six productions—did stage managing while also playing a Marine in Rain and the juvenile lead in The Kibitzer. George Cukor was not there; he had just been lured to Hollywood, which was hastily converting to sound while importing noted stage actors and directors. This was a bad omen for the theater, especially for regional stock companies, but hardly noticed by us; we played to packed houses and for Rain had to run four matinees. In mid-July the company began its annual hot-weather hiatus, so I said farewell and left for New York and Fortune. Its editor, Parker Lloyd-Smith, welcomed the idea of my working two months and then leaving for Europe. He said it would make me more valuable on my return. My job would be waiting for me. For two months, sharing an office with Dwight Mac-Donald, I joined him and others in turning out practice articles that for the moment went into the files instead of to press; the first issue *of* Fortune *was still six months off. In September my travels began. I learned about* pension *life in Paris, the* soukhs *of Marrakech, the hills and byways of Italy, the wine gardens of Vienna. I visited museums, met people, caroused, and for several months, on invitation, joined the Max Reinhardt theater school in Vienna, which operated in the old imperial theater of Schönbrunn Palace. I was scarcely conscious of the New York stock market crash and the Depression that followed. I itched to get back. Having tasted only briefly the life of working America, I wanted to plunge in fully.*

But when I returned, I found the world changed. The Broadway theater seemed dead or dying. Almost all regional stock companies had disappeared; Rochester's Temple Theater had become a movie house equipped for sound films. Almost all businesses seemed to be suffering. Parker Lloyd-Smith, first editor of Fortune *magazine, had jumped from a twenty-third-floor window to his death. The magazine had duly opened in February 1930 but things hadn't worked as he planned. He had thought to assemble a group of "industrial amateurs," bright people fascinated by the business world but ready to look at it with critical intelligence; this would be no "puff magazine." It hadn't proved a winning formula. A new team was taking over. It was a clean sweep. Visiting the office, I found no one I knew. I gathered I was out. Settling back in my parents' apartment at Columbia University, looking for a job for five months, I began to feel equipped for nothing.*

In a speakeasy I came across a girl I had known from Princeton days. When she asked me what I was doing I told her I was unemployed. She said, "Why don't you go into advertising?" I told her I had never thought of it, knew nothing about advertising, knew no one in advertising. She said her husband was in advertising. "He's sitting over there. He's with Erwin, Wasey & Company, one of the big ten agencies. He's head of radio. They've just won the Camel account."

So she introduced me to her husband, Charlie Gannon, who phoned two days later and asked me to see him at his office in the Graybar Building. He had once been a singer in a radio quartet but had evolved into a suave entrepreneurial figure who wore pince-nez. In spite of this Victorian touch he was clearly all business. He told me of the agency's great new coup, winning the Camel cigarette account, with proposals that had included a radio campaign. "They're ready to go on the air!" Plans for the radio series were pretty well set but they needed to staff it. For one thing, they would need a director. How much salary would I need to come aboard?

Students graduating from Princeton in those days generally expected to begin at twenty-five dollars a week. That is what I had received in Rochester. At *Fortune* I was paid thirty dollars a week, which had seemed remarkable. So I told him I could probably live on thirty dollars. Gannon said, "We wouldn't do anything like that to you, Erik." (When I got my first check, I found I was getting sixty-five dollars a week, enough to leave home for a midtown flat. I would also have an expense account.)

The absurdity of the situation did not sink in until later. Network radio, nationally organized, was only about four years old and had exploded so rapidly that no pool of knowledgeable personnel existed. Gannon himself probably owed his position to this fact. So, faced with the need to hire a director, he had settled for a contact made in a speakeasy.

So I got the job. Almost as an afterthought Gannon said, "You know music, don't you?" I told him I didn't know much about music. "Well, you wrote the Princeton Triangle show, didn't you?" I explained I had written the book and lyrics—with a collaborator. He waved the problem aside. "You know enough about music."

I had never had a radio so bought one and listened to it all weekend. I felt I should come in with some good ideas. On Monday I began work and was started on a tour of the agency's radio programs. The first, created for Chiclets, featured Les Reis and Artie Dunn at a piano singing cheek-by-jowl in close harmony. Their theme song:

> When you're feeling kinda blue
> And you wonder what to do,
> Che-e-e-e-ew Chiclets, and che-e-e-e-er up!
> When you've lost your appetite
> Here's the way to set it right,
> Che-e-e-e-ew Chiclets, and che-e-e-e-er up!
> (FADE OUT FOR OPENING ANNOUNCEMENT)

Another series produced by Erwin, Wasey & Company, for Forhan's toothpaste, featured the astrologer Evangeline Adams. Listeners sending in a Forhan's carton with date and time of their birth received a horoscope reading. She encouraged accompanying letters about personal crises; the most striking were discussed on the air, with advice on how to make best use of astral conjunctions. Other writers got printed advice via mail. The theme song was "Ah Sweet Mystery of Life," played at opening and close by a string trio. The commercials were read by a golden-voiced David Ross, who also had a poetry series titled *Poet's Gold*. On a more encouraging plane was a *Maxwell House Hour* with the Donald Voorhees orchestra and guest stars, including John Charles Thomas, and a Philco Symphony series under Howard Barlow. I learned that someone from the agency (*director, producer, production man*—the terms seemed to be used interchangeably) was on hand for each agency program and was in charge. Any request he might make from network personnel seemed to get prompt attention. There was no doubt who was calling the tune. And the talent was on the agency's payroll—to be billed to the sponsor, plus a commission.

The program that was to be my special domain, sponsored by the R. J. Reynolds Tobacco Company, was to have multiple scheduling. Titled *Camel Quarter Hour*, it would be on the Columbia Broadcasting System six nights a week, Monday through Saturday, 7:45–8:00 P.M. for the Eastern part of the country, repeated live at 11:30–11:45 P.M. for the Western states. Thus there would be twelve performances a week. They would feature the singer Morton Downey accompanied by the music of Jacques Renard's orchestra, which had been winning late-evening audiences with lush orchestrations by Ray Sinatra (cousin of Frank). The fourteen-piece band at one time or another included trombonist Tommy Dorsey and pianist Claude Thornhill. To these elements Erwin, Wasey & Company had made an unusual and curious addition: Tony Wons.

I was told—everyone else seemed to know all this—that Wons had built an enormous audience at WLS, Chicago, reading poems. He was one of those who had discovered and exploited radio's possibilities for extreme intimacy. Speaking in a low, well-modulated voice less than an inch from the carbon microphones of the time, he began each of his programs with "Are you listenin'?" His poetry reading and the brief philosophising that went with it attracted floods of letters, mostly from women, in which many poured out their intimate problems. He was said to have become a soulmate to millions. He began publishing collections of the poems he had read, under such titles as *Tony's Scrap Book* and *'R You Listenin'?* *

---

* Reilly & Lee, Chicago, published editions of *Tony's Scrap Book* in 1931, 1932, 1933 and *Three Tony's Scrap Books in One Volume*, copyright 1930–31.

CBS offered him a daily morning spot coast-to-coast in exchange for a cut of his book revenue. Thus Tony became, in a sense, his own sponsor. His poem selections ranged from public domain selections to poems sent in by listeners. Each *Camel Quarter Hour* was to feature at its center a poem read by Wons, backed by violin music of Jacques Renard. Twice on each program Wons would also read, in the same intimate manner and backed by similar mellow music, a message about Camel cigarettes (in newly introduced cellophane wrappers), said to be "as fresh as the dew that dawn spills on a field of clover." Contrasting sharply to the shouted commercials of Lucky Strike programs of the time, which were delivered by an announcer known as "thundering Thorgensen," the mellow approach was felt to be a shrewd countermove, certain to be welcomed by many, especially women.

As the premiere approached, I kept wondering what I was supposed to do. I had been given a stopwatch, and realized that one requirement was to get each program off on time—exactly 14:30 minutes from its start. I also realized that for each program a "continuity" was prepared by our office personnel, reproduced in dittoed copies. Afterwards one copy was to be filed by me with attached report form noting any glitch or disaster, technical or otherwise, that might affect our payments to the network or our billings to the sponsor. All this seemed reasonable. But I kept feeling there must be more that a "director" was expected to do. I dared not ask too many ignorant questions; however, I did cautiously question another agency staff member. He said, "Well, if you feel the orchestra balance is off, you get it fixed. You may want to move the drums, or the string section, or the mike. Or whatever. Or, if you feel that at a certain point there ought to be a choir of woodwinds, maybe close up, you say so." The advice petrified me. I could not imagine making any such judgments. Fortunately I discovered that the production man assigned by CBS to assist, and who looked to me for instructions, was already a radio veteran and was knowledgeable and ambitious. He and the engineer loved moving instruments around for better balance. And at the end of a program he loved to stand, stopwatch in hand, motioning to the engineer to fade the music down for the announcer's final "This . . . is the Columbia Broadcasting System!" (The word *system* was to land exactly at 14:30, being a signal to stations throughout the country to cut away for "station identification.") I let him have his head, while I occasionally nodded approval. I realized I might learn the studio business from the top down.

If an artist or technician asked my opinion of something, I generally said it sounded good. Actually, I seldom had an opinion. Again, I was a stranger in a foreign land with mysterious rites and criteria. I was an oddment, trying to get in step. Once, praising Jacques Renard for a violin cadenza, I may have overdone it. He shrugged. "I play a whorehouse fiddle." Renard, whose family hailed from eastern Europe, went in for Yiddish-style self-deprecating comments.

Downey, the main attraction—billed as the "Camel Minstrel"—had a remarkable pure-sounding tenor voice. A Connecticut Irishman, he could always draw fan mail with "When Irish Eyes Are Smiling" or "Ave Maria." Off-mike he relished vulgarities. Always restless when not performing himself, he had a liking for practical jokes. During a late-evening "repeat broadcast" he stood in front of the announcer just before his ritual sign-off and suddenly dropped his pants—a challenge to the announcer to keep his composure. A bit rotund himself, Downey liked to tease Renard about his huge bulk, which Renard took in good humor. Ribbing the musicians was another Downey specialty. Exuding admiration over a musician's new suit, Downey said, "Hey, that's really something! Beautiful!" Then, earnestly: "Tell me, do you like that better than what they're wearing now?" Downey led the chorus of laughter.

Downey had been "discovered" by William Paley, the young cigar manufacturer who had bought the ailing Columbia Phonograph Broadcasting System just three years earlier. In Philadelphia Paley had experimented with a "La Palina Girl" on local radio to promote the cigar named after the Paley family and noted the jump in sales. Acquiring his network ("Phonograph" was dropped from the name), Paley invested in more singers. Scheduling Bing Crosby and Kate Smith in daily spots, he built them into major attractions; Downey came next. A few months on CBS, with "Wabash Moon" as his theme song, groomed him to become the "Camel Minstrel"—with "Carolina Moon, Keep Shining" as his theme song. In this role he was reported to earn six thousand dollars a week.*

My occasional meetings with Gannon were a bit intimidating. His pince-nez and easy assurance seemed to dominate the encounters. And I had a sense of getting by with a certain amount of fakery. One day he asked casually, "Erik, does it ever occur to you to say a nice word to Downey about his singing?" I was puzzled. It had not occurred to me.

---

* *New York Times*, July 19, 1931, sec. 9, 13-1.

Did Downey lack for praise? Gannon said, "I'd consider it, if I were you. It's important for you to keep on good terms with him." He implied that Downey had been heard to make a snide reference to me. "Why don't you take him to dinner once in a while?"

A few days later I did find myself telling Downey that his rendition of "I Surrender, Dear" had been splendid, and he reacted with a warmth and delight that surprised me. A few days later we began an occasional dinner together, in the interval between the early and late broadcasts. During this time I usually ate dinner at a small restaurant on the ground floor of the CBS building at 485 Madison Avenue, for about two dollars, sometimes three. I charged this on my expense account as authorized and felt I was awarding myself a salary raise. On the first of my Downey dinners, at a restaurant suggested by him, the bill came to eighty dollars. I was horrified. I could not imagine putting eighty dollars on my expense account, and said so. Downey seemed amused. "How much would you dare to put down? Forty dollars?" I felt I could risk that. Downey said, "We'll split it." I was greatly relieved. A few days later Gannon and others at the agency knew all about the incident—from Downey—and it caused hilarity. It apparently did not hurt my standing at the agency, but it gave me a somewhat unworldly image among fellow workers.

Tony Wons was a sharp contrast to both Downey and Renard, physically and otherwise. A sober, reedlike, ascetic-looking figure, Wons seemed detached from his surroundings. When not at the microphone he sat on a straight chair against the wall, awaiting his next turn. He never showed either disdain or approval of what was going on around him. In this I tended to identify with him. He minded his own business. He arrived and left alone.

His poetry selections (entirely his decision) seemed to me better than I had expected. They ranged from anthology classics like Elizabeth Barrett Browning's "How do I love thee? Let me count the ways . . ." to sentimental inspirational poems. Occasionally he featured Americana items by "hobo poets" like Bruce Carman, Richard Hovey, and others, writers I had not encountered in literature courses. One such poem, which he repeated a number of times, began somewhat as follows (I quote from memory, having been unable to find it in *Tony's Scrap Books* or anywhere else):

The moon is up and the stars are out and the breath of night is sweet,
And this is the time when wanderlust should seize upon my feet,

But I'm glad to turn from the open road and the starlight on my face
And leave the beauty of out-of-doors for a human dwelling place. . . .

It ended:

I never have known a wanderer who really liked to roam
All up and down the ways of the world and never have a home.
The tramp who slept in your barn last night and left at the break of day
Will wander on until he finds another place to stay.
For the only reason a road is good, as every wanderer knows,
Is just because of the homes, the homes, the homes to which it goes.

I gathered that Wons was something of a wanderer himself. He mentioned having done some ranch work and a variety of factory work. In the 1920s, falling ill (tuberculosis, I assumed), he was told he had less than a year to live, so he thought he might as well do something he enjoyed and offered to read poems at a radio station. Success led to further success, and his health improved. Programs like his seemed to have a special meaning in the Depression years, when people who had ceased to go to the movies or to travel found in radio a continuing link to humanity. I learned that a quirk in the copyright law made such programs possible. Poets controlled exclusive rights to "publish," "adapt," or "translate" their poems, but not the sole right to "perform" them—a right presumably surrendered by the act of publication. The word *perform* was not mentioned in the passage relating to poets, which differed in this respect from provisions relating to dramatists and lecturers, who under copyright law specifically controlled performance rights. The difference had given rise to the rash of poetry programs in early radio. Most, like David Ross's *Poet's Gold*, sounded cultured and were read in mellifluous tones. Wons sounded earthy and Midwestern, with a pleasant dry timbre. The law was subsequently revised to give poets full control of performance rights; an immediate result was to drive most poetry programs from the air.

The quick success of the *Camel Quarter Hour* led to events that astonished me. Radio-Keith-Orpheum expressed interest in booking the program on its vaudeville circuit. Vaudeville had almost vanished but remained as an adjunct to movies. While one-time greats of vaudeville—Eddie Cantor, Ed Wynn, Jack Pearl, Jack Benny, Fred Allen, George Burns, Gracie Allen—had moved into radio (attracting sponsors by the scores and listeners by the millions), surviving vaudeville interests looked to

Camel Quarter Hour (CBS) on tour, 1933. Tony Wons, Morton Downey, and Jacques Renard. (State Historical Society of Wisconsin)

rising radio talents to bolster their circuits. Double features were a fix-ture at most theaters, but a few movie palaces looked to single features backed by one or more vaudeville acts. Thus it was that in 1932 the *Camel Quarter Hour* embarked on a thirteen-week Radio-Keith-Orpheum tour of major cities. It became an astonishing part of my U.S. education. In most cities we were to do three performances per day—four on Satur-days and Sundays—along with our twice-daily Monday through Saturday broadcasts, which were to be done from local CBS outlets. It created a dizzying schedule. Downey (the tour was said to double his earnings) hired an advance man who in a number of cities arranged police escorts to rush us between theater and radio station, creating a turmoil over our presence that was considered invaluable. Downey's friendship with New York mayor Jimmy Walker (who had once visited our studio) proved a further asset: in some cities we were received by the mayor, apparently at Jimmy's suggestion. Day after day the theater was jammed. The theater marquee generally featured Downey but sometimes mentioned both Downey and Wons. Watching the crowd—we always photographed the line of people at the box office just before opening, when the line looked longest—I wasn't sure whether Downey or Wons was the greater draw. In some cities the marquee said "Camel Quarter Hour." It all appeared a bonanza for the R. J. Reynolds Tobacco Company, which had approved the tour but had no financial involvement in it. On the stage every music stand resembled a large Camel package.

The tour soon developed a steamy atmosphere. A Ziegfeld Follies road company sometimes intersected with our travels. After our late-night broadcast our troupe tended to spill into nightclubs, often with Ziegfeld girls in tow. Even the obese Jacques Renard, to everyone's surprise, was seen squiring a tall and extremely beautiful Armenian showgirl. He seemed to be worried about his sexual stamina; one morning over a cup of coffee he moaned, shaking his head sadly, "Last night—I practically had to use toothpicks."

A burlesque circuit also crisscrossed our tour, and was featuring "Peaches" Browning, famous from tabloid headlines because of her legal tussles with real estate tycoon "Daddy" Browning, from whom she had won a fine settlement. Her burlesque act opened with the song "Now Everything Is Peaches and Cream." I conferred regularly with Downey about songs to be scheduled on future programs, and one day found Peaches Browning in his suite. He introduced us, then said, "Erik, she has the fattest pussy you've ever seen! Look, I'll show you." He started to lift her skirt. I was a bit flustered, but she giggled and pushed him away, chiding, "Mort!"

A trunk of orchestrations—it took four men to lift it—traveled with us, and each week more orchestrations arrived from Ray Sinatra in New York. A clearance procedure with ASCAP (handled by CBS) was also involved. We traveled from city to city by Pullman. In our Pullman car

Downey and Renard had their own bedrooms, so that their wives could join them if they wished. (Barbara Bennett, Downey's wife, turned up briefly; Mrs. Renard, perhaps alerted by rumors, arrived from Boston.) The musicians had uppers and lowers. I shared a room with Tony Wons and got to know him better, but only slightly so. He was always considerate. He would arrive at the Pullman with two oranges, and urge one on me for my health. "It will flush out your system." Tony continued to keep to himself, not mixing with others. He made no nightclub visits. No one knew what he did in his spare moments.

In the theater performances both Downey and Wons got thunderous applause and had fans waiting later for autographs. The total theater act took twenty to twenty-five minutes. It began and ended with Downey numbers. The middle consisted of an orchestral number with violin solo by Renard and the Wons portion, which included two readings—unchanged throughout the tour. The first poem was a fail-proof tearjerker by Jill Spargur that was filigreed with violin music played by Jacques Renard. Some hundred hearings of it implanted it forever in my neurons, so that key passages still haunt me. Read quietly, intimately—but amplified—it included the following lines:

> I always wanted a toy balloon, it only cost a dime,
> But ma said it was risky, they broke so quickly,
> And besides, she didn't have time,
> And even if she did, she didn't think they were worth a dime. . . .
> I only went to one circus and fair,
> And all the balloons I ever saw were there!
> There were yellow ones, and blue ones, but the kind I liked best
>   were red,
> And I don't see why she couldn't have said
> That maybe I could have one, but she didn't. . . .

It ended:

> I got a little money saved,
> I got a lot of time.
> I got no one to tell me how and where to spend my dime.
> Plenty of balloons, but—
> I don't want one
> Now. (MUSIC UP)

Tony followed this unexpectedly, shrewdly—and boldly, it seemed to me—with a passage from Shakespeare's *Merchant of Venice*, Shylock's attack on prejudice.

> Hath not a Jew eyes? Hath not a Jew hands, organs, dimensions, senses, affections, passions? Fed by the same food, hurt with the same weapons, subject to the same diseases, healed by the same means, warmed and cooled by the same winter and summer?

It startled the audience, and held it firmly. Wons wanted no background music for this. The theater was hushed.

The final Downey number always had a big finish—a "Publix" finish, the musicians called it—in which Mort let out all the stops. He could for such passages produce impressive volume. But I began to worry about his voice. After only a few weeks he often woke up voiceless. A doctor joined the tour, and every morning began with a throat-spraying session in an effort to restore the voice. Mort began to sing cautiously during broadcasts, preserving it for the theater. Even here he sang less and spent time in often tasteless banter with the orchestra. I felt his voice was losing its bell-like quality.

One day I received a frantic call from Charlie Gannon at Erwin, Wasey & Company. A usually unruffled executive, he sounded panicky. It had to do with our sponsor. "Erik, I'm going to send you a list showing the R. J. Reynolds representative in every city on your tour. The first thing you've got to do when you arrive in a new city is get hold of the R. J. Reynolds man and keep him happy. Whatever that calls for, do it! Never mind the cost! Take him to a nightclub, get him drunk. If you have to get him laid, do it! But keep him happy!"

It was a long phone call. I gathered that R. J. Reynolds had asked its representative in each city to look at the vaudeville enterprise and advise them what it meant for Camels. What impression was it making? This had put each R. J. Reynolds man into the role of theatrical critic. What comments or advice this had produced I never learned, but it had clearly created alarm over our "million-dollar account." My task was damage control.

Until then I had begun each arrival with a visit to the CBS outlet accompanied by our regular CBS studio engineer, "Westy" Westover, who was traveling with us. We felt a need to meet station personnel, including the local production man assigned to assist us (CBS had not sent the New

York production man), and especially we wanted to study the studio and its acoustics. Westy would walk around the studio clapping his hands, listening to the reverberations. In some cities studios were still primitive—revamped ballrooms or garages or warehouses—and raised problems of orchestra placement. Westy would now have to do all that alone: my first move as we arrived in St. Louis was a phone call to Mr. Applegate, first name on my list. I felt totally unprepared for the sort of task now facing me, but I reached him by phone and invited him to lunch at our hotel. He seemed pleased.

He proved an affable person. He was enthusiastic about the *Camel Quarter Hour* and was sure it was helping the Camel cause. He looked forward eagerly to seeing the theater show. All this was encouraging. I told him there would be a pass for him at the box office.

Over coffee I finally edged into a question I had been rehearsing internally. "Is there anything we can do for you, Mr. Applegate?" It sounded as though I was positioned to bestow a variety of favors; he did not seem to reject this notion. He smiled and looked a bit embarrassed. Clearly something was on his mind. Finally he said that yes, there was something. I waited anxiously.

He explained that he was a scoutmaster, with a scout troop that met every Saturday morning. It would be just a wonderful thing if Tony Wons would meet with his troop on the coming Saturday and be inducted as an honorary member. It would be an unforgettable day for all the boys.

I felt relieved beyond words. No Princeton course had prepared me for the art of pimping. I assured Mr. Applegate that I would do my best, and felt reasonably sure Wons would agree. I would ask him that evening.

When I found occasion to broach the idea to Tony Wons, his reaction was immediate. "Hell no, I can't do that." He explained that in every city he had arrangements with bookstores and department stores to sign books. A new *Tony's Scrap Book* was just coming out, the second in two years, and he was to sign copies at a department store that Saturday. He showed me a small ad in the morning paper. "I can't change that. Besides, I sell a lot of copies that way."

I was taken aback. It all seemed so logical, but no one in our tour had taken the slightest interest in this other life of Tony's, or even been aware of it. The revelation put me momentarily in a panic. But next morning I hurried to the department store for desperate negotiations. The upshot was that on Saturday Mr. Applegate's troop lined up for attention in the book department of the store. The event attracted a large crowd of the curious. Tony was formally inducted into the troop; then he signed books. He was busy for over an hour. The store was delighted, Tony was happy, Mr. Applegate was ecstatic. It was a big day for poetry.

The tour went on, a blur of crises. Among family letters I find one I wrote to my sister Elsa, dated April 3, 1932, from the Ritz-Carlton Hotel in Boston. I remember well the opulent musk smell in the hotel's elevators and the fact that I paid five dollars for my room in that Depression year. I wrote her:

> This is the town where Jacques Renard rose from the ghetto. He has thirty to forty relatives continuously at his heels, and conducts himself in a very lordly fashion. Tonight I have to go to a testimonial dinner in his honor.

I also wrote:

> The *Camel Quarter Hour* is still breaking records here and there. We have been to seven cities now and have six more ahead of us. I, the scribe, send voluminous reports to Erwin, Wasey. . . . I am also preparing a long, detailed, glowing account of the tour which will be presented to the R. J. Reynolds Tobacco Company; it will describe all the exploitation schemes, the reactions of audiences, the lunches with mayors in various cities, and especially all the free advertising that Camels have derived from the trip. It will be a good-sized volume.

These client-relations efforts turned out to be in vain. The deterioration in Downey's voice became all too obvious in the last weeks of the tour, especially on the air. I was not very surprised that, on our anniversary, the series was canceled. Camel campaigns continued unrelentingly, but via another agency. It was not the only major account we lost that year.

It took me a long time to sort out my feelings about the Camel caper and to sense what the *Camel Quarter Hour* was all about. In the 1920s few women smoked. Cigarette makers became beguiled by the thought that if women could be persuaded to smoke, that would double the market. A bonanza of this sort was the thought behind Lucky Strike's campaigns built around movie and opera queens. For Camels it was the vision behind Downey's silvery tenor, Renard's lush music, and especially Tony Wons, soulmate to millions of women. He was counted on to bring them into the fold.

At Erwin, Wasey & Company I never heard such strategies mentioned; perhaps medical reports already discouraged discussion. And I am sure no one on our tour was thinking of such matters. For all, the job was the focus. It was good to get a show off on time, get a good review, win a good rating, see your name on a marquee, get a police escort, move an audience, be received by the mayor, write a good report. These were enough. To any larger implications we were as oblivious as our audience. The obliviousness was a gold mine, and we troupers received our share of its yield. Along with our salaries each one of us received, each week, a free carton of Camels. We were content. Could Tony Wons himself—once scheduled for early death—have had any inkling of what his role might mean?

Health data eventually made clear the dimensions of the story. Cigarette advertising was finally barred from U.S. broadcasting; U.S. sales began to dwindle. But other territories became available. The countries of East Asia—Japan, Korea, China, Taiwan, Hong Kong—entered a boom in the 1980s and offered cultures where smokers included millions of men but few women—or children. Proven strategies were put into play by the leading cigarette companies. For the United States it was a time of woeful trade imbalance, but by 1990 Clayton Yuetter, President Bush's secretary of agriculture, was telling a press conference, "I just saw the figures on tobacco exports here a few days ago, and my, have they turned out to be a marvelous success story." A U.S. tobacco executive confirmed this. The outlook for the Chinese market alone, he said, "confounds the imagination." [*]

[*] Stan Sesser, "Opium War Redux," *The New Yorker*, September 13, 1993, p. 79.

BILLY HALOP

"I was a fourteen-year-old
boy for thirty years."
—Mickey Rooney

Erwin, Wasey & Company seemed to be coming apart. One of its account executives, Atherton Hobler, took the Maxwell House account and all our other General Foods advertising over to Benton & Bowles, a gift so splendid that he was made president of Benton & Bowles, allowing both William Benton and Chester Bowles to jump from advertising into political careers—one becoming a U.S. senator, the other governor of Connecticut. Our Philco account likewise went to others; we began to look like a second-class agency. For a time all employees were on half-time, half-pay. But the battle for new accounts went on and bore fruit. I had no contact with those efforts, but I was delighted that some of the new accounts wanted drama, not music. It was a trend of the moment, a hopeful one for me. By the mid-thirties I found myself producing and directing three dramatic series: (1) True Story Court of Human Relations—a Friday night half-hour series on NBC for Macfadden Publications, sampling sleazy confessions from True Story magazine; (2) Forum of Liberty, a Tuesday half-hour series on NBC for Macfadden's Liberty magazine, offering each week a dramatized history of a U.S. industry plus words of wisdom from one of its leading tycoons—an effort (successful) to persuade his company to advertise in Liberty; (3) Bobby Benson of the H-Bar-O Ranch, a daily fifteen-minute juvenile serial with a Western locale scheduled on CBS 6:15–6:30 P.M. My family was able to remain fairly oblivious to all this; I did not urge them to listen. I sensed that none of it would fill them with pride. My name was not heard on the air so I was pursuing this career almost incognito. But I told myself I was extraordinarily lucky to have landed in an industry that, instead of suffering from the Depression, was thriving on it. I was earning a good living, learning something

new, and involving myself in something thoroughly American. Perhaps,
before long, I would feel at home in it.

Both NBC and CBS had lounge areas where hundreds of actors circulated
or sat about, waiting for their next program or rehearsal. Adjacent to
these were the many studios—large and small, each with its own control
room—from which a fantastic array of dramaturgy was suddenly being
spewed across the country: women's serials, children's serials, mysteries,
melodramas, folksy rural dramas, romance, comedy, dramatized history,
dramatized news. New York was radio's programming capital, and these
NBC and CBS studios were the heart of it. All network broadcasts from
here, including repeat broadcasts, were "live." These "major" networks
banned recordings except for sound effects. This was not a legal stric-
ture: most individual stations and regional hookups relied on phonograph
records and syndicated recorded programs for at least part of their programming. But NBC and CBS leaders felt that listeners to national networks must always have the sense that what they were hearing was going
on at that moment. Otherwise the idea of a network would lose its meaning, prerecorded material would soon dominate, and listeners would be
confused and easily misled.

Some two thousand actors supplied the voices for the programming
glut. They swarmed in and out of the lounge areas; to make my way
through the swarm, as I had to do constantly, could be a daunting experience. I knew many of the actors. Like other directors, I held "general auditions" and had built a file of hundreds, noting vocal qualities,
quirks, accents. I admired many and had given encouragement where it
seemed due. So why, they wondered, hadn't they received a phone call?
The truth was, most weeks I had less than a dozen roles to cast, but I
had to know the available gamut. Couldn't they understand that? Pretty
ingenues crisscrossed the lounge with expectant looks. Each week there
seemed to be new arrivals from all parts of the country. Child actors sat
with their mothers, who kept a watchful eye for directors. Some mothers
would rise, moving steadily forward; I sensed I must keep on the go, avoid
eye contact. Some actors would buttonhole you en route, or "acciden-
tally" meet you in the washroom. And at the office I would find notes,
cute notes, notes with clippings on recent performances, notes from the
mothers with photos of their children. "Just a reminder."

Reaching the studio I could feel safe, momentarily relieved of guilt feelings. And here were riches to play with. For *True Story* I had a thirteen-piece orchestra for bridges and backgrounds. Sound effects were always a fascination. Many sound effects were now available on recordings; a special delight was to play them at various wrong speeds and note the results. You could create unlikely worlds, dream worlds. A director was king in the studio and necessarily made instant decisions. There was no time for meetings and discussions; the pace was relentless. If a scene didn't work, I could cut, add, rewrite as I pleased. It was all very educational.

Occasionally Charlie Gannon entered the studio, piloting a sponsor. He would point out the sound effects gadgets, explaining the wonders. He kept the sponsors out of my hair. At NBC, from an upper gallery, large groups of tourists would occasionally look down on us, led by an NBC page conducting the forty-cent Radio City Studio Tour. (Gregory Peck got his start here, as a page.) The tourists were behind glass; we couldn't hear them but they could, via monitor speakers, hear us. Actors signaled each other when the "forty-centers" loomed above us. It meant, "Keep it clean."

Before launching *Bobby Benson of the H-Bar-O Ranch*, Erwin, Wasey & Company decided that open auditions should be held for the main running roles. A successful series could go on for years, so choices were crucial. With freelance writer Peter Dixon, who would write the series (and for a time direct it), I listened to an array of candidates for the title role. We tried them in various scenes and situations. Gannon and other agency people joined us from time to time.

Bobby was supposed to be about twelve years old, a bright young city kid who had inherited a ranch. It was called the H-Bar-O Ranch—meaning, as millions of kids would soon know, that its cattle were branded H–O. This was (as kids would likwise know) the name of a cereal, H–O Oats, sponsors of the program. The premiums we would send out for boxtops—hats, rings, scarves, pins, and more—would also be "branded" H–O. It was considered essential to "merchandise" a series.

The relation of Bobby to the ranch hands—Tex, the foreman; Windy, the funny cowboy; and all the rest—was a key element in the program. They would call him Little Boss. He consulted them on ranch management problems, listened earnestly to their advice, asked questions, then made decisions. The right Bobby would never be bossy about this, but eager for more information.

The moment we heard Billy Halop, we felt we wanted him. He had a natural, unspoiled sound. Most of the youngsters were from the Professional Children's School and many had a very self-assured sound, which we didn't want. Bobby had to remain curious about everything—ranch life, the cattle, the West, the Indians, the horses, the roundup, the desert and its wildlife. He had to be ready to listen.

Billy Halop had strong competition. An impressive rival was Walter Tetley, a midget in his twenties. An alert performer, highly intuitive, he had begun a very successful career playing children's roles on radio. He later became a regular on the Fred Allen comedy series. Some of the agency people urged us to choose Tetley. They pointed out that his voice would not change so we could be set for years. Also, there would be no problem with child labor laws relating to working hours. And no constant problem with stage mothers. These were persuasive arguments, but Peter Dixon and I held to our first instincts. We picked Billy Halop. For Polly, Bobby's younger sister, we picked Florence Halop, Billy's sister.

During this process we got to know a number of stage mothers, a fascinating breed. Mrs. Halop was, at the moment, the most successful. Whenever the dramatized news episodes on the radio *March of Time* series (predecessor to the screen *March of Time*) involved a child role, Billy or Florence generally got the call. Mrs. Halop watched tenaciously over her two charges—their schooling, clothing, manners, physical training. She herself was said to have been a dancer, which was hard to believe, because she was large and bulky, a dominating presence. The other mothers circulated unpleasant rumors about her, which we ascribed to jealousy. In the lounges some of them sat together; she sat alone. They were furious that we had given Mrs. Halop a *Bobby Benson* monopoly. The mother of a girl who had competed for the role of Polly was especially distraught— and incredulous. I tried to placate her, telling her that we had indeed been impressed by her daughter; if there was a chance to use her on one of my other series, I would do so. A few weeks later I cast her in a *True Story* part. Afterwards I received from the mother a thank you note enclosing a five-dollar bill. When I gave this back to her, explaining that that was unnecessary—"We don't go in for that sort of thing"—she was flustered. She said Mrs. Halop had advised her that was the thing to do. I was nonplussed. It seemed to me one of the mothers was guilty of a nasty maneuver—but which one?

In view of the high-pressure atmosphere surrounding this competition, we were surprised and pleased with Billy's easy naturalness. It did not wear off. He remained the eager questioner, ready to learn from the cowhands. Their loyalty to the Little Boss was readily understood. In the studio the group chemistry was splendid. The older actors all considered Billy a "nice kid."

The series was built around crises, and the solutions generally brought Western lore into play, articulated by Tex the foreman or one of the cowhands. All this was a delight to me. I had never read a Western. My American experience had begun at a junior high level, so everything before that tended to be a void. *Bobby Benson* was beginning to fill that void. My coworkers would hardly have suspected that I was learning something every day. When Bobby Benson thought he had discovered gold and learned it was only iron pyrites, "fool's gold," it was old stuff to them, new to me. The cowhands told yarns about old Western heroes and bad men—all new to me. The singer Tex Ritter (not yet a famous movie star) became one of our cowboys and sang little-known campfire songs— all new to me, as to Bobby Benson. He and I were learning together.

I admired the resourcefulness of Peter Dixon's writing. A resident of suburban Scarsdale, New York, he had organized a neighborhood Junior Council that met regularly and provided him with *Bobby Benson* feedback. He tried out ideas on them. Because there had once been an effort to introduce camels into the Western desert, on the assumption they would thrive there and provide a means of transport, Dixon had his cowboys find a camel wandering on the range, apparently descended from the old experiment. A week of programming was devoted to the ranch's efforts to figure out how to manage the camel and what to do with it. It was both humorous and informative. Another sequence of programs concerned a rattlesnake infestation. In one of them the ranch pig—an animal despised by the cowhands—becomes a hero, despatching a rattler with its hoofs. We learn that the pig's layer of fat protects it from the snake's venom. For another episode a snake handler brought an actual rattler in a box. By gently stroking its stomach (while firmly holding its neck) he could make it rattle on cue—an astounding, frightening sound. When a cowboy "shot" the rattler, the handler grabbed the rattle an instant later, quashing the sound. Bobby and I learned a lot about rattlers. After the sequence the snake vomited.

In the first weeks of the series Dixon wrote and directed while I served as agency "production man." But Dixon soon approached nervous exhaustion and it was decided I should direct. I looked forward to each episode.

Billy Halop's acting retained the unspoiled quality that had drawn him to us. Role and actor seemed a perfect fit: Billy identified totally with Bobby—perhaps too much for his own good. The end of each episode left the ranch in a crisis, a cliffhanger, that sometimes seemed to pose an insoluble dilemma. Billy agonized over these crises. Again and again he would say to Peter Dixon, "How am I going to get out of this?" Peter would smile and say, "You'll find out." Dixon felt that if Billy knew the details, it might detract from the credibility of his acting. On this principle he refused to divulge future plotting. At times he may himself have been undecided about future events; his scripts, which came to the office for duplication, sometimes arrived only a day or two before broadcast.

Billy persisted in agonizing—as I began to learn from his mother. She took me aside. Billy had trouble sleeping at night, she explained. He kept tossing, wondering how he could solve the latest crisis. She wanted me to take charge of this problem—make it clear to Billy that fiction was one thing, reality another. She had talked to him about this, but it didn't seem to help. Now it was up to me, she said. "He admires you, he looks up to you. Talk to him."

I did talk to him. I spent time with him. I even went horseback riding with him in Central Park. Occasionally we talked about storytelling and its perilous fascinations. Whether I made headway, I wasn't sure. I had other crises to cope with.

Our *True Story* program faced a bizarre problem, brought on by its sponsor, Bernarr Macfadden. His magazine empire had prospered on body building, spicy confessions, and unsolved mysteries, but he broke into the news regularly with new ventures odd enough to seize attention. In the depth of the Depression he started in downtown New York a one-cent restaurant where coffee was made by pouring boiling water over a cluster of raisins. All dishes cost one cent and, it was said, offered the unemployed a balanced diet. Then, early in 1936, he announced his candidacy for the presidency of the United States. The Erwin, Wasey agency was notified that he expected his *True Story* series to take due notice of this event. This seemed such a preposterous idea that I was sure the agency would in some way sidestep it, but not so. Management decided that the client should be accommodated; I was to work out the details. Discussing

the problem with our *True Story* liaison, I suggested that Bernarr Macfadden himself appear on the *True Story* program to make a pitch for the
Red Cross drive; our introduction of him would take care of the presidency matter, as follows: "And now, a word from the renowned publisher
Bernarr Macfadden, often mentioned as a possible candidate for president of the United States." This plan was accepted, and so I had the honor
of receiving our sponsor at the studio and, at the proper moment, conducting him to the microphone to speak his piece. He was smaller and
frailer than I expected. The political world showed no sign of noticing
the event. The agency probably felt a bit surer of its Macfadden account.

Another Erwin, Wasey program had been launched on CBS with quick,
explosive success—a fifteen-minute advice program titled *The Voice of
Experience*, broadcast daily at noon. Since I spent hours daily at CBS, the
series was handed over to me to supervise. It was essentially a sinecure.
M. Sayle Taylor, who broadcast as The Voice of Experience (his name was
never used) was a solo performer. He was sponsored jointly by a number
of Erwin, Wasey's drug clients: Musterole, Haley's M-O, Haley's CTC,
and others. Troubled people were their market, and his audience. They
were soon sending him up to fourteen thousand letters a week. Some
wrote of astounding, fascinating problems. The Voice answered a few of
them on the air in strong, well-modulated tones. Others were answered
by mail—#24, #16, #72, and so forth—sent from The Voice's office. This
was the same procedure as Evangeline Adams had followed, but it was
now handled far more efficiently. My task was to report any program
mishaps or glitches but there didn't seem to be any.

The broadcasts became strange, sobering intervals in my daily studio
routine. They did begin to get under my skin. But it was difficult to imagine, or think about, those fourteen thousand people, just as it was difficult
to think about ten million unemployed. I lived daily with Bobby Benson
problems. Peter Dixon, approaching exhaustion, was told by his doctor to
take a long rest from his *Bobby Benson* writing. John Battle, a droll Texan
who played the part of Windy—a great favorite with our audience—said
he could turn out "stuff like that." We let him try, and he quickly proved
it. His scripts had a zany, reckless streak that was difficult to restrain.
This sometimes worried the agency people. But our ratings kept climb-
ing. In the end, Battle and Dixon took turns writing and having nervous
breakdowns. After six or eight months each began to feel the need for
relief.

Battle was responsible for one of the most extraordinary of all *Bobby Benson* sequences—one with complex ramifications. He decided to have a group of H-Bar-O cowboys come to New York "for the rodeo." New York's Madison Square Garden (at that time located on Eighth Avenue) hosted an annual rodeo run by one Colonel W. T. Johnson. Battle said he would invent some New York adventures for the cowboys, and meanwhile there would be talk about one or two of them competing in the rodeo. It would give the series an exciting timeliness and capitalize on the rodeo's popularity. Battle said he had fascinating and amusing information about rodeos that he wanted to use.

But his plan kept growing. One day he explained to me that most cowboys riding in the rodeo represented ranches, but others were freelancers, who competed on their own. "So here's what we should do," said Battle. "Cowboys love silk shirts—good, heavy silk. A cowboy will do anything for a silk shirt. So we should have some silk shirts made—three or four hundred dollars per shirt—with big letters on them: H–O. I'll take those over to the Garden. I'll say to a freelance rider: 'Here. Keep this shirt, it's yours. Wear it in the rodeo.' I'll explain about the imaginary ranch, but he won't care about that. He just wants the shirt."

We had the shirts made. As rodeo riders arrived in the city, Battle circulated among them. Soon he reported success. Meanwhile the program had references to an H-Bar-O cowboy named Slim being scheduled to ride on opening day. (A minor character named Slim had appeared in an early sequence of the *Bobby Benson* series, played for twenty dollars per program by Henry Fonda, temporarily down on his luck. The character hadn't appeared since. Now Slim would merely be an off-stage character. We would not even need to cast him.)

During this buildup for the rodeo, other plotting was needed. Battle had Windy and Waco go sightseeing. They marveled at the Brooklyn Bridge and bought it from a bystander for a very fair price. They quickly recouped their investment by setting up a toll barrier and collecting ten cents per car. Then they were arrested and hauled off to jail. What will happen to them? "Listen tomorrow."

Billy asked Battle, "How can we possibly get them out in time for the rodeo?"

Battle said, "You'll see." The cast was getting a bit bored with Billy's worrying.

In the next day's episode Windy and Waco came before a judge, who proved merciful. He let them off on condition that their ill-gotten wealth be donated to charity, which was promptly done in Battle's script. Meanwhile listeners were not allowed to forget Slim, who was to ride the following day.

In Madison Square Garden a large crowd was on hand. After several contests came a moment when the official public-address announcer proclaimed that the next rider in the bulldogging contest would be "Slim Cassidy of the H-Bar-O Ranch!" A wave of high-spirited screams and cheers swept over the arena. It accompanied the rider as he triumphantly achieved his task. He seemed inspired by the warm support. Afterwards other riders approached John Battle behind the scenes. "Can I get one of those shirts?" In the next few days further laurels were won by "H-Bar-O riders." The victories were duly noted and celebrated on the 6:15–6:30 programs via last-moment revisions. Erwin, Wasey and the H–O Oats people were enthralled. This was "merchandising" of the grandest sort.

Then the rodeo management intervened—in a totally unexpected way. Colonel Johnson wanted to know, "What is this ranch? Where is it? Who is this Bobby Benson?" Battle was summoned for a talk with the colonel. What the colonel learned seemed utterly bizarre to him. But he became intrigued. "Can the boy ride?"

On the final day of the rodeo, an extraordinary event—well set up by dialogue on the *Bobby Benson* series and announcements on the Madison Square Garden public-address system. Closing rituals brought a moment when the loudspeakers proclaimed: "And now, none other than Bobby Benson of the H-Bar-O Ranch!" In rode Billy as a great roar rose up from the crowd. It followed him as he twice circled the arena, waving his cowboy hat. He rode fast, in fine style. He looked ecstatic. As he reached the exit he wheeled, gave the crowd a final wave, and was gone. Watching him, I was sure it would always be one of the great moments of his life.

Shortly afterwards Billy Halop, by then fourteen years old, was cast for a major role in a Broadway production—*Dead End*, by Sidney Kingsley. He was to be the leader of a gang of slum kids, soon known as the "Dead End kids." It became a resounding success. The play presented such an authentic picture of a turbulent dockside area that the producer was rumored to have rounded up an actual gang of East Side toughs and put them to acting. *New York Times* critic Brooks Atkinson made some inquiries and corrected the rumor in his column: "Billy Halop, as the leader of the mob, is Bobby Benson of radio, famous these many years." Atkin-

Billy Halop as Bobby Benson, "Little Boss" of the H–O ("H-Bar-O") Ranch, 1935. (State Historical Society of Wisconsin)

son praised him—and the play—extravagantly.* When I myself went to see it, I felt that Billy's part was totally at odds with his nature, but that he carried it off like a trouper. He shouted, blustered, threatened with the best. His voice had changed. For years thereafter he was known as "leader of the Dead End kids."

Bobby Benson went off the air, to return later with a different Bobby.

---

* *New York Times*, October 29, 1935.

The ranch was renamed the B-Bar-B Ranch and won other sponsors. Peter Dixon still wrote it. John Battle was reported to have moved to Hollywood, becoming a writer for the Disney studio. *Dead End*, after two years on Broadway, became the movie *Dead End*, a Goldwyn smash hit of 1937. A studio release announced that "prospective Public Enemy No. 1 of the Dead End kids" would again be Billy Halop, "better known among his own generation as Bobby Benson." The release added: "When he appeared on Colonel Johnson's rodeo as a special added attraction in Madison Square Garden he was greeted with more penetrating whistles than even the bronco riders." This became a burgeoning studio legend. A later imaginative release had it that Colonel Johnson had been so impressed by the boy's virtuoso riding in the rodeo that he presented Billy Halop with a horse.* Hollywood's *Dead End* generated clones with such titles as *Angels With Dirty Faces*, *Crime School*, *Little Tough Guy*, and *They Made Me a Criminal*, always "with the Dead End kids." Billy's parents joined him in California. Florence married a Hollywood agent. Billy remained leader of the toughs. A Universal Pictures release said that Billy Halop "has played nothing but 'tough kids' on the screen but has never been in a fight in his life." With the coming of war, the genre vanished, replaced by war movies. After that Billy's name seldom appeared in the news. I read that he had joined the Signal Corps; after the war, that he had married an actress, Helen Tupper. Seven months later they were reported to have divorced. In 1954 he was reported jailed on a drunk charge after calling the West Los Angeles police station threatening suicide. In the late 1960s a radio series titled *Whatever Became Of . . .* (later followed by a series of books of the same title) featured an item on Billy Halop. He was reported to have become a "registered nurse specializing in pediatrics. . . . He still would like to act but turns down parts which still identify him as a Dead End kid." In another interview, he said that he would like to own and run a ranch.

In the early 1970s, shortly before I retired from Columbia University, I had a phone call from him. He was in New York; I invited him to come to my office for a chat. I hardly recognized him. He was thinner, wore steel-rimmed glasses, and was rather stooped. I asked what he was doing and he said, "Nothing much." He just thought he'd like to see me again. We reminisced.

---

* Halop file, New York Public Library theatre collection.

In 1974 he told a *National Enquirer* reporter that he had had no work for ten months. He had joined Alcoholics Anonymous. He was almost broke, living at a friend's house, and driving a 1962 Ford convertible.* In 1976 he was reported to have died in his sleep on November 9 at the age of 56. Obituaries appeared in *Variety*, the *New York Times*, and many other papers. I felt sure that the death had not been wholly involuntary.

* *National Enquirer*, October 12, 1974.

PEARL S. BUCK

"All of life is a foreign country."
—Jack Kerouac

Rumor had it that Erwin, Wasey & Company's partners were at odds. To quash the rumor, the company announced a unity dinner, with all employees invited. Big plans were afoot. I was not well known to top agency people, but they were aware of me as someone who spent most of his time at network studios. So it must have seemed logical to ask me to arrange entertainment for the dinner. I felt flattered but perplexed. It occurred to me to ask The Voice of Experience (an agency success story of the moment) to record a fifteen-minute program in his regular format, with "desperate" appeals for advice from various top agency people. We would use initials, not names. To prepare the "problems" I visited secretaries of various account executives and found them delighted to help; they suggested a range of annoyances relating to office routine, home, hobbies, and client relations. The Voice too was ready to cooperate; he recorded the program in his CBS studio after a broadcast.

The dinner, at a downtown hotel, was splendid, and included toasts to a glowing future. Then my recording came on the p.a. system. I hardly knew what to expect. Again and again, the "letters" drew salvos of laughter, as did the "comforting" replies by The Voice. At times the laughter was boisterous, even savage; we had clearly touched raw nerves. I was worried, but reassured by comments afterwards. With a chuckle, many people said it was "great." I sensed I had acquired a new standing among agency people. The banquet was pronounced a success. But a few weeks later came word that one of the agency's partners, Arthur Kudner, was leaving to form a new agency, Arthur Kudner, Inc., taking with him such crucial accounts as Buick, Goodyear, Fisher Body, National Distillers, and Macfadden Publications. To his new agency Kudner decided to take *with him Charlie Gannon (he became a vice president), and Gannon took me. Ensconced in a glossy corner office on the thirty-second floor of Radio City's new International Building, I went right on directing the* True Story Court of Human Relations. *I was also assigned to a short series sponsored by Goodyear during the 1936 presidential campaign, based on the* Literary Digest *poll. It featured conservative commentator John B. Kennedy, who on each program reported the magazine's accumulating evidence (based on telephone surveys) that FDR would be routed by Alf Landon. The agency people were ecstatic over the prospect; many would crowd into the control room to relish the latest figures. In November, when FDR carried all states except Maine and Vermont, the* Literary Digest *folded. (Its problem: many FDR supporters didn't have telephones.) At Kudner business went on as usual.*

One day the following spring Gannon called me into his office. He explained that Kudner was about to move him to higher duty—New Business. Gannon's thought was that I should move into his slot. By now, he observed, I knew all about studio activity and should be ready to take over at the office, looking after the clients. I went to my apartment and ruminated. I was appalled. For the first time I faced the question of where this work was taking me.

Soon afterwards I resigned, went to a lake in Maine, slept, and read books. My younger brother Victor joined me. He was trying to start a career as an artist. He was outraged about the Spanish Civil War and events in China and Ethiopia. We did a lot of talking.

At Maranacook, Maine, in August, a telegram arrived: "CALL ME UNIVERSITY 4 3200 EXTENSION 502 TODAY 1:30 OR TOMORROW 1:30 IN REGARD TO TEACHING RADIO COURSE AT COLUMBIA UNIVERSITY NEXT FALL. REVERSE CHARGES. HATCHER HUGHES." I phoned him, and a day later left for New York.

Professor Hatcher Hughes, winner of the 1924 Pulitzer Prize for his play *Hell-Bent for Heaven*, was in charge of a group of Columbia University drama courses. He had been persuaded by a young production man on the staff of the Rudy Vallee variety hour—*Vallee Varieties*, produced on NBC by the J. Walter Thompson advertising agency for Fleischmann's Yeast—to let him teach a course on radio writing. It was announced in a 1937 fall catalogue. In August the young man informed Hughes that he— and the whole *Vallee Varieties* staff—were being transferred from New

York to Hollywood, a more fruitful locale for guest stars. Hughes, who had never taken an interest in radio, was baffled as to where to turn. He happened to live in the same Columbia University apartment house as the Barnouws and had heard that someone in our family had something to do (he wasn't sure what) with radio. He inquired about my whereabouts and sent the telegram.

I had never had a high opinion of how-to courses, yet it seemed worth a go. I myself had written very little for radio (writing mainly in emergencies) but I felt I had learned the requirements of a producible script. My parents were delighted with the change in the wind. They saw it as at least a step toward respectability. My father thought I might, while teaching a course or two, take up graduate study. I thought so too.

My attitude toward writing courses changed rapidly. The quality of the students was one factor. I also discovered that it was an auspicious time to start a course on radio. Though advertising agencies and their clients controlled the choicest hours—as I knew too well—something of interest was happening in the other hours, the unsold periods, which still comprised more than half the schedule. The networks had for years filled these with miscellaneous music ground out by staff musicians. Economy fillers of this sort were called "sustaining programs." But network leaders were becoming alarmed over the rising tide of denunciations, especially from government and academia, describing radio as a "pawnshop" (Senator Burton K. Wheeler), a "huckstering orgy" (Lee de Forest), a "pollution of the air" (Senator Harry Hatfield), a "sickness in the national culture" (Dean Thomas Brenner, University of Illinois). The powerful Senator Robert F. Wagner of New York had even introduced a bill calling for cancellation of all existing station licenses to set the stage for a whole new allocation of channels under new priorities—a New Deal in radio. The zeal of the early FDR days favored its passage, and in fact it came close to passage—too close for network comfort. It seemed to be a time for drastic action.

CBS saw in the unsold periods an opportunity to create a new impression without upsetting lucrative business. A significant CBS move was the creation in 1936 of its *Columbia Workshop*, a series that invited writers to experiment with the medium. It was announced as "not available for sponsorship." Among the first to respond to CBS's "workshop" invitation was Archibald MacLeish, who sent in a "verse play for radio" titled *The Fall of the City* (1937). It violated all accepted wisdom about what radio could do. Broadcast by CBS from a New York armory with masses of New York City College students contributing crowd effects, and narrated by a little-known young actor, Orson Welles, it warned against movements like Hitler's, which a number of prominent Americans saw as "the wave of the future." When Hitler marched into Vienna shortly afterwards, taking it over without firing a shot, the MacLeish play seemed in retrospect a work of prophecy. MacLeish followed this triumph with a manifesto published as a preface to the printed play, calling on poets to recognize the wonders of this new medium. He asked whether they were really satisfied with "the thin little books to lie on the parlor tables." He told them the poet could, via radio, once more speak to the many instead of the few.

Other poets responded—Stephen Vincent Benét, Alfred Kreymborg, and later many others. Norman Corwin, just hired by CBS as a production man, turned playful radio poet with *The Plot to Overthrow Christmas* (1938) and an angry one in *They Fly Through the Air With the Greatest of Ease* (1939)—clearly referring to Mussolini's aviators in Ethiopia and Spain, one of whom had compared the beauty of a bomb's landing to "a rose unfolding." These ventures, low-budget successes, won Corwin a larger CBS budget to create an Americana variety hour, *The Pursuit of Happiness*, which drew a wide spectrum of contributions from writers known and unknown. CBS followed this by scheduling *Twenty-six By Corwin* (1941), a move unprecedented for radio in putting the spotlight squarely on the writer—who also directed. NBC countered with *Arch Oboler's Plays*, likewise featuring a writer-director, who had won attention with bravura science fiction on the late-evening series *Lights Out*.

All such activities influenced students joining my classes. A high school English teacher in Brooklyn, Bernard Malamud, was one of my earliest registrants and got an A. I recommended him to a producer, which seemed to amaze Malamud. (When his novel *The Natural* appeared, it sidetracked his temporary interest in radio.) The following year brought Eslanda Robeson, scholarly and articulate wife of the great singer Paul Robeson. He had just scored a resounding success (November 1939) on Corwin's *Pursuit of Happiness* series, introducing "Ballad for Americans," submitted by Earl Robinson and John Latouche. The flood of admiring letters had prompted CBS to schedule a rebroadcast (1940), and she felt that her husband had a splendid career awaiting him in radio. The problem was how to present him; she planned to work on possible for-

Columbia class gets CBS studio demonstration, 1939. The author is at left, and in the last row, second from right, is Dorothy Beach, later Mrs. Barnouw. Note: CBS's WABC, New York, was later renamed WCBS. (Courtesy CBS)

mats. At the moment, the future looked encouraging to the Robesons— and to me.

One day, in a telephone call, a pleasant secretarial voice asked whether I would be available to have lunch with Pearl Buck. Scarcely believing, I murmured that I would, and noted the details. The lunch was to be the following Monday at noon, at the office of her publisher (and husband) Richard J. Walsh.

What could it be about? Was it a hoax? Pearl Buck was, at this time, at the zenith of the literary world. In 1938 she had won the Nobel Prize for literature, having earlier won the Pulitzer Prize and numerous other honors for her first novel, *The Good Earth*. Though born in the United States, she had spent most of her life in China with her missionary parents, talking Chinese more often than English, playing with Chinese children, thinking of herself as Chinese. They, in turn, seemed to accept her as one of them. They sometimes asked if her pale color was the result of too much soap. Immersed in Chinese village life and lore, she had eventually returned to the United States bursting with stories and with the manuscript of *The Good Earth*. Its publication in 1932 made her at once a world celebrity. Along with its sequels it was read throughout the world in innumerable translations. She shunned the limelight. Overwhelmed by invitations to speak, she seldom complied. All such requests were carefully screened by husband/publisher Walsh. Why was this extraordinary lady inviting me to lunch?

The special quality of her fame was epitomized by the Will Rogers episode. He had won celebrity as a homespun philosopher. He had starred in the *Ziegfeld Follies* delivering one-liners—often political—while twirling a lasso, and he was later given a box on the front page of the *New York Times* and other papers, which millions were said to read even before turning to the sports or financial sections. Books were scarcely a Will Rogers domain, yet one day his box read:

Mr. Rogers Turns Book Critic and Highly Recommends One

Don't tell me we got people that can read and they haven't read Pearl Buck's great book on China, *The Good Earth*. It's not only the greatest book about a people ever written but the best book of our generation. Even in China, the Europeans and the Chinese say it's absolutely true, and there is few books written about people where they say it's good themselves. I had an engagement to fly up and meet her but it stormed that day so I missed the treat. So go get this and read it. It will keep you out of some devilment and learn you all about China, and you'll thank me.

Yours, Will Rogers.

America is said to have stampeded to the bookstore. Each new award renewed the stampede.

Arriving at the office of Richard Walsh, I discovered that the lunch party consisted of Pearl Buck, Walsh, and me. We sat in the board room, each with a sandwich and a salad.

Pearl Buck had a relaxed, easy-moving manner. She was handsome in a wholesome way, with a somewhat ample figure. After only a few preliminaries she came quickly to the point. She told me she would like to register in my course in radio writing at Columbia University. Would this be permissible?

I could think of no basis to declare her unqualified. I said yes, it would be fine. She then said she hated a lot of fuss and did not want to be the center of attention. Could this possibly be avoided?

I felt that if she registered simply as Mrs. R. Walsh, it might solve the problem. I suggested also that someone else might be willing to go through the registration line for her. She appreciated this idea. (The university had no IDs at this time.) She then explained that the U.S. state department had asked her to write a series of programs to be beamed by shortwave to China, where the Chinese-Japanese War was in full fury. She wanted to do this, but not until she had studied radio and had confidence in what she was doing. She added that she was fascinated by the medium and hoped later to do a series for broadcast in the United States, to get Americans thinking more about Asia.

I explained that my writing course had been split into two sections, one on Monday evenings, the other on Tuesday evenings. She said Monday was not possible for her but Tuesday would be fine, except that she would have to miss the first class. This seemed to worry her excessively; she said she meant to work hard and would attend regularly. I reassured her, telling her that I would send her material that would bring her up to date.

My mother volunteered to go through the registration procedure as "Mrs. R. Walsh" and carried off the deception without a hitch—to her own great delight. No one else was told about the Pearl Buck enrollment— except the girl who had just become my wife and who had likewise been an early student. Dorothy (Dotty) Beach was a Vermont girl who had won extraordinary teenage successes as a dancer and singer and become a two-year scholarship student of Metropolitan Opera diva Louise Homer, but she had decided to leave all that behind her. When she registered she was interviewing theater celebrities over WINS, New York. We began a fifty-year adventure together.

For me, the plunge into marriage reflected a decisive change in my outlook on life. My advertising agency years had often had a look of success, but had sapped my self-esteem. My Columbia earnings were a fraction of my former salary, but things were happening. My first-year course notes had quickly evolved into a *Handbook of Radio Writing* that Little, Brown & Co. had decided to publish and that was soon adopted in radio writing courses springing up throughout the country.* It was

---

* Erik Barnouw, *Handbook of Radio Writing* (Boston: Little, Brown, 1939).

crammed with excerpts from scripts that I had picked up in NBC and CBS studios, abandoned by actors after broadcasts. The novelty of the book, giving a close-up of the flood of programming disgorged by radio, won it surprising attention. "For career-seeking cubs and ink-stained old-sters," said *Time*, "U.S. bookstalls last week had a handbook compiled by a radio veteran . . . Holland-born, Princeton-built ('29), author, drama-tist, summer-stock trouper who might have become a matinee idol (*see cut*) had he not chosen backstage radio." To my surprise, this brought me commissions to write scripts—for series that especially interested me. George Kondolf of the defunct Rochester stock company, whom I had served as assistant stage manager a few years earlier, had now become producer of *Cavalcade of America*, sponsored by Du Pont, and was estab-lished at its agency, Batten, Barton, Durstine & Osborn. He invited me to write an episode on Benjamin Franklin as diplomat in Paris, a richly satisfying assignment that was soon followed by others. This series was considered less "commercial" than other sponsored series, being con-cerned with company image rather than merchandising. It seemed to be a constant celebration of good citizenship. Then Norman Corwin at CBS, having written a glowing "jacket statement" for my textbook, invited me to join his *Pursuit of Happiness* staff as a writer and editor. I had not dreamed that a textbook could produce such results. It even had an im-pact at Columbia's graduate school, which was willing to accept the book as my master's essay. (However, I never completed the degree.)

I sent Pearl Buck a copy, along with items related to the course. A reply came from the farmhouse she had bought in Perkasie, Pennsylvania.

> Thank you very much for the registration card and I am looking for-ward with the greatest eagerness to come to your class. . . . I have read the book twice and found it of great interest, and have been reading everything else you sent and that I could get my hands on besides.

The Pearl Buck development was both exhilarating and nerve-wracking. The Tuesday class turned out to be a lively and articulate group, but as its second meeting approached, I kept wondering whether Pearl Buck would actually turn up. I began to doubt it. Yet at the last moment, there she was. With hat pulled down tightly over much of her face she walked quickly to a seat in the back of the room. She became the most punctilious student I ever had.

Pearl S. Buck, the most punctilious student enrolled in Radio Writing u2, 1940. (Courtesy Edgar Walsh)

I set up a series of deadlines when students were expected to hand in a script, synopsis, or series proposal. She never missed a deadline. I often spent part of a class reading and commenting on material handed in, but hesitated to do this with Pearl Buck's scripts. All dealt with Asia—China, Korea, or Japan—and the dialogue often had the quasi-biblical sound of *The Good Earth*. I was afraid a class reading might expose her presence. Instead I mailed her a detailed critique on each script, generally focusing on radio technique and form. On each occasion she followed by promptly handing in a revision, always marked "corrected copy." She was an avid experimenter. Radio was turning away from theatrical all-dialogue drama to more narrative forms, and she responded enthusiastically to this. In fact, I began to feel that her talent was in narrative rather than in dialogue.

I became aware of how rigorously her life was organized. She said she began each working day by reading her mail and dictating replies. By nine o'clock she was ready for her writing. First she would read what she had written the day before and "correct" it. By nine-thirty or ten she would be ready for new work. This apparently flowed out with extraordinary speed—perhaps too readily for her own good.

I learned much later that she was also devoting regular time, attention, and funds to developing a home for retarded children, prompted by her experience with her own retarded child by her first marriage. She had been married to the missionary Lossing Buck, a renowned expert on Chinese agriculture. The marriage had not been a happy one and had ended in divorce.

One evening a week was now reserved for movies, which she and Mr. Walsh always attended together. I began to realize that although the Nobel award and the style of The Good Earth had given her a quasi-classic image, she was obsessed with popular media. As a young child she had read and reread all of Dickens, but somewhat clandestinely. She had found a set in a corner of the missionary quarters assigned to the family, but it was not considered suitable reading. The recommended reading was the Bible (which her father was forever translating into an improved Chinese version) and the Christian Observer and other church publications. Her own first published work appeared in the Christian Observer, which came from Louisville, Kentucky. Her contribution began, "I am a little girl six years old. I live in China." She told of her two younger brothers who had died early and gone to their "real home." It was titled "Our Real Home in Heaven." Her mother was too exhausted with missionary and wifely duties to keep a close watch over Pearl, while her father came and went on missionary travels, so she spent time with her amah, who often took her to low-brow Chinese theatrical shows in which the girl took unending delight, enveloped in the waves of response from the crowd.

She told me that when she first came back to the United States and entered a movie theater, she felt almost suffocated—by the odor of people whose diet relied heavily on beef and milk. The Chinese had often spoken to her of the smell of most Westerners. The overwhelming consciousness of this beef/milk smell had disappeared after some months in the United States; she said she could no longer notice it. She had become Westernized.

Columbia University never learned that a Nobel Prize author was registered in my radio writing course. We kept the faith. But one curious incident occurred. Late in the course she wrote me about having to miss a class because of some unavoidable matter. She wanted to tell me this in advance because she did not want me to think her interest was flagging. Later she mentioned with amusement and delight that a member of the class had mailed her a summary of what had happened in the meeting she had missed. This student did not later speak to her about it and remained anonymous.

Pearl Buck's extremely respectful attitude toward me often seemed to me slightly unreal, or of another world. It was as though an old Chinese image of teacher and pupil controlled the situation—even though the pupil was older than the teacher. Years later, in her memoir *My Several Worlds*, she wrote:

> What else do I remember? One winter I was charmed by radio, and planned a novel written for that fine medium, so new to me then, and I went quietly to a class at Columbia taught by an excellent radio writer, and there, unknown among young men and women green to the craft, too, I learned and wrote my assignments until the professor's sharp eye picked me out, and then he told me I had learned enough and that there was no more he could teach me. I never wrote the novel, but I wrote a few radio plays during the war. . . . Meanwhile, I learned not only from the professor but from those young men and women who were my fellow students.*

The project that had brought her to Columbia—a series to be beamed to China—was duly accomplished. Under the title *America Speaks to China*, six plays were shortwaved. Written by her in English, they were translated by a Chinese specialist of the Office of War Information. She also wrote, for a war relief drive, a script titled *Will This Earth Hold?*, which I later included in an anthology I compiled for Farrar and Rinehart, *Radio Drama in Action*. It concerned an episode related to her by a traveler from China, about people in a village, hundreds or perhaps thousands of them, helping to level their entire village, homes and all, using the most primitive tools, to make a landing strip for the B-29s that were to arrive for the bombing of Japan. Its broadcast in 1944 over a New York station occasioned a distressful telegram from Pearl Buck about changes she had not authorized. Did the producers, she asked, have any right to do that?

I wrote her a long letter explaining that under the helter-skelter way in which radio had evolved, writers had been welcomed but had almost never had control over their work. It was an uncomfortable issue for

---

* Pearl Buck, *My Several Worlds* (New York: John Day, 1954), p. 458.

me, conscious as I was of how cavalierly I had treated writers during my Erwin, Wasey directing period. I was now seeing writers' problems more and more from a writer's point of view. I told her that a Radio Writers Guild had recently been formed under the aegis of the Authors League of America, with the hope of improving the situation, and mentioned that I had become active in it.

Her completion of the writing course did not end our relationship. In 1942, a few months after Pearl Harbor, she embarked on an ambitious project that would absorb energy and funds for almost a decade. At a gala at the Waldorf-Astoria attended by innumerable American and Asian notables, including Nehru—many in colorful garb—she launched the East and West Association to develop the relationship she saw as central to the future well-being of the world. She once explained to me that the Chinese symbols for *east* and *west*, when placed together, signify "good." Dotty and I attended the inaugural. Pearl Buck then asked me to serve on the public relations committee of the new association. A zealous East and West staff was soon booking visits by Asian scholars and artists to campuses and broadcasting stations and arranging special courses and seminars. After the war it began sponsoring visits by Asians to America and by Americans to Asia—at first, with considerable U.S. government encouragement and support. Pearl Buck had withdrawn from the missionary world but was more missionary than she knew.

Her East and West agenda kept expanding. *Pearl Buck: A Woman in Conflict*, the fine biography by Nora Stirling, relates how Pearl Buck was invited to Harlem to an exhibition of work by black artists, and came on images for which she was not prepared and which she found shattering— black bodies swinging from trees, charred remains of houses, bewildered faces of black children. She asked the artists to explain what these meant, and thus she found another world opening to her. During her Chinese years America had seemed to her a place of cleanliness, a place that had its problems but was surely moving toward the light. The very presence of Western missionaries in China implied that they represented a better and more enlightened world. The wrenching experience of her first Harlem visit was to have a long-range effect. At the East and West Association understanding between peoples was to mean not only between nations but between groups within nations.

She hardly knew where her widening agenda was taking her. The internationalism of wartime gave way rapidly to cold war. In this everyone was expected to take sides; the uncommitted were suspect. To Senator Joseph R. McCarthy and his cohorts, Pearl Buck's wide-ranging sympathies were suspicious in themselves. Who were these Asians being sent to our schools and imperiling our airwaves? One of McCarthy's major financial angels, the importer Alfred Kohlberg, was also the main backer of Washington's powerful China lobby, which made support of Chiang Kai-shek, as the hallowed leader who would save China, a litmus test for loyalty to the United States. Waverers on this issue (Pearl Buck was one of them) were readily assumed to be crypto-communists. To J. Edgar Hoover of the FBI, interest in Negro rights was a similar symptom. Lists of suspect individuals and organizations began to dominate government and media in the postwar years. A concert by Paul Robeson in Peeksill, New York, was turned into a violent riot by American Legion demonstrators, and in consequence he became a fixture on such lists—a case of the victim being blamed for the assault. Considered "controversial," he was no longer welcome on CBS. The name Pearl Buck likewise began to appear on lists.

My role in the East and West Association led me to mention to friends at CBS Pearl Buck's interest in writing a "novel for radio." Vice President Davidson Taylor seemed galvanized by this idea, which, as he saw it, might lead to a new era in daytime drama. But his interest cooled quickly after he had explored the matter with upper echelons.

A powerful influence in the book field was the radio series of Mary Margaret MacBride. Her interviews with authors were credited with selling books by the thousands or millions. She had a unique gift for putting authors at ease and drawing them out. They often said more than they intended to and enjoyed themselves hugely. Pearl Buck had appeared on her series. MacBride was the first network interviewer permitted to interview *ad lib*. In the early days of network broadcasting all interviews were first held away from the studio, days before a scheduled broadcast. On the basis of notes a script was then created, reviewed and edited for "policy," and finally performed "live" in a studio broadcast. MacBride's success on a local station had enabled her to short-circuit this absurd procedure, and she had acquired numerous sponsors. As the blacklists got started, sponsors occasionally mentioned people they hoped she would avoid, names they felt should not be associated with their products. Most were authors in whom she was not interested—but not all, as she confessed much later in her memoir *Out on the Air*. The advertising manager of one of the companies phoned her one day, to say he had just been coping with a delegation of indignant women, who had confronted him with a list of "suspect people" who had appeared on her series, some more than once. MacBride writes in her memoir:

> And lo, Eleanor Roosevelt led all the rest! Then Pearl Buck, Carl Van Doren, Fannie Hurst, and many more of my best friends. . . . I confess it shamefacedly . . . I finally yielded to pressure and turned down several who were on the committee's lists. . . . It is the blackest memory of my radio life.

In her memoir, MacBride's remorse seemed to be transmuted almost immediately into satisfaction as she added:

> We lost only one sponsor that I know of as a result of the witchhunt, and that place was filled at once.*

Along with witch-hunts, it was a time for self-preservation. In *My Several Worlds* Pearl Buck deplored the "strange atmosphere that has pervaded my country since 1946." It had made it impossible for the East and West Association to function, and in 1951 she reluctantly dissolved it. In later years we occasionally exchanged letters, but seldom met.

---

* M. M. MacBride, *Out on the Air* (New York: Doubleday, 1960), p. 146.

WILLIAM A. HART

"For nothing can seem foul to those who win."
—William Shakespeare

After Pearl Harbor it was musical chairs in the broadcasting field. A phone call from NBC informed me that its script editor had suddenly departed, lost to a navy commission. Would I take over, supervising the editing of all NBC public service programming? Indeed I would. A turbulent fourteen months followed. Still teaching two evenings a week, I spent my days in an office in Radio City's RCA Building at the end of a corridor of staff writers' cubicles. From here emerged dramatized series and specials on the war, its progress and home-front problems. Then suddenly . . . a phone call from the Pentagon from novelist Paul Horgan, now Major Horgan of the Army Information Branch. It had in a few months created the extraordinary Armed Forces Radio Service (AFRS), serving troops throughout the world via some three hundred outlets, some operating from Quonset huts, all receiving from the United States a weekly package of recorded programs on long-playing sixteen-inch disks. These featured all the most popular comedians, singers, and dramas, mostly drawn from network programming—an important morale factor. One major problem, said Horgan: A congressional hearing was pointing out that the legislation that created and financed the system had stipulated that "information and education" of the troops was the main purpose— so that those fighting the war would have some sense of why. Would I quickly form and head an AFRS Education Unit to supply the crucial, neglected ingredient? Indeed I would.

I moved to a seedy Washington hotel, commuting to New York weekends to be with Dotty and our first child, Jeffrey, born in 1940. Within months, working from the Pentagon, I got the unit organized, and the weekly packages of programs flown to the troops began to include in-

formational programs, some drawn from network public service series, others created within AFRS. But then, suddenly . . . VE Day brought a change. As troops streamed back from Europe, some continuing eastward for the Asian climax while others were held for U.S. duty, the Pentagon ordered all its civilian employees replaced by uniformed returnees wherever this was feasible. I resettled in New York and once more found George Kondolf entering my life. Still at Batten, Barton, Durstine & Osborn (BBD&O) producing Cavalcade of America, *he had lost its script editor to Pacific war duty. Could I take his place at least temporarily? He mentioned what seemed a grandiose salary. By all means, I said. Dotty and I were expecting a second child and contemplating a move to the suburbs, so the money would be welcome. I had not expected ever again to enter the advertising world, but here I was, at BBD&O, serving the interests of E. I. Du Pont de Nemours & Company.*

I had for years had a high regard for *Cavalcade of America*, the only continuing coast-to-coast series about U.S. history. It was a boon to history teachers, who could use it as "assigned listening." It had won many prizes such as those given annually by the Institute for Education by Radio at Ohio State University. *Cavalcade* had given me some of my earliest and most interesting freelance commissions, on such topics as Benjamin Franklin, Andrew Jackson, Thomas Edison, early railroad history, and medical subjects like Rocky Mountain spotted fever and the Children's Hospital in Boston—all helping to fill huge gaps in my knowledge of U.S. history and institutions. Each assignment had meant a feverish boning up on relevant data. I got along well with Frank Monaghan, the genial Yale historian who was the series consultant and came to New York for rehearsals, sometimes discussing script details with the writers. Now I was to become part of the program's inner machinery, more aware of its working principles. This would mean acquaintance with a shadowy figure who seemed to hover over all aspects of the series, and whom I had often heard mentioned—William A. Hart, Du Pont advertising director. In Wilmington, Delaware, he was part of a hierarchy of which the BBD&O people knew little, but when he came to New York he was The Sponsor.

When I joined the *Cavalcade* team, Kondolf mentioned that Hart had thought well of my writing. I soon found that not everyone at the agency thought well of Hart. Much time was spent anticipating Hart's objections to topics, plots, or script details, during which the epithet "that bastard" was used regularly. No identification was needed. The dislike illuminated a bizarre argument that took place soon after my arrival. Hart planned a long fishing trip and wanted Arthur Pryor Jr., head of BBD&O's radio department, to accompany him. Pryor was a true-blue company man and willing to go in the line of duty, but protested the BBD&O personnel department's assumption that this should constitute his vacation. After doing his duty he said he would need a real vacation with Mrs. Pryor, and he finally won his point. It was officially determined that a fishing trip with Hart was an ordeal rather than a holiday. The fact that a sponsor would look to his company's advertising agency to supply a fishing companion seemed to me at least curious.

Hart came from Wilmington each week for rehearsals and sat in the "sponsor's booth" with our BBD&O group, holding discussions that generally led to revisions. He exerted his authority with obvious self-assurance; everyone at BBD&O seemed hesitant to disagree with him. Hart also came for conferences at which future topics were decided. I began to realize that these sessions were the most crucial in determining the overall nature of the series. Proposals from various sources were discussed, but Hart's word was decisive. A range of taboos came into play.

One taboo was familiar to *Cavalcade* writers. On a *Cavalcade* program no shot could be fired; even the sound of an explosion was for many years taboo. This policy related to the origin of the series. In 1935 the Du Pont company had been traumatized by hearings held by Senator Gerald P. Nye of North Dakota on World War I munitions profits, which revealed that Du Pont had made 40 percent of the explosive powders used by all the Allies, earning $237,908,339.64 in war profits and sending Du Pont stock from $125 to $593. The revelations had popularized the phrase "merchants of death." Immediately after the hearings Bruce Barton of BBD&O, considered a master strategist in corporate public relations, recommended to Du Pont that it go on the air with a series on U.S. history to be titled *Cavalcade of America*, stressing idealistic aspects while ignoring all military events. *Dos* and *don't*s were carefully planned; William Hart became their custodian and interpreter. The name Du Pont would henceforth be identified—especially for youthful audiences—with explorations, inventions, and humanitarian progress. Improvements in the lot of women would be stressed, and commercials would remind listeners of the company's contributions to these via "better things for better living"—to which Hart was credited with having added the words "through chemistry."

Subsequent studies by the Psychological Corporation, commissioned by Hart, indicated that favorable opinion toward Du Pont increased significantly by the end of the 1930s—a turnaround that Bruce Barton ascribed to *Cavalcade* and nylons. The findings helped to make *Cavalcade*, with Hart at the helm, a radio perennial and later a television series, a longtime bonanza for BBD&O.

The "no shooting" rule amused writers and was in no way troublesome to them. From the start it attracted idealistic young writers like Arthur Miller and Norman Rosten, who had been fellow students at the University of Michigan. There many students had signed the Oxford Pledge never to bear arms; Miller and Rosten themselves leaned toward pacifism. Thus the public relations interests of a munitions manufacturer dovetailed for the moment with the social concerns of young writers of liberal and even leftist bent. Like-minded writers who similarly became *Cavalcade* contributors included Arthur Arent, Norman Corwin, Robert Anderson, and Peter Lyon—who all became my friends and whom I considered among radio's best writers. Lyon was among several who had come to *Cavalcade* from the *March of Time* radio series, which likewise required writers with a historical and social sense. Occasionally *Cavalcade* recruited more celebrated writers for specific assignments: Robert Sherwood, Maxwell Anderson, Carl Sandburg, Stephen Vincent Benét, and others. All seemed ready to answer the call.

As *Cavalcade* editor at BBD&O, I discovered that topic selection involved other taboos of which writers tended to be unaware, inasmuch as writers were never involved in the selection process. The taboos were not codified but seemed clear in the mind of William Hart, who could amplify them as needed. The BBD&O people understood the general pattern but could still be surprised. Anything to do with unions, strikes, or labor relations was out of the question. I should assume, I was smilingly advised at the agency, that American history stopped around 1880 except for science and the advancement of women. In fact, the improved lot of women was looked on mainly as an achievement of science.

Another restriction concerned race. In its first ten years *Cavalcade* had never focused on a black leader. This had been mentioned by the agency as a possible Du Pont p.r. problem, but the matter had always been shunted aside. In 1948, when the series would finally take the step, the leader chosen would be Booker T. Washington, who felt the Negro should "keep his place" until better educated.

Still other mind-set problems came to light. In a meeting I suggested that the Tennessee Valley Authority might make an interesting topic as a science and engineering achievement. A word from Kondolf let me know I had made a mistake: that was "socialism." A similar issue arose in my own script on Rocky Mountain spotted fever and the development of a vaccine for it. Professor Monaghan, at the urging of a doctor involved in these events, said we should mention the role of the U.S. Public Health Service in this breakthrough—to the intense annoyance of Hart, who said that *Cavalcade* had not been created to promote socialism.

Andrew Carnegie, with emphasis on his worldwide funding of libraries, was at one time approved as a topic. Carnegie had once said that there was nothing wrong with getting rich, but it was a sin to die rich. When this comment turned up in the script, the topic was promptly scuttled. Hart's curious explanation: "People might think we're trying to defend rich people."

It was often difficult to distinguish sponsor and agency views. In an agency discussion about possible recruits to the staff, the impressive writer Morton Wishengrad was mentioned, but a BBD&O executive said that hiring him would not be fair to Wishengrad himself. I was puzzled. To *Wishengrad?* Yes: as a Jew, he would not be able to work on the Du Pont account, so his career would be blocked. This seemed to be the standard BBD&O view in 1945—although not long afterwards a Jew became president of Du Pont.

All such restrictions seemed to be regarded as consistent with a positive, hopeful outlook on American society. History was not looked on as a probing of problems, but as a celebration. It dealt with heroes. A program generally ended with the Donald Voorhees orchestra rising to a triumphant crescendo; the words should justify the crescendo. I recall a script comment from Arthur Pryor: "It needs more come-to-Jesus."

It puzzled me that I had not, before joining the *Cavalcade* staff, noted how selective its version of American history was. Like other listeners, I had experienced it one program at a time, and each was likely to be impressive, often moving, and—as certified by Professor Monaghan— reasonably accurate. I could now see that the series added up to an extremely distorted and misleading panorama of American history. Should I be worried about this—about all we were *not* doing? How could I affect

the situation? It was clear that schools and teachers embraced the cele-
bratory history. As "assigned listening" it offered no political risks. The
series still kept winning prizes. And liberal, idealistic writers continued
to accept its commissions, usually with alacrity. *Cavalcade*'s roster of
writers seemed to me to epitomize the high status it had won.

Ironically, this roster became a target in the postwar period, as groups
armed with lists went into action. Typical was American Business Consultants, three former FBI agents who in 1947 began offering their services
to sponsors as "security" consultants. Their lists of suspected subversives
(*commies, fellow travelers, dupes*—the terms were used interchangeably)
were bolstered by "citations," for example quotes from the *Daily Worker*
to the effect that a listee had once attended a rally for the International
Brigade in the Spanish Civil War, or against segregation in the U.S. armed
forces, or against the FBI itself. Such citations were all considered tip-offs
that, wittingly or unwittingly, listees were doing the work of "international communism" and were, for all practical purposes, "traitors." The
consultancy business apparently thrived, generating rival groups with
ever longer lists. At a Radio Writers Guild meeting I learned of a group
claiming that *Cavalcade* and BBD&O were particular hotbeds of subversives. This seemed so preposterous that I could hardly imagine anyone
taking it seriously.

When I had been at BBD&O only a few months, dramatic news came
to me from Columbia University. I was proposed as a full-time faculty
member, to teach two courses and supervise others, dealing not only
with radio but also with television. Dr. James Rowland Angell, former
president of Yale, had become NBC public service counselor and had persuaded NBC to propose a Columbia University–NBC teaching program,
to include workshop courses at NBC studios in both radio and television.
Television had been dormant during the war, so a paucity of trained personnel loomed as a problem for the months and years to come, which
were expected to be boom years in both media. My background at both
Columbia and NBC had apparently made me the choice to supervise this
venture. I explained to Kondolf that this was an opportunity I could not
ignore, and he agreed. But he wanted me to continue as a regular *Cavalcade* contributor, which I welcomed. In taking a larger academic role,
it seemed to me important to remain in evidence on the air. I at once
agreed to write a program about President Millard Fillmore, a subject that
for some reason was important to William Hart. I knew absolutely noth-

ing about Fillmore; I still felt embarrassingly ignorant on many phases of American history, and the Fillmore assignment was another chance to fill a gap.

As I began my Columbia tasks I completed the Fillmore script, titled *The Oath*, and saw it winding its way, via occasional conferences and revisions, through approvals by Monaghan, BBD&O, and Du Pont. I learned that William Powell had agreed to play Fillmore. The program was scheduled to be produced in Buffalo, which was Fillmore's home town and also the site of a Du Pont factory. Thus the broadcast would be an occasion for intense public relations activity—the reason for Hart's close involvement. The broadcast would take place on the stage of a Buffalo theater, with many city dignitaries and hundreds of Du Pont employees as an invited audience. Afterwards there would be a gala reception at a country club. High-level Du Pont executives would be on hand. It was emphasized that my presence was expected at the Buffalo rehearsals, the broadcast, and the follow-up reception. A hotel suite would be provided. I assured Kondolf—and Hart—that I would be there.

Then a complication arose. The Radio Writers Guild, in which I had become deeply involved (a nominating committee had even proposed me as a candidate for president), was to meet the day after the broadcast; I could be there by taking a New York Central sleeper scheduled to leave Buffalo a few hours after the Fillmore broadcast. In the light of this schedule, it seemed advisable for me to skip the country club reception. Others of the BBD&O group and cast were staying overnight to attend this affair, but I considered this an added amenity rather than a duty. I mentioned this thought to Kondolf, who seemed apprehensive. He felt he must tell Hart. During a rehearsal he did discuss it with Hart, who appeared to take the news in stride. But Hart insisted that I at least appear at the country club for an hour or so, after which they would get me to the train in plenty of time. He would see to it personally, he said. Kondolf, always the pragmatist, felt I should go along with this. It seemed to be a crucial client-relations matter.

Before the broadcast I checked my suitcase at the station. I was nervous about the arrangements but Hart kept reassuring me. After the broadcast we were all dispatched to the country club in a series of limousines. At the club a lavish buffet supper unfolded. An orchestra played. At one point I asked Hart whether a taxi might be ordered for me, but he would not hear of it. "I'll take you myself. We'll see that you get to your meeting!" As he moved about, surveying the event, checking details, I could hardly believe that he would find time for my problem. But he kept offering assurances. He seemed to be in a surprisingly affable mood.

Finally I was notified that Mr. Hart was ready. I was led to a driveway where a limousine was waiting, with Hart himself at the wheel. I got in. He had the air of a gracious host. We sped toward town with small talk en route: he had been delighted with the broadcast; William Powell, in spite of failing health (and a recent colostomy), had been splendid. We pulled to a stop at the station with time to spare. He reached in front of me to open the door, and I got out. When I turned to thank him he called out, "Remember me to your communist friends!" and slammed the door. He drove away quickly. It was the last glimpse I was to have of William Hart. As it turned out, *The Oath* was my final *Cavalcade* commission: a housecleaning was under way.

LYNN FONTANNE

"I am acquainted with no immaterial
sensuality so delightful as good acting."
—*Lord Byron*

*Columbia University had become my base of operation, and this began
a wonderfully fruitful period. The NBC–Columbia University joint cur-
riculum was an almost fail-proof arrangement, which would continue for
half a dozen years. Hundreds of returning GIs, with the blessings of the
GI Bill of Rights, poured into the courses intent on reconnoitering the
coming media world, revolutionized by television, FM, and the tape recorder. Supervising, I too learned. Like our students, I was unsure where
my future lay.*

*Meanwhile I wrote. Teaching and writing formed a rich combination,
each reinforcing the other. Phone calls and commissions no longer came
to me from* Cavalcade of America, *but they came steadily from* Theatre Guild on the Air, *sponsored by U.S. Steel. Though this was another
BBD&O corporate client, the series was produced differently—by an independent producer rather than by the advertising agency itself. Major
production from advertising agency offices had become overly cumber-
some (and was a questionable arrangement to begin with). Increasingly,
production was delegated to another entity at a package price. Thus
the venerable Theatre Guild, Broadway's most patrician institution, had
turned "packager." For a time it was treated with utmost deference by
agency and sponsor. The list-bearing harpies carried little weight at the
Theatre Guild. The driving force of the list-bearers came mainly from
makers of consumer goods, many of whom feared boycotts at department
stores and supermarkets.*

Theatre Guild on the Air *had begun in September 1945. Soon afterwards I had been commissioned to adapt* The Silver Cord, *to be broadcast
with Ralph Bellamy and Estelle Winwood. Then came* Little Women *with*

Katherine Hepburn, Our Town *with Thornton Wilder,* I Remember Mama *with Mady Christians, and* Mary, Mary Quite Contrary *with Gertrude Lawrence. Then, wonder of wonders, three programs with Alfred Lunt and Lynn Fontanne. During school years I had often stood in line at Gray's Drugstore on Times Square, where vacant seats to Broadway shows were sold at discount prices in the final hours, hoping above all for a Lunt-Fontanne ticket. Even now, I was awestruck.*

The year was 1947. Television had begun, but radio still held the nation spellbound. I was asked to adapt *The Great Adventure* by Arnold Bennett. A telephone summons said I should see Armina Marshall about it immediately. In the rotation worked out by the three Theatre Guild partners, it would be her turn to supervise. She explained that this was a crucial assignment. The play had been scheduled at the suggestion of Lynn Fontanne, who had seen it in England as a young girl just starting her career. It had apparently made an everlasting impression on her, still vivid after many decades. All her life she had been determined some day to perform *The Great Adventure,* playing the role created by the extraordinary music hall idol Miss Wish Wynne. Arnold Bennett himself, in his journal, had referred to Wynne as a "genius." Now, a half-century later, Fontanne had apparently decided it was her time for this role. Armina Marshall wanted me to keep all this in mind as I approached my task. It gave me a somewhat uncomfortable sense of responsibility, and I was glad I had several months to do the job.

I read the play that evening. My first reaction was one of consternation. It seemed creaky, static, and unsatisfying in its resolution. Finding that it was based on Bennett's own novel, *Buried Alive,* dramatized by Bennett himself, I got a copy of the novel from the university library. On reading it, I felt much better. It has action missing from the play and, moreover, an entirely different ending. In both versions of the story a world-honored painter, whose spreading fame had made him more and more a recluse, is apparently interred in Westminster Abbey amid all the pageantry that is his due. Actually his valet, who happened to have a heart attack in his master's bedroom, had been interred in the Abbey while the painter himself, fleeing the dreaded hubbub, is sheltered by a warmhearted widow in Putney, who begins to cure him of his shyness. The artist now lives in blissful obscurity. Eventually, enterprising reporters get wind of what has happened; in the play the scandal is successfully quashed to avoid embarrassment to the British Empire, but in the novel it is not and leads on to a far more amusing climax.

I asked the Theatre Guild if I could use material from the novel. The first answer was no; it would involve a different copyright owner and new, probably difficult negotiations. But I happened to notice in the Columbia library copy of *Buried Alive* that there was no copyright notice. The novel had apparently been published in the United States without copyright protection. It represented a period in publishing history when the United States refused to recognize international copyright agreements and had become the bad boy of the literary world, thriving on piracy. As a result, European classics had become widely available in the United States and had played a part in the gentrification of the U.S. middle class. In any case *Buried Alive*, published without copyright, was in the public domain so far as the United States was concerned. Theatre Guild counsel studied the matter and saw no legal reason to bar me from using it along with the play, for which rights had been negotiated by the Guild.

What evolved was an adaptation that used passages from the play but a structure more like that of the novel—a loose structure suitable to radio. In radio, changes of scene cost nothing. I even used a radio device that had seldom been used on the stage: first-person narration passages for both Lunt and Fontanne, so that parts of the story would be experienced from his point of view, others from hers. I realized it would be a new departure for the Lunts.

Some weeks after I delivered the script to the Theatre Guild, an urgent call came from Homer Fickett, director of the *Theatre Guild on the Air* broadcasts. He came straight to the point: "I think we're in trouble." The Lunts, just back from Genesee Depot, their Wisconsin retreat, had read the script. Lynn Fontanne wanted to discuss it with us. We were to go for a breakfast meeting the following Sunday at the Lunts' East Side apartment.

Homer Fickett, a monumentally calm director, was accustomed to crises and approached the Sunday meeting with bonhomie. Breakfast was served on a low table in front of a fireplace, with a fire going. Homer and I sat on a couch facing the Lunts, who occupied a similar couch. We had orange juice, eggs Benedict, toast, jam and coffee. Homer quickly got the Lunts reminiscing, and this became what seemed to me a dazzling performance, not unlike the Lunts' stage performances. They constantly interrupted each other, teased each other, talked through each other's speeches (as they did on the stage), while always allowing the other's key lines to come through clearly. They constantly supplemented (and amended) each other's account in a way that involved both rivalry and partnership, and always wit and warmth. It was unforgettable.

As I watched, hardly saying a word, I kept wondering about the script. After more than an hour of performance, it seemed we should either talk business or leave. So I asked Lynn Fontanne if there was something she wanted to say about the script. She shook her head and smiled reminiscently. She mentioned having just reread the original play. After a while she said: "I was wrong; I thought I remembered a play. I didn't at all. I remembered a performance." She then said my script would do very well indeed.

On that note we departed. The Lunts seemed, to our astonishment, to be accepting the script as written. And that is how it went into rehearsal. Since the Lunts had approved, no one at the Theatre Guild dared tamper with it. During the following week I had the amazing experience of seeing it take shape in the Lunt-Fontanne manner. On the first day, when lesser members of the cast tended to give their all, to show what they could do, the Lunts held back, seeming to *think* their way through the scenes rather than to act. A U.S. Steel representative, a dignified gentleman known to me only as Mr. MacDonald, usually came on the first day to sit in the sponsor's booth and listen to a run-through. He was taken aback by the unspectacular Lunt-Fontanne reading and had to be reassured by Armina Marshall that they would indeed be magnificent when the time came. Mr. MacDonald accepted the reassurance. He seldom disputed the Theatre Guild partners on any matter relating to drama. (Already a television devotee, he was a *Kukla, Fran and Ollie* fan; the Theatre Guild had arranged to have a television set on hand in the green room, so that he would not miss his favorite show.)

At later rehearsals the cast worked without executive observers, and it became clear that the Lunts had been working things out in minute detail at home. Especially in the Lunt-Fontanne scenes, a marvelously intricate interlacing of their performances evolved day by day. Narration passages were a new experience for them. Lunt at first commented that they made him feel "lonely," but after a while he seemed to enjoy them. When the broadcast came, the acting seemed to me the most brilliant I had heard on radio. In response to demand, the Theatre Guild rescheduled the program two years later, with the Lunts repeating their performance live. Broadcasts from recordings were still taboo at NBC and CBS.

During this two-year period, while the Lunts were appearing on Broadway in *O Mistress Mine* (which I would adapt after its Broadway run for a *Theatre Guild on the Air* broadcast), I received a letter with the return address "Empire Theater". That is where *O Mistress Mine* was playing. The impeccably typed letter, signed by Lynn Fontanne, read:

> Empire Theatre
> New York City
> May 5, 1947

Dear Mr. Barnouw:

We have often received a letter from Mrs. Bennett over the years asking if we wouldn't care to revive "The Great Adventure" and it has always seemed to us as it did when we came to do the radio script, that it was a little anemic for the kind of thing that is expected now in the theatre. But since your wonderful revision of the script and your knowledge of exactly what to do with it, I have been thinking ever since that if you would consent to try and write a whole play, ignoring Bennett's dramatization and taking your play directly from the book, you could do a magnificent job of it for present-day consumption.

If this would interest you and we get the consent of Mrs. Bennett, then you can see Mr. John C. Wilson and have a talk with him about what financial arrangements you would like to make. If you do agree to it, I would be very much obliged if you will keep the proposition a secret, as I am doing this off my own bat without mentioning it to my husband, the idea being to delightfully surprise him. So don't even mention it to the Guild or anybody. It will be between us and John C. Wilson.

> Yours sincerely,
> Lynn Fontanne

To a young university instructor, the arrival of such a letter from a reigning queen of the theater was indeed an event. While overwhelming, it stirred also a confusing mixture of thoughts. What was the meaning of the secrecy request? Was Alfred Lunt likely—or not likely—to share her enthusiasm for the idea? More serious was my own doubt that the idea was

Lynn Fontanne. (Courtesy The National Broadcasting Company, Inc. and Billy Rose Theatre Collection, New York Public Library for the Performing Arts—Astor, Lenox and Tilden Foundations)

feasible, at least for me. For over a decade I had lived and breathed radio. I had begun to dabble in television, and the advent of the tape recorder was making me deeply interested in the possibilities of the documentary. The theater was no longer nagging at me; I was heading elsewhere. And I was sure that what I had contributed to the broadcast of *The Great Adventure* had much to do with my knowledge of radio, while only a little of it was applicable to the theater. In fact, I had no slightest notion of how to approach the project.

At the same time, I was sure that to anyone in the broadcasting or theater worlds it would seem insane if I did anything other than what I now proceeded to do. I wrote to Miss Lynn Fontanne, c/o Empire Theater, expressing my delight and saying I looked forward to hearing from Mr. John C. Wilson. A reply came promptly.

130 East 75th Street
New York 21
May 16, 1947

Dear Mr. Barnouw:

I am so delighted that you are interested.

Mr. Wilson is, at the moment, in London but we are expecting him back any day and as soon as he comes I will tell him of your willingness to try a script.

Meanwhile I am sending you a copy of a letter I have had from Mrs. Bennett, which I cannot make head or tail of. Perhaps you can but I do hope that when deciphered it is not discouraging.

We are off to the country on June 1st and shall stay there all summer long, but you will hear from Mr. Wilson soon after he lands.

Yours sincerely,
Lynn Fontanne

The enclosed letter from Dorothy Bennett was long. The first thing I noticed about it was the surprising address from which it came: 606 West 116th Street, New York 27—across the street from my office in the Columbia University School of General Studies. I had earlier taken a graduate course in modern English literature with Professor William Y. Tyndall, who had devoted a lecture to Arnold Bennett and had made references to Dorothy Bennett. But he too, I learned, was unaware that Dorothy Bennett was living at the edge of the Columbia campus. Her letter began:

606 West 116th Street
New York 27
May 11th '47

Dear Miss Fontanne,

Thank you so much for your very nice letter. As to what you say of "The Great Adventure," in the first place I am most interested to learn that you and Mr. Lunt have always thought the play would suit you. I could not agree more fully. You would be merely perfect, and would re-create the characters in fullest richness and the story with its vital truth—given the right script. . . .

But respecting the idea of making an entirely new script: would not this have the very serious disadvantage of losing many of the facets of the characters as revealed in the existing dialogue, and also much of their "basic essence"; and of blurring, or changing, the play's intellectual theme and argument? . . .

There was more urging of this sort. She fervently hoped the Lunts would consider doing the original play, with a few needed revisions, and drop the idea of commissioning a new work. Finally, she raised serious practical obstacles to Lynn Fontanne's plan:

> Now I must explain that, although I own the play (which by the way was written by Mr. Bennett alone) by a deed of gift, the book ("Buried Alive") belongs to the Bennett Estate. Due to the fact that another legatee has a life interest in it, the Estate is managed at present by the Public Trustee, London. Therefore, authorization for a new dramatization of the book would have to be given by him; although he, no doubt, would have first to consult me, as owner of the existing dramatization. . . .

Dorothy Bennett, though referred to by Lynn Fontanne as Mrs. Bennett, was not Bennett's wife. She was the actress long known as Dorothy Cheston, who had legally changed her name to Dorothy Bennett so that she and Arnold Bennett could travel together without embarrassment. The arrangement had been established in punctilious fashion, as described in Margaret Drabble's fine biography of Bennett. Bennett's interest in Dorothy had begun years after his legal separation from his wife. After discreet teas and dinners with the actress, he had explained to her his agonizing dilemma. His wife had adamantly refused a divorce, and there seemed no legal way to dissolve the marriage. But Bennett declared to Dorothy his love and devotion. He could not offer her a ritually sanctioned marriage, but if she could accept a less formal relationship, he would do all he could to make her happy. She had thought it over for a time, then agreed. They had honeymooned in Paris, and lived there much of the time. Among their literary friends the arrangement was readily accepted, and meanwhile the couple led a very domestic life. One of Bennett's chief worries concerned Dorothy's future. In the legal separation from his wife, it was stipulated that the income from all his literary properties would go to her after his death. Bennett, interpreting this as applying only to his books, decided to deed to Dorothy the very successful play *The Great Adventure*. This was contested in court by the wife, who became increasingly vindictive after Bennett settled down with Dorothy, but the arrangement survived the legal challenge, and the play became Dorothy's property. Understandably it remained of crucial value to her, and not only for financial reasons. She herself had appeared in a 1923 revival of the play in Britain. To press the Lunts, she soon followed her first letter with another. It began:

May 26, 1947

Dear Miss Fontanne:

An offer has come up from a manager who wants to do "The Great Adventure" for a week at the Greenwich summer theatre, but who is asking for an option on a N.Y. production of the play. He wanted my answer at once, but I replied that I cannot let him know before the beginning of the week as to the N.Y. option. . . . .

Dorothy Bennett therefore asked the Lunts for a firm commitment of some sort. Could she be assured they would do the play, with whatever revisions might be needed, "in about 2 years time?" If so, she would "refuse to grant any options elsewhere." A copy of this came to me with another Lynn Fontanne letter from the Empire Theater:

May 27, 1947

Dear Mr. Barnouw:

I have tonight received another letter from Mrs. Bennett, a copy of which I enclose.

So I think perhaps we had better let it go, as she seems on the tiresome side, don't you think? I have written her, telling her it is impossible for us to make a decision at the moment and advising her to take the offer from the manager of the Greenwich summer theatre, including the New York option.

I am so terribly sorry. And I am very grateful to you for your kindness and willingness to work on it.

Yours sincerely,
Lynn Fontanne

This seemed, at the moment, to end matters—to my simultaneous relief and disappointment. But Dorothy Bennett quickly wrote again, reversing direction. "As long as you have started things rolling," she wrote Lynn Fontanne on May 28, "I beg you to go on, or rather to let them stay rolling. I shall not grant any option elsewhere for a New York production." This brought me another Empire Theater letter.

Dear Mr. Barnouw:

It looks a little bit now as if Mrs. Bennett was being a bit too business-like and trying to hurry us. I am enclosing her letter.

Please do whatever you think about it. I will be with you either way.

My address after Saturday of this week will be Genesee Depot, Wisconsin.

Sincerely,

Lynn Fontanne

P.S. John C. Wilson will write you—and you can talk it over with him.

But instead of John C. Wilson, manager of the Lunts, I heard from the Theatre Guild. Its attorney, H. William Fitelson, was taking charge; the matter had become a Theatre Guild venture. His first problem was to clear the rights. He wrote to me to say: "That is going to be a problem because it not only concerns the Estate and Mrs. Bennett, but also Twentieth Century-Fox." I had a series of meetings with Fitelson. It was the first time I had breathed of the matter to anyone but Dotty.

The problem was that a film titled *Holy Matrimony*, starring Monte Woolley and based on *Buried Alive* and *The Great Adventure*, had been made by Twentieth Century-Fox, and that its lien on the screen rights still had years to run. Clearing this problem was essential. One of the rewards of a Broadway success—for its producer, writer, and sometimes others—was a share in the large sum that might come from the sale of screen rights to a Hollywood studio. A Broadway production was not likely to materialize without this possibility. And the relevant rights must be available internationally. *Buried Alive*, in spite of its dubious copyright status in the United States, was still fully covered in Europe and elsewhere; screen rights to *Buried Alive* must be included in the package. The difficulties seemed immense, but Fitelson was prepared to explore them with Twentieth Century-Fox.

It was many months before I heard more, in a further meeting with Fitelson. Amazingly, he had obtained an agreement, but with many provisos. Twentieth Century-Fox had accepted the idea of "merging" the screen rights in my unwritten play with the screen rights in the script written for *Holy Matrimony* and owned by the studio. This meant that the author's share of a new film sale would go partly to me, partly to

Twentieth Century-Fox. Since the total author's share might be substantial, this did not seem too serious. But there were other conditions. The deal would be void unless, before a stipulated deadline—about two years away—the play was approved by the Lunts and accepted for a Broadway run in a Theatre Guild production starring Alfred Lunt and Lynn Fontanne.

Fitelson helped me review the risks. If I had trouble getting the necessary acceptances before the time limit, my efforts would have been wasted. If either of the Lunts fell ill, my efforts would also have been wasted. If the deal lapsed, I would have on my hands a script without underlying rights, and virtually unmarketable. Worse yet, was it not likely that the Lunts might meanwhile be offered some other script much to their liking? Lunt-Fontanne successes tended to have three-year cycles—a season on Broadway, another on the road, another in England. My wife and I had, by this time, a daughter, Susanna, as well as a son. We were paying off a mortgage and able to do so because of continuing freelance commissions, which I would have to set aside to tackle this play. I told Fitelson: "I don't think I can afford to do this." He agreed. "It had to be your decision." He would inform Lynn Fontanne. She was disappointed. She thought it was somewhat "naughty" of me.

It turned out that the Lunts did find a script that launched them on a new three-year cycle—a final major theatrical triumph. Ironically, it came to them from another Columbia faculty member. *The Visit*, adapted by Professor Maurice Valency from the work of Friedrich Dürrenmatt, became the next Lunt-Fontanne vehicle.

Near the end of the Broadway run Dotty and I went to see *The Visit*. I had not seen the Lunts for some years. Afterwards we went to the stage door and I sent in my card, without any idea of what to expect. Almost at once, word came that we were to be admitted. As we went in, both Lunts came bursting from their dressing rooms and greeted us as if we were long-cherished friends. It seemed astonishing, as our relationship had always been so formal: the famous couple and the young instructor—Mr. Lunt, Miss Fontanne, Mr. Barnouw. But we chatted gaily, and reminisced. Then Lunt made an extraordinary statement.

He said something along this line: "You know, that thing you did for us, *The Great Adventure*—we listen to that now and then, in Wisconsin. We have a recording of it. The theater is a very strange business. You work in it for half a century, and you have nothing to show for it. Oh, we have clippings, and stills, and posters, things like that. But that recording, that gives us an idea of what we were like. I'm going to have an LP made of it."

Today great performances can be preserved via magnetic tape and numerous other processes. But the career of the Lunts belonged largely to an earlier era, when performances indeed vanished into thin air. I don't know if Lunt had an LP made from his recording; I hope so. His was an off-the-air acetate recording, very perishable, on sixteen-inch disks now obsolete. I had such a recording too, and deposited it for preservation in the National Archives in Washington.

DWIGHT D. EISENHOWER

"People don't choose their careers;
they are engulfed by them."
—John Dos Passos

Columbia was experiencing an interregnum. For decades President Nicholas Murray ("Miraculous") Butler had been an unchallenged autocrat who could create or abolish schools, departments, and programs. On the side he was a periodic Republican candidate for U.S. president, going to national conventions as New York State's "favorite son" candidate, which made him a national personage. He was a fund-raiser par excellence. This was not yet a science of computerized assaults on the consciences of alumni young and old, rich and poor; it was, rather, a matter of the right word at the right moment to the right tycoon. But by the mid-1940s Butler was no longer himself; after a period of decline and indecision, he was persuaded by friends to step down. The venerable secretary of the university, Dr. Frank Fackenthal, became titular acting president, under whom decisions tended to be made at lower levels. A presidential search committee went into action. The name of Eisenhower began to be mentioned. Which Eisenhower? No, not the educator. The hero, of course. The General of the Armies. For months it was just a rumor, then a sure thing.

Meanwhile, on campus, jurisdictions and lines of authority grew fuzzy. The decline of centralized authority created confusion—and opportunities.

To my office in the School of General Studies (I shared it with three other lower-level faculty members) came a surprise visitor—Dr. E. Gurney Clark, professor of epidemiology at the university's School of Public Health. He brought with him T. Lefoy Richman of the U.S. Public Health Service in Washington, who had a project to discuss. Dr. Clark, having learned that the School of General Studies had a section concerned with broadcasting, had decided to bring him to me. It was the fall of 1947.

Richman explained that his work at the PHS had to do with syphilis; this involved a problem on which I might be helpful. (This baffled me—I could not imagine the connection.) The topic, Richman observed, was unmentionable in most media. So far as he knew, no major network had ever allowed the word to be spoken. The term *syphilis* seemed to be feared as though the word itself could transmit the spirochete. Most large-circulation magazines would not print it. The Hollywood code had specifically banned the subject of "social diseases" from the screen.

A medical development had prompted U.S. Surgeon General Thomas Parran to state that the disease (in its later stages a cause of blindness, insanity, paralysis, heart failure, and death) might actually be eradicated if it could be talked about—on radio, for example. Since radio was obligated to serve the "public interest, convenience, and necessity," should it not lead the way? Richman asked how I felt about that idea. I said it sounded fine.

Would Columbia perhaps be interested in a federal grant or contract to produce a series of recorded programs for distribution to stations all over the United States to bring the subject into the open? Before I could answer, Richman and Clark began to fill in background information. The talk grew increasingly clinical.

The room had four faculty desks, crammed closely together, serving various instructors of the School of General Studies, the university's adult education branch. I was relieved that no colleague was at the moment holding student conferences. Our talk did not sound like a radio or television agenda.

A treacherous thing about syphilis, I was told, is that early visible symptoms such as a sore, and/or a rash, may hardly be noticed, and in any case *always* disappear of their own accord, no matter what. As a result, the disease encourages quackery and self-medication: whatever nostrum is tried seems to work, so the patient thinks he or she is fine. Then begins a long period—it may be ten or twenty years or even more—when only a blood test can show the presence of the germ. At the PHS some statisticians were estimating that three million Americans were infected without knowing it. All were prime candidates for late syphilis and its horrors, which could come suddenly and were irreversible.

Clark emphasized that throughout the "latent" period a cure was possible. Until recently the prevailing treatment had taken eighteen months and was painful; most patients never finished treatment but drifted away. Control efforts had looked almost hopeless—until lately. In 1943 Dr. John F. Mahoney of the PHS, stationed at a U.S. Marine hospital on Staten Island, had experimentally treated four servicemen—syphilis patients—with injections of the new drug penicillin. After a week of injections blood tests showed that all four were cured. It was astounding, seemingly opening a whole new era in the struggle. During the war supplies of penicillin were reserved for the military, for diverse medical uses. But now, at last, full attention could go to the nation's syphilis problem, including the unsuspecting three million. Congress had authorized and funded a gigantic PHS hunt to find the untreated and bring them to treatment.

It was, Richman insisted, a hardheaded, dollars-and-cents proposition. The United States was spending some $20 million a year maintaining the syphilitic blind and insane in public institutions. Each year the cost went up. It made no sense: many of the unsuspecting could be saved, remaining in many cases breadwinners and taxpayers instead of becoming public charges. So—the campaign. Was I interested?

I hardly knew what to say. The job for which Columbia had hired me was to teach courses and supervise others in radio and television. How far could that stretch? Job descriptions had not yet taken over academia. I felt excited but nervous. A high school course on "hygiene," with its climactic scare lecture, had been my main introduction to this new challenge. Richman was zeroing in on the details.

A random blood-testing of tens of millions was obviously out of the question, he said. A more democratic procedure was planned. It called for a series of recorded programs, to be tested first in one region, that would so tellingly make clear the patterns of syphilis that any listener with reason to suspect infection would come forward for a blood test and treatment if needed. The PHS had numerous "rapid treatment centers" where treatment could be completed in a week or so. The PHS would soon decide who should produce the proposed radio programs. Richman hoped it might be Columbia University, but that would have to be decided via competitive bidding. The PHS would identify half a dozen universities with radio units comparable to ours. Within days all would receive a written description of the project and an invitation to bid. Could a bid from Columbia be expected?

Without any reason to suppose I had authority to say yes, I said it.

Eisenhower in academia: "To help Columbia help America." (Columbia University)

Within a week the promised material arrived in the mail. I filled it out. It called for a budget. I had never constructed a businesslike budget, much less a government budget, but sought advice and muddled through. Who could sign the document? Officials of the School of General Studies doubted if it could be deemed a suitable School of General Studies project. I ended in the office of the university provost, Albert Jacobs. He seemed intrigued. He examined the budget, making sure it had adequate provision for "contingencies" and "indirect costs." He quizzed me on talent pay rates. Then he said, sure, he would sign it for the university. The document was dispatched. A week later, on the date set for the opening of the bids in Washington, a phone call came, informing me that Columbia had been the only bidder. The other universities may well have been baffled by the bidding invitation, accompanied by government syphilis brochures. We were awarded the contract. My life went into a turmoil of action as hectic as the Camel cigarette days. But this time I relished every moment. I controlled a "credit line" of some twenty thousand dollars. I signed myself "Director, VD Radio Project"—a hastily invented entity. (For administrative purposes the evasive "VD" seemed sensible at this stage.) On December 17, 1947, *Variety* carried an item headed: "Columbia U to Aid VD Disk Series."

Having become president of the Radio Writers Guild the previous month, I inserted a note in the guild's membership bulletin about the VD Radio Project. Writers were invited to submit proposals. A meeting to brief those interested was announced, to be held at a Radio City projection room. More than a hundred writers turned up. Messrs. Richman and Clark performed and riveted the group's attention. Script proposals began to pour into my office.

About this time the announcement came that General Dwight D. Eisenhower had accepted appointment as Columbia University president, to take office in the spring. In Washington, returning from a European tour of duty, he fielded reporters' questions about his Columbia future. He said he would soon talk to university officials and "get some advance inkling of what a college president is up against." He admitted knowing little about it but understood he would not be involved in "burdensome administrative details." Seeking to define his role, he said he would try to "devote my energies in providing internal leadership on broad and liberal lines."* After a visit to the campus he pronounced himself "appalled" at the complexity of the institution, with its "countless numbers" of graduate and professional schools and programs. He hoped he could "help Columbia help America." The university's upper echelons appeared agog over the appointment. Mutterings were heard at lower levels. Some resented the choice of a symbolic figurehead without academic experience. Many predicted that the campus would be a mere stopping place en route to the White House. I was too busy to worry about these arguments. I did not think the coming of the V-E hero had any bearing on me or the VD Radio Project.

By the time the general took office, fantastic progress had been made on our contract. We had auditioned test pressings of a number of programs for PHS officials, and the reactions were enthusiastic. My favorite NBC director, Frank Papp (he also taught one of the Columbia University–NBC radio courses), had done most of the directing. Under a rental arrangement, we had used NBC studios for our recording sessions. Most of the programs ran 14:30 minutes, a prevalent radio length of the time. Various genres were included. No one could answer such questions as What

---

*S. E. Ambrose, *Eisenhower* (New York: Simon & Schuster, 1983), vol. 1, p. 471.

is the favorite programming of people who have syphilis without knowing it? or How does one get the attention of such people for a program on syphilis? Informed that the rural South and industrial cities of the North would be important target areas but that no group was immune, we elected a range of program genres: soap opera, documentary (using the newly invented tape recorder to interview patients in rapid treatment centers), short spots, and programs we dubbed ballad dramas or "hillbilly operas" in which narration was sung by figures like Roy Acuff, Red Foley, and Tom Glazer. Such programs were proposed by folk music specialist Alan Lomax, who also wrote many of these programs and became deeply involved in our project. There were also straight dramas, some with stars. Their agents had generally proved unfriendly, determined to protect their clients from moral pollution. The stars whom we could approach directly behaved differently. Lomax had readily obtained the cooperation of Acuff, Foley, and other singers. I recruited actors connected with my earlier activities—Henry Fonda of University Players days, Eddie Albert from the NBC days. Eddie, in turn, brought in his wife, Margo, an eager volunteer. George Hicks was known to me from *Theatre Guild on the Air*, on which he performed U.S. Steel institutional commercials. He had won fame during the war for his running account of the Normandy landings, spoken into a wire recorder amid the upheaval and aired soon afterwards (after censorship review), an event that began a rapid erosion of the network ban on recorded programming. We now persuaded Hicks to take a tape recorder into rapid treatment centers, where his low-key questioning of patients proved extraordinarily effective in drawing out their personal narratives.

As we built enthusiasm, the PHS people began to talk about a second contract. They were considering Tennessee, a border state, as a possible test area. But additional programs seemed to be needed for saturation campaigns in crucial areas. There was talk of establishing a $50,000 revolving fund at Columbia for the production of programs ("on syphilis and other public health subjects") to be syndicated to state and city health departments. The PHS planned to encourage states and cities to organize "case-finding" drives, for which it would make financial grants, including money earmarked for "informational materials"—such as they would find available from Columbia. It seemed to me a neat plan, providing stimulus to both the production and the use of needed materials. But as I broached at Columbia the possibility of a new and larger PHS contract,

I found a sudden skittishness. No one was willing to consider a further syphilis involvement until "the General" had arrived and reviewed the whole matter. I was not sure what had caused the alarm. I was aware that a Catholic spokesman had lately blasted the PHS idea of bringing the subject into the open via broadcasting. The plan was denounced as immoral as well as indecent, a threat to the family. I had not, at the time, taken this very seriously.

But Richman felt I should know about an earlier problem that had proved damaging. It involved the advertising industry. Soon after Pearl Harbor the industry had set up the War Advertising Council (later re-named Advertising Council) to channel war messages into advertising. Various government units suggested themes (avoid rumors, save cans, don't waste, learn first aid, be an air raid warden), which advertising agencies then incorporated into various media. Inasmuch as syphilis education had been established in the armed forces, the PHS felt that the general public should also be ready for it and proposed a War Advertising Council campaign on the subject. The council agreed; it was seen as beneficial to war industries. Ads were prepared to appear in *Saturday Evening Post, Colliers,* and other leading periodicals. At this point an association of Catholic advertisers had rallied opposition. It prepared a series of ads that it proposed to run in the same periodicals—assailing the council and the PHS if they should decide to go ahead with their abhorrent and immoral plan. Richman had obtained proofs of these protest ads and showed them to me. They had achieved their purpose. Amid wide consternation, the campaign was canceled by the Advertising Council.

It seemed to me that this setback may well have been one reason why the PHS, in its postwar efforts, looked to academia rather than the advertising industry. And I wondered if echoes of this history had reached the university and set off the new nervousness.

Eisenhower settled at Columbia in mid-June 1948, shortly after commencement. A grand reception was scheduled for July 6. But even before that, on June 21, I was instructed to appear at his office in Low Memorial Library to explain the VD Radio Project. I was astonished that this venture, so puny in the scale of university undertakings, should have such priority. I asked Dr. E. Gurney Clark to go with me for medical and moral support. I took sixteen-inch test pressings of several programs and a portable disk player. We waited only briefly in the anteroom before being ushered in. The general, at his desk, rose with military briskness and came to shake hands with us. I explained about the equipment I was carrying, and all three of us began groping along the baseboard for an electric outlet, finally found behind a curtain, and for a place to put the disk player. When all this was resolved, we settled down.

After brief explanation of the public health problem (by Clark) and of the radio project (by me), the general was ready to hear a program. He looked very serious. I dropped the needle on *Unborn Child*, starring Margo and movingly written by Sandra Michael, writer of *Against the Storm*, a daytime serial that had won numerous awards. *Unborn Child* was a fifteen-minute program. It struck me as odd, even bizarre, that the conqueror of the Nazis, liberator of Europe, should now be sitting before me with furrowed brow, listening to this dialogue. But there he was.

The program concerned an expectant young mother. To her astonishment, her doctor's routine blood test reveals a syphilis infection, apparently contracted from her husband. The infection threatens child as well as mother. But we learn from the program that penicillin treatment early in pregnancy can cure the mother and at the same time assure the child will be free of the infection. In *Unborn Child* a healthy child is born. The husband too is treated and is meanwhile interviewed by a trained "contact tracer," leading to treatment of others. Did the wife forgive him? Did the marriage survive? We are not told.

Eisenhower seemed ready to hear more, so I dropped the needle on *They Never Even Suspected*, excerpts from George Hicks's interviews with patients under treatment in various stages of syphilis. Hicks's interviewees included people from diverse walks of life. There was an auto mechanic and an advertising executive. Also, a rather high-sounding lady who had apparently had syphilis for years and kept saying, "I never dreamed I could have such a thing." Most cases had been diagnosed as a result of routine blood tests during treatment for other ailments. Most could look forward to restored health. This did not apply to the final patient on *They Never Even Suspected*, who had passed into the late syphilis stage. Questioned by Hicks, he babbled long replies, apparently unaware that his speech had become almost incomprehensible. Damaged and disrupted by the germ, his speech mechanisms were out of control. He could be cured of syphilis but normal speech would never return.

I had brought another program, a ballad drama starring Roy Acuff, but—unsure of the reaction—I had left it till last. To my relief, Eisenhower indicated he had heard enough. He said he liked the first program better than the other. Then he turned to Dr. Clark and for the next ten minutes reeled off in rapid succession a long series of questions. It was as though he had been cataloguing problems in his mind and was ready for this catechism. I was impressed with the range of the questions, which dealt with treatment, length, hazards, side effects, follow-up investigations, cost, recent history, legal issues, relations with radio stations, procedure at treatment centers. Clark answered concisely. Occasionally I chimed in. We explained that in every city, each program would be followed by an address where free blood tests would be available. Treatment would be available at a PHS rapid treatment center. Several dozen such centers were in action across the country, ready for the drive.

Having finished his questions, Eisenhower leaned back in his swivel chair and seemed to relax. "Well!" he said, decisively. "I'm *delighted* we're doing something that isn't *way up* in the academic clouds!" He put his hands up over his head and moved his fingers as though to symbolize academic clouds. Then he stood up and congratulated us. "If there's anything I can do, let me know." We shook hands and left, his assurance singing in our ears. It meant, we felt sure, that it would now be clear sailing at Columbia. But it seemed to mean more. It had a bearing on another problem, which had been worrying Richman for some months.

There would soon come a moment, in city after city, when a radio station manager would be visited by a local health official with a packet of recorded programs. Asked to broadcast them, to help combat an old scourge, what would he answer? We had assumed, because of the war years and the historic opportunity offered by penicillin, that at least some station managers—perhaps many—would be ready to ignore the old taboo. *Would* they? Richman was determined to prepare as carefully as possible for the crucial encounters and proposed the following. At PHS expense, we would invite a dozen station managers, representing large and small stations in various parts of the country, to a dinner at Columbia. An enclosure would explain our project and the reasons for it. At the dinner we would seek their advice. We would pay for travel and overnight accommodations.

The invitations went out and acceptances came from most of the executives. A few regretted on grounds of business pressures. One, J. Leonard Reinsch, manager of a powerful Georgia radio station and author of a book on *Radio Station Management*, did not answer our letter nor a follow-up telegram, which we had sent with the answer prepaid. This made me uneasy, but the proportion of acceptances was encouraging. The group met on a Friday evening in a private dining room of the Faculty Club, along with Richman and Clark. It was congenial. We talked about current entertainments in New York (most of the men were making weekend visits out of the occasion) and then about syphilis. They all said we were doing a fine thing—important, no question about it. So Richman finally put the question. What would they say to the local health official with his packet of recordings? Would they say yes and put them on the air? All looked thoughtful.

Finally, one said he wasn't sure. A station depended (for its very life, he said) on the various groups in the community. He would have to check with them—businessmen, religious leaders, educators, government people, even the mayor. He hoped his station would be able to cooperate, but he couldn't say. He hoped so. Others had similar comments. We seemed quickly to reach a stalemate.

Then, one had a suggestion. Why not get a network to take the lead? That would make it much easier. Others chimed in enthusiastically. Of course! A network precedent—that would be the thing.

A unanimous recommendation couldn't well be brushed off. But I had a feeling that we had put our heads into a noose. Our project seemed to hang on a very chancy proposition. The station managers departed with renewed praise for our enlightened work.

My ties to NBC seemed to indicate we should start there—giving NBC, as Richman put it, first chance to do the pioneering. NBC decided promptly: It would not be an appropriate NBC venture. I then reminded myself that CBS, the number two network, had the more impressive public service record, and was probably a better bet. I met with Davidson Taylor, its public affairs vice president, whom I had known for some time. He had at first been responsive to the idea of a Pearl Buck "novel for radio." But CBS's answer came just as promptly, via a phone message the next day: No possibility.

That left ABC, which was considered the also-ran network. It had come into existence just five years earlier, carved out of NBC through antitrust pressure, with a line-up of former NBC stations—the weaker ones, technically and financially. It existed precariously with many hours of unsold time. But that saved the day for us. ABC Vice President Robert Saudek, in charge of public affairs, seemed at once to welcome our topic-of-ill-repute. He had begun devoting unsold prime-time hours to documentaries on controversial subjects, hoping for more press and audience attention. He also saw our problem as solving a crisis he faced at the moment. He had earmarked 9:30–10:30 P.M. on April 29, less than four weeks away, for a documentary on the history of the Communist Party of the U.S.A. But the script department was going through hell trying to get the script into shape. It seemed a legal and political nightmare. Saudek had become convinced the script could not be ready in time. He said he would cancel communism and substitute syphilis on April 29, if I could produce a script by mid-April, fully approved by the U.S. Public Health Service. The deal was made. I wrote the script that week. Dr. E. Gurney Clark made himself constantly available. Richman came from Washington. On April 14 Saudek released the news to the press. The subject for April 29 would be *VD: The Conspiracy of Silence.* (The program would say *syphilis* but we would work up to that gradually.)

The script presented three fictional, interweaving case histories. The role of silence was a factor in all three. In one, a bus driver dates a girl who rides his bus one day. An intermittent voice-over narrator quietly notes that car cards on the bus offer him advice on bad breath, tooth decay, body odor, dandruff, colds, hemorrhoids, arthritis pain, blood pressure— not a word on syphilis. The case histories are punctuated by flashbacks on the history of the disease—its historic role as the illusive "great imitator" that baffled science for centuries. At the end is a sample of George Hicks's "actuality" interviews with current patients in treatment centers.

Rehearsals, directed by Martin Andrew, began in a nervous atmosphere. We learned that Mark Woods, ABC president, was already getting protesting letters and telegrams. He was persuaded to stand firm. But Saudek kept dropping in on rehearsals to reassure himself. The "controversial" nature of the subject now became our greatest asset. Never again would it have the notoriety and attention value it had on Tuesday evening, April 29, 1948. Years of foolish terrors had set the stage. It brought us a large audience and many reviews in newspapers and magazines. They drifted in for weeks afterwards. Only a handful were critical. Most used such phrases as "a notable and important advance in the educational use of radio" (*New York Times*) and "a milestone" (*Variety*). Equally helpful were letters—from (among others) teachers, lawyers, doctors, clergy. One was from a high school principal who had with some trepidation urged his student body to listen, and was glad he had; it was what he had hoped for. There was an eloquent letter from a mother. She had been wanting to tell her daughter certain things but hesitated; she herself was so fuzzy about the facts. So she and her daughter had listened together and were grateful. Some weeks later the Institute for Education by Radio at Ohio State voted *VD: The Conspiracy of Silence* the outstanding program of the year.

At the PHS, Richman organized his ammunition. By the end of June he had designed a brochure addressed to broadcasting station executives, to be carried by the health officer with his packet of programs. It featured pictures of the program stars and quoted reviews and letters that one such program had evoked. In July the brochure acquired its finishing touch. Under the words "A Job That Needs You," addressed to station managers, was a message from the former General of the Armies.

> The American people must learn of the menace and cost of venereal disease, and of their opportunity to eradicate it. American radio, with its widespread and diversified appeal, is perhaps better equipped to convey this message of warning and of hope than any other medium of information. This is an unparalleled opportunity for the broadcasting station to join with doctors, clergy, and other community leaders in a vital public service.
>
> Dwight D. Eisenhower

The general had signed it without hesitation. Later he appeared at a university press conference giving the campaign a further send-off. Ad-libbing an addendum to the university press release, he said the programs concerned a "repulsive subject" that had to be faced. A p.r. expert would not have chosen this phrasing, but Eisenhower gave it a ring of righteous determination.

One could hardly have anticipated the bandwagon effects these moves apparently generated. In Jackson, Tennessee, site of the first local drive, every station within earshot carried *all* our programs, and some added offerings of their own. Newspapers and billboards joined in. In some of the later statewide drives, all stations within a state participated. Our programs were carried in all states except Maine (which said it did not have a syphilis problem). The taboo appeared to have vanished. Meanwhile we began to receive statistics on "bloods taken," "positives found and treated," and other illuminating data. Each patient was asked what had brought him or her: newspaper story? radio? poster? word from a friend? routine checkup? other? Based on the findings, the Tennessee health department concluded that in 1949, 18,032 cases in Tennessee had been brought to treatment through radio programs.* At one time more than a fourth of its syphilis patients said that radio had brought them. Many patients could identify a specific program. The first local drive, focused on Jackson, gave us dramatic evidence of which programs, which genres, were the main catalysts there. Only three "hillbilly opera" programs were ready for use in Jackson, but these were mentioned respectively by 33, 31, and 29 people, outscoring all other genres. The five "straight dramas" in the program cluster were mentioned by 15, 14, 12, 11, and 9 people respectively. All six of the actuality documentaries, featuring patients under treatment, were mentioned by a total of 6 people. Why this result? Students for whom I played the recordings generally assumed that the actualities, because of their unvarnished reality, would bring in the most patients. At the VD Radio Project we concluded that the actualities had fascinated an audience interested in syphilis as a public health problem, whereas the music drama programs reached people whose interests ran to sex, music, and success, with the crucial information riding in on their momentum. Because of the clearcut results, the PHS commissioned further such programs, for which we recruited Woody Guthrie, Hank Williams, Merle Travis, Sister Rosetta Tharpe, and others. Many of the programs were written by Alan Lomax. Their impact was similar in all parts of the country. Lomax's advice had proved spectacularly right.

Toward the "eradication" of syphilis the PHS reported the following: Admissions of the syphilitic insane to public institutions dropped from 6.6 per 100,000 population in 1939 to 2.1 in 1951; deaths from syphilis dropped from 11.1 per 100,000 population in 1939 to 3.7 in 1952. Dr. Gurney Clark said it was becoming difficult to find cases of late syphilis to demonstrate to medical students. Health officials were increasingly optimistic.

The successes had an impact on my role at Columbia. Grants and contracts began to come from diverse sources: the Anti-Defamation League, U.S. state department, Social Security Administration, National Educational Television, World Health Organization. The projects involved not only radio but film, television, comic books, and animated films. The VD Radio Project was transformed into the Center for Mass Commu-

*Digest of Proceedings, 9th semiannual venereal disease control seminar, PHS, 1950.

nication (CMC) and was merged into Columbia University Press, which sometimes defined the new unit as its "mass media division."

The surge even took us into the jukebox field. In 1949 a Tennessee health officer asked why our syphilis project had ignored jukeboxes. He had talked to a jukebox entrepreneur who said he would be delighted to cooperate, given the right material. It seemed crazy—but, at home with a cold, I began to play with the idea, and a lyric of seven stanzas emerged. I sent it to Tom Glazer with a note: "I'll phone you about this." When I did phone he said, "I hope you wanted me to write music for it, because I have."

At CMC we decided to invest a few hundred dollars of our public health revolving fund in a recording session. Glazer assembled and rehearsed a small combination. On our first run-through we found that the song ran exactly three minutes, the right length for a ten-inch 78 RPM disk. A few days later we had our test pressing of "That Ignorant, Ignorant Cowboy." It went as follows, sung by Glazer and chorus. The short line in each stanza was spoken. A chorus of "cowboy" voices sang the italicized refrain.

An ignorant cowboy went out on a spree
And oh what an ignorant cowhand was he.
He had a few drinks and his head was a-whirl
And he ended up in the arms of a girl
Called Katey—
That ignorant cowboy,
That ignorant, ignorant cowboy.

Now that cowboy was awfully handsome they say,
As I'm sure he could tell from his mirror each day,
But many weeks later one morning he saw
A rash on his face and he cried with a roar,
"What is it?"
That ignorant cowboy,
That ignorant, ignorant cowboy.

That cowboy was worried and fretted and frowned
And he went to his medicine chest and he found
Some wonderful tonic that must have been hot
Supposed to be good for whatever you got

And he took it—
That ignorant cowboy,
That ignorant, ignorant cowboy.

Now that cowboy each morning he washed at the sink,
And then came one morning when what do you think?
The spots on his face they had all gone away,
He looked and he shouted, "Ti-yippi-ti-yay!
I'm cured!"
That ignorant cowboy,
That ignorant, ignorant cowboy.

That handsome young cowboy was happy once more,
'Cause nobody ever had told him the score,
But the germ that had got him was still there inside,
'Cause this is a treacherous germ that will hide
Inside
An ignorant cowboy,
An ignorant, ignorant cowboy.

Now pardners, it surely is sorrowful strange
To think of that cowboy a-riding the range
Not knowing some day he'll be surely struck down
By the germ that he caught when he went up to town
On a spree—
That ignorant cowboy,
That ignorant, ignorant cowboy.

A ranch on the range isn't likely to find
Much use for a cowboy who's dead, lame or blind,
So if you've known Katey, please listen to this:
Only a doctor can cure sy-phi-lis!
Don't be
An ignorant cowboy,
An ignorant, ignorant cowboy.[*]

A few days after our recording session a phone call came from "Mitch" Miller, later a popular television personality but at that time a Mercury

[*] "That Ignorant, Ignorant Cowboy" © 1949 by Erik Barnouw and Tom Glazer.

Records executive in charge of A&R—artists and repertory. Glazer had played "Cowboy" for him. Miller wanted to take over our master and bring out the record under the Mercury label, with royalty payments to Columbia University Press. I quickly agreed. Our staff had not the faintest notion how to market a phonograph record.

Events now moved with dizzying speed. ABC, abandoning the long-standing network taboo on recordings, was introducing the disc jockey to network radio—bravura style, with a roster of celebrity disc jockeys. It had publicity value but was also a spectacular cost-cutting measure. Eddie Cantor became a disc jockey. Even Paul Whiteman agreed to assume the disc jockey mantle. In 1924 Whiteman had made musical history by introducing George Gershwin's "Rhapsody in Blue" at a New York concert. Twenty-five years later he decided to introduce "That Ignorant, Ignorant Cowboy" to a coast-to-coast radio audience, advising listeners, "Now listen *very* carefully." "Cowboy" became another nine days' wonder. *Billboard*'s charts gave it a favorable rating: "Should get good juke and jock activity." * Gene Autry, protesting, was quoted as saying, "Cowboys are not ignorant." A Brooklyn businessman sent a furious letter to his congressman, who forwarded it to U.S. Surgeon General Leonard A. Scheele—who, however, had already endorsed the record. Celebrities were being asked to comment on the to-do; most responded enthusiastically. Only Thornton Wilder demurred. (In a note to me he apologized for his "cranky" reaction. He preferred "straight" medical advice. He was just back from a Goethe meeting, which "made us all eagles for standards!") Robert J. Landry, *Variety* editor, contributed: "Should get through where tracts and lectures fail." In Chicago a public health officer approached George A. Miller, president of the Music Operators of America, an association of jukebox operators who had broken away from mob-dominated pinball machine operators and wanted respectability. He offered to send postcards to all his members coast to coast, urging them to carry "Cowboy." He said this was the first time a government agency had ever asked for jukebox cooperation. To him, the syphilis campaign seemed a step toward improved status.

In New Rochelle, New York, near my Larchmont home, I visited a music store to ask for "Cowboy." The salesman gave me a quizzical grin, as though I had asked for some disreputable under-the-counter item.

* *Billboard*, October 15, 1949.

"Been a lot of trouble about that, you know." I asked him what trouble, but he declined to elaborate. No, he did not carry the record. I was unable to track down the apparently covert "trouble." Area jukeboxes remained pure. "Cowboy" went on a rampage in a few cities but remained unknown in most, despite George Miller's efforts.

At Ohio State University the Institute for Education by Radio bestowed on "Cowboy" a "special award." Academics seemed to take to him. They were beguiled by the information that the word *syphilis* stemmed from 1530, when it was used by the physician and poet Fracastoro in a Latin poem about a shepherd (named Syphilus) who had caught a mysterious disease, which Fracastoro described as communicable and dangerous. Our cowboy seemed a logical successor to the old shepherd.

"Cowboy" won its most spectacular successes in San Francisco, where, according to informal reports, jukeboxes wore out some fifteen hundred disks in a matter of weeks. This brought Dwight D. Eisenhower back into the situation. He received a letter from a San Francisco father, whose daughter, Katey, had been about to enter Barnard, Columbia's women's college. But she had been so mercilessly teased about what she had done to a poor cowboy that she could not possibly face the campus where all this had started. The letter was forwarded to me by the president's office with a request to draft a reply for Eisenhower's signature. I did so as best I could, but painfully. I heard no more.

By 1953, when the general had left the campus for the White House, there was great euphoria among syphilis crusaders. This set the stage for one of the earliest acts of the Eisenhower administration, in keeping with Republican views. The media-driven hunts seemed no longer warranted and were discontinued. It seemed time for the government to "get out of the business." All PHS rapid treatment centers were closed and treatment "returned to the private physician." The syphilis problem was privatized. There were few protests.

But warnings of danger were heard. Treatment centers had been the base for "contact tracing." Each patient treated could lead to others— sometimes many. Under the new arrangement, physicians were supposed to report any syphilis case to a health department so that contact tracing could be done as before. But a new factor had entered the situation. A laboratory break-through had developed a slow-release form of penicillin that could cure syphilis in one massive dose—replacing the earlier weeklong series of injections. A physician finding symptoms that *might* mean syphilis—or flu or any of a number of other conditions treatable via penicillin—appeared to have a new option. The one-dose treatment would do it, no matter what. No diagnosis meant no contact tracing. No one dared to suggest publicly that this was happening. If it was, syphilis would soon be on the rise again. But with the decline in contact tracing, available statistics on this subject were not as voluminous as they had been. Within a few years available evidence made clear that syphilis was increasing, and rapidly. But by that time health departments were over-whelmed by a new drama—AIDS—for which the syphilis battle seemed to have been only a rehearsal.

By this time syphilis was seldom a focus of public attention. For a few brief years it had excited the mass media. Now it seemed a stale sub-ject. At a Radio Writers Guild annual dinner, Abe Burrows was asked to entertain as stand-up comic. He chose to do a sardonic disquisition on documentaries. It began: "A documentary—is usually about syphilis." It got a good laugh.

The campaign had had different meanings for different participants. One radio writer said: "I'm not interested in syphilis. But if we can knock out one stupid taboo, we can wipe out others." I too had that feeling.

The syphilis crusade had begun at about the same time as my nego-tiations with Lynn Fontanne. My fascination with the new challenge was one of the reasons why I decided *not* to plunge into a risky Lunt-Fontanne venture. I did not mention this to Bill Fitelson, the attorney who had spent so much time ironing out the details. And I certainly never mentioned it to the queenly Lynn Fontanne. Would she have understood how syphilis—and the documentary genre—could lure me away from the theater?

Soon after Eisenhower departed from Columbia, I had a visit from my Princeton classmate Noel Busch, who had been a fellow contributor to the *Nassau Lit.* He was now a writer for *Life* and was doing a long piece on Eisenhower. Busch was anxious to know how I assessed Eisenhower's Columbia regime. I said that I had been very pleased—that even at my modest level I had had dealings with him and received solid support. Busch said, "Damn, I can't find anyone who'll say anything against him." He had interviewed a number of deans; all apparently said he'd given them great support.

It became clear later that this wide-ranging support had produced a number of jurisdictional problems at Columbia. The university found it necessary to appoint a Committee on the Future of the University to sort out all the confusions—while the general was in Washington giving solid support to other plans proposed to him, including covert ventures in Iran, Guatemala, Cuba, and Vietnam. Thinking in terms of global adventures and tactics had become easy for him, as it had for a whole generation.

FRANK AND ANN HUMMERT

"I do fear that make-believe makes belief."
—David Rintels

My Columbia work was now all-consuming and hugely satisfying. But I was still president of the Radio Writers Guild. In 1948 RWG was heading into a dangerous confrontation with radio's major powers. I felt like a fish out of water and hoped I could finish my one-year term without disgrace. When I confided to the RWG lawyer that I was not sure of my qualifications for the job, he said, smiling: "You give us respectability."

My predecessor had been the able Peter Lyon, knowledgeable about union matters. He had written scripts for the CIO for use on two joint AFL-CIO radio series—the wartime Labor for Victory *and the postwar* Labor-USA. *I admired his clear writing and had included a script of his in my 1945 anthology,* Radio Drama in Action: Twenty-Five Plays of a Changing World. *At RWG he was a hard act to follow.*

Lyon had piloted the guild to contracts with the major networks, mainly covering staff employees writing nonsponsored programs. This was a crucial achievement, yet only a beginning. The knottiest problem lay ahead: to win a contract for freelance writers, the bulk of our membership, who wrote the sponsored programs that comprised about half of network radio and were controlled by hundreds of corporate sponsors scattered around the United States, produced for them by scores of advertising agencies, sometimes via independent production units. For a decade this complex alignment had given us a skillful runaround. Geographic dispersal made the sponsors elusive. Their agencies said they couldn't commit their clients to anything, being merely agents. They sometimes said they doubted the legality of our demands, which included pay scales, particularly minimums. That, they said, would be a price-fixing conspiracy in violation of the antitrust laws. Some used an unsavory tactic, advising writers to shun RWG on the ground that it was "communist-dominated." The more they said this, the more they apparently believed it. And it suited the political climate. In resisting our demands they were donning the mantle of patriotism as well as serving "the bottom line."

Outraged by such tactics, almost all radio writers had gradually joined the guild. By 1948 it had some twelve hundred members—most in New York, many in Los Angeles, a smaller number in Chicago. All were increasingly impatient. Endless New York-Chicago-Los Angeles telephone calls buzzed about the need for militant action. Finally, a few weeks before the expiration of my term, I found myself presiding over an especially jam-packed, uproarious New York meeting. The sole agenda item: a strike vote. The result was overwhelming. Only two members shouted "Nay!" Parallel meetings in Los Angeles and Chicago reported similar results. A strategy committee was to set the date. A few days later ("Let's not change horses in midstream") I was reelected president. To my horror, I found myself in charge of an impending nationwide strike. Our membership had resolved to stop writing, picket studio buildings, and shut down big-time radio.

How had I gotten into this! How would Columbia University react! What about NBC, its colleague in radio-television instruction! On campus I was surprised to find things going as usual. Few people seemed to have noticed the brief news items about the strike vote. Colleagues were interested, but seemed to assume it was no big deal. I was terrified that it was.

The writers could not understand why even major sponsors—companies like General Foods, General Motors, Du Pont, U.S. Steel, R. J. Reynolds, American Tobacco—were resisting our demands, which seemed to us modest, too much so, many thought. Committees had codified our demands and embodied them in proposed contracts. A few small independent production units had signed them, but most companies held firm. On some sponsored series, especially in prime time, writers were receiving fees considerably higher than our proposed minimums, and a number of series had begun to give on-the-air credit, another of our major goals. So why the resistance?

We had expected resistance, but mainly from special segments of the industry. Most daytime serials, for example, paid far below our proposed minimums. Most also refused to give on-the-air credit. In one prelimi-nary meeting with an advertising agency, RWG representatives were actually told that mention of writers was out of the question for day-time serials because "it would spoil the illusion—our listeners believe these stories are real." In the guild's view, the most formidable opposition would come from the Hummert empire, controlled by the mysterious Frank and Ann Hummert.

They were responsible for an amazing lineup of programs, including the largest block of daytime serials. These were sponsored by promi-nent household products that had apparently thrived on the relationship. Many of the serials had been on the air for ten years and showed no sign of decline. For women listeners the Hummerts offered *Backstage Wife, Betty and Bob, David Harum, John's Other Wife, Just Plain Bill, Lorenzo Jones, Ma Perkins, Our Gal Sunday, The Romance of Helen Trent, Stella Dallas, Young Widder Brown.* For children they had *Little Orphan Annie.* New serials were constantly being tested on local stations, candidates for future network scheduling. All offered five fifteen-minute episodes per week, all written anonymously.

Frank Hummert had been a partner in Blackett, Sample & Hummert, a leading advertising agency for more than a decade. In 1935 he married his assistant, Ann Ashenhurst, and they withdrew from advertising to form a company called Air Features, to which Blackett, Sample & Hum-mert delegated the production of all its serials. The Hummerts moved their new company to midtown Manhattan. Their operation was soon compared to that of the elder Alexandre Dumas, in that the Hummerts themselves were said to do all the plotting while engaging others to "fill in the dialogue," as the Hummerts put it. These writers—all RWG mem-bers—received $25 per episode, $125 per week. On serials produced by other companies, writers earned as much as $1,000 to $2,000 per week. The disparity was staggering. To bring the Hummerts to a higher level was one of our main aims.

But the Hummerts were a difficult target. They made their home in Greenwich, Connecticut, from which they did most of their supervising of Air Features programs. I found no New York writer who had met Frank Hummert; only a few had ever met Ann Hummert. The Hummerts dealt with writers largely through intermediaries and through written syn-opses and memoranda. The plotting was done far ahead. Dialogue writers were not allowed to deviate. The task offered a livelihood but involved a frustrating relationship.

Most of the series were built around insoluble dilemmas. *Backstage Wife* looked at marriage from the point of view of a woman whose husband moved constantly in more glamorous circles than she did, always encountering women who represented potential threats. Could she hold her central role in his life? *John's Other Wife* used essentially the same formula except that the husband was a major business executive, with secretaries ready to cater to his every whim. The series formula was in some cases articulated at the start of each episode, as on *Our Gal Sunday*—"the series that asks the question: can a girl from a little mining town in the West find happiness as the wife of a wealthy and titled Englishman?" While some series featured perpetually troubled characters, others—*Ma Perkins, David Harum*—featured helping-hand characters, aiding people in trouble.

Most critics disparaged "soap operas," but scholars had begun to take an interest in them. Herta Herzog, a social psychologist, had published a report titled "On Borrowed Experience," which appeared in *Studies in Philosophy and Social Science.** Herzog, in the course of innumerable interviews with serial listeners, had found many who seemed to accept the stories as real, or at least spoke as though they did. Referring to a soap opera doctor who had helped a character through a medical crisis, one listener said wistfullly, "I wonder if he could cure me." Many looked to the serials for guidance in their own problems. An unmarried woman said: "I like family stories best. If I get married, I want to get an idea of how a wife should be to a husband." Some listeners addressed letters to serial characters, offering advice on their problems, sometimes warning against plots by other characters. Such letters delighted advertising agencies and were cited as bolstering their ban on authorship credit.

Herzog threw further light on the "reality" aura. The Hummert serials were said to draw fifty million letters a year, many enclosing boxtops or coupons in response to merchandise offers, which were sometimes related to story events. One character invented a type of can opener, later offered for boxtops. Garden seeds were a frequent offer, enabling a housewife to say, "Look at my Ma Perkins peonies—they're doing fine." Serial

* *Studies in Philosophy and Social Science*, 9, no. 1 (1941): 65–91.

listeners were found to be a special group who did not listen to news-oriented programs. The average serial listener followed 6.6 serials. None listened to fewer than two; one followed twenty-two. Almost a third spoke of planning the day around "my programs." Some expressed a dire dependence on serials. This was the world where the Hummerts reigned supreme—and to which we were about to lay siege.

The strike date was set: October 26, 1948. Many writers had stopped writing. A strategy committee was in action, headed by Peter Lyon, former president. Volunteers prepared picket signs. Some writers (including me) were aghast at the idea of picketing, but others seemed ready, even eager. A feverish spirit developed. All major radio studio buildings were to be targeted. There were endless committee meetings and coast-to-coast phone calls. I made daily trips from Larchmont to the city, then shuttled between the campus and the downtown RWG office on Thirty-Eighth Street. The office was managed by a paid executive secretary, in frequent consultation with our attorney, known as a "labor lawyer."

Arriving at the office the day before the strike date, I received a phone call from the U.S. Conciliation Service—something I had never heard of. A J. R. Mandelbaum was on the line and sounded authoritative. He requested that I keep pickets off the streets until he had had a chance to talk to "both sides." With no notion of what our obligations or rights might be, I promptly accepted. To me it seemed a blessed reprieve. I informed the members of the strategy committee, some of whom were furious. They phoned the West Coast, where more fury erupted. That evening the Los Angeles members met until almost midnight (their time), after which they phoned me at my home—at 3 A.M. our time. They protested my action. What right had I to ignore the strike decision? I explained that the strike was still on, that we were merely postponing the picketing. This brought scorn. What was a strike without pickets?

Next day Mr. Mandelbaum met with our strategy group and officers. A man of imposing physique, neatly tailored, he assumed a take-charge manner. He stayed on his feet. "I want you to put out a press release immediately. I'll tell you what to say—take this down. Quote. Through the intervention of J. R. Mandelbaum, U.S. Conciliator, the Radio Writers Guild has agreed to keep its pickets off the streets temporarily until he has had an opportunity to confer with a committee representing sponsors and their advertising agencies. Unquote." He explained to us, "When I talk to them, I want them to sense that only through me are pickets staying off the street—at least for the moment. That will make them listen to me."

Next day our press release appeared in a few trade papers, while Mr. Mandelbaum conferred with the "other side." A day or so later another release appeared in trade papers. "Through the intervention of J. R. Mandelbaum, U.S. Conciliator, a committee representing sponsors and. . . ." As he continued his shuttle diplomacy, each news item seemed to begin with the name J. R. Mandelbaum. He had made himself the man in the middle. At the guild office some of the fury subsided while we waited for results. But many considered him a pompous egotist. A seething restlessness continued.

At this point another surprise message greeted me at the RWG office. Mr. and Mrs. Frank Hummert wanted to meet with me. The message suggested lunch at a Park Avenue restaurant near the Air Features office. I wondered what they were up to. I asked Peter Lyon, as chairman of the strategy committee, to go with me. He seemed as puzzled as I was. Some members felt we should not meet with the Hummerts and argued that industry wide, not piecemeal, negotiation was needed. But we returned the call and agreed to the suggested time and place.

Unlike most of our members, I had once encountered Mrs. Hummert—not via script writing but through my teaching. For the 1938–39 academic year I had received approval for a survey course, with a budget that included fifty-dollar fees for some two dozen guest lecturers representing all phases of the broadcasting industry, including preparations for television. The project (one of the lecturers smilingly called it a "vaudeville course") proved extraordinarily useful to my education, and justified itself by attracting fifty students. Among those who accepted my invitation and performed impressively were Frank Stanton of CBS on research, Eddie Cantor on producing comedy programs, Norman Corwin on radio as a poetry medium, Howard Barlow on preparing music for radio's *March of Time*, Cesar Saerchinger on radio news, John Royal on NBC's preparations for a television era, and Ann Hummert on daytime serials. Her acceptance especially delighted me. I was curious.

The Hummert serials evoked a cliché small-town America. Ann Hummert turned out to be chic, petite, alert. She seemed highstrung, intent on the job at hand. Introduced for her talk, she paced up and down restlessly while talking. She spoke without notes, never hesitating. After talking for about forty minutes, she answered questions in the same brisk manner, seemingly ready for every question. Some of the questions were challenges.

Many people, she said, considered the serials "escapist," but not so. They were real. That's why people loved them. They saw themselves and people they knew. Critics who called them escapist just didn't know America. To illustrate, she talked at some length about *Just Plain Bill*, which seemed to be a favorite of hers. Members of the class seemed particularly interested in this portion. One of the members later decided to write an article on "soap operas," to be sent to *Harper's*. Wanting to quote her directly, he phoned Air Features and asked for an opportunity to check the quotation with Mrs. Hummert, to ensure its correctness. She came to the phone and said, "That's no problem. I'll send you a copy." She had apparently prepared for the lecture by writing it in full and memorizing it. Her public appearance, so unusual for the Hummerts, must have seemed crucial to her—perhaps an occasion to answer stinging criticisms. The typescript duly arrived and showed the following passage on *Just Plain Bill:*

> So we put this man from the Middle West—the fact that he was from the Middle West makes him a great favorite; people seem to like characters from that section best—in this situation. Here he was talking to his assistant: "My daughter is coming home today. I haven't seen her in eighteen years. She's been east with her aunt, in fine finishing schools, and doesn't even know I'm her father. Is she going to be too good for me?"

Here, as in *Backstage Wife, John's Other Wife,* and *Our Gal Sunday,* the Hummerts had begun with a basic dilemma, a social gap, around which years of program sequences could be spun. She had no hesitation in calling it "real."

When Peter Lyon and I arrived at the designated Park Avenue restaurant, we learned that the reclusive Hummerts had a special table in a corner masked by potted palms, preventing others from observing them. We were led there and found the Hummerts already present. My immediate impression was the contrast between them. She, as before, was stylish and a bundle of energy. He was tall, gangly, with a folksy, bucolic character. He was also older and seemed a bit sallow-looking. Together they seemed to epitomize a Hummert serial formula. Could a folksy geezer from the Midwest find happiness with a svelte, dynamic secretary in suburbia? Perhaps she was right; perhaps it was all more real than one supposed.

We ordered lunch. Lyon and I each ordered a solid lunch. Mrs. Hummert ate something sensible. Hummert's choice was something strange. Perhaps it was shredded wheat with hot water poured over it. My main recollection is that it was odd, and ascetic.

Mrs. Hummert led a few minutes of small talk, then looked to Mr. Hummert. It was clear that she was yielding the spotlight to him. He began a leisurely monologue—the apparent purpose of the encounter. "If there is anything I hate, it's lawyers. If lawyers get involved in a thing, it poisons the whole business. Now this matter of the writers' contract, and the strike, and all that—the only people likely to gain from it are the lawyers. So that's no good."

We agreed about the lawyers. Hummert paused a moment, then went on.

"So here's what we would like to do, Ann and I. We would like to join the Radio Writers Guild. We want to be able to say to our sponsors, 'We're union members. There's been this strike vote. We have to go along. We have no choice.' Is there any reason we can't join?"

We were flabbergasted. Nothing like this had occurred to us as a possibility. The implications were not immediately clear, but his question had to be answered. Lyon had a briefcase with assorted RWG papers—proposed contract, press release, membership forms. He assured the Hummerts they were eligible and would be welcome. Hummert looked briefly at an application form. He said they would fill out applications right away and have them delivered to the guild with the membership dues.

All this had been accomplished so swiftly that we were, for the moment, nonplussed. Then Lyon took a further step. Casually he asked, "Now about our contract. Could you sign it on behalf of Air Features?"

Hummert drawled, "Well—that's what you'll have to take up with Air Features." I was baffled. Was this a new runaround, a trap of some sort?

Hummert went on, "You probably think I own Air Features. That's what everybody thinks. I don't own it. I'm just an employee. I set it up that way, on purpose. The president of Air Features is Jim Sauter. That's the fellow you'll have to talk to." It all sounded like a maneuver by the shrewd, foxy hero of the Hummerts' *David Harum* series.

Lyon asked, "Well, would you introduce us to Mr. Sauter?"

"Sure, why not? After lunch, let's walk over there and say hello."

And that's how it happened. At Air Features we walked straight through the secretarial area to the inner office of "J. Sauter, President." Hummert strode right in and we followed. Sauter rose from his desk. Hummert said, "Jim, these are the folks from the Writers Guild. They have this contract. You know about it. Why don't you sign it?"

Sauter looked at it. "Oh yes. Yes." And he signed it. It covered a large chunk of network programming.

It was extraordinary news at RWG. Some members were incredulous. We were not able to observe the impact of the Hummert defection on the sponsors, advertising agencies, and independent producers, but it became clear a day or two later, when Mr. Mandelbaum reappeared at the guild office, obviously in fine fettle over the news he brought us. The opposing forces had caved in—earlier than he had expected. He obviously considered it a triumph of his shuttle diplomacy. They had agreed to negotiate a contract and were prepared to start talks in early November. The "other side" had engaged a well-known attorney to work out a peaceful settlement.

The meetings began impressively at the Waldorf-Astoria. On one side of a long table sat our lawyer and our executive secretary, flanked each day by a delegation of writers available that day. On the other sat the sponsors' attorney (his fee was reported to be twenty-five thousand dollars) flanked by a formidable array of advertising executives. By the spring of 1949 the Minimum Basic Agreement covering employment of freelance writers was complete. In 1951, after the National Labor Relations Board had held a vote of all writers covered, the agreement went into effect.

The writers' strike of 1948 was no great labor crisis. But in the business affairs of American writers it marked a fateful turning point. The writer is one of two professions selected for attention in the U.S. Constitution. It empowers the Congress

to promote the Progress of Science and useful Arts, by securing for limited Times to Authors and Inventors the exclusive Right to their respective Writings and Discoveries.

The Founding Fathers clearly considered it important to strengthen the independence of writers and inventors by giving them control, at least for a time, over uses made of their work and revenue from it. Copyright legislation was duly enacted by the Founding Fathers and became the Magna Carta of writers. It remains so for the Authors League of America.

But a strange thing happened en route to modern times. In 1909 the Congress passed a new copyright law, which served the rising managerial class of the day by simply amending the meaning of the word *author*.

The word "author" shall include an employer in the case of works made for hire.

Thus at the dawn of the new mass media the support that the Constitution had earmarked for writers was quietly handed to their bosses. Copyright law became *their* Magna Carta. It encouraged new media corporations—in film and then in broadcasting—to deal with writers on an employer-employee basis, presumably settling all questions of ownership and control. The mere use of the word *employ* in a contract, or in the check signed by the writer, seemed to give the company carte blanche to do as it wished with the writer's work. For writers it had curious results. In a catalogue of copyright entries in the Library of Congress, I came across a reference to my first script written for *Cavalcade of America*. The entry read: "Dr Franklin Goes to Court by Erik Barnouw. Author: E. I. Du Pont de Nemours & Company." The script had been written at home, commissioned on a freelance basis. But the language had made me an employee and meant I owned nothing beyond my original fee.

When the RWG was first organized, its freelance writers clamored for the guild to put an end to employer-employee contracts. But then something new entered the picture. The New Deal's Wagner Act, passed in 1936, gave *employees* the right to bargain collectively, even on pay scales, without being in violation of antitrust law. And a strike could be a legal step in the bargaining process. So when RWG went to war for its freelance writers it went not as a guild of independent contractors but as a union of employees. The employee status, though hated, had provided clout. It now enabled the guild to win precious rights for radio writers: to receive writer credit; to be present at rehearsals; to be paid for repeat uses; to be paid for adaptations to other media; and, in case revisions were needed, to have the first chance to make them.

What writers could not control was the final form of their work. This was galling to many writers but, ironically, was the key to the new clout. The new collective bargaining agreement included a clause approved by the National Labor Relations Board:

> *Persons covered.* This agreement shall cover freelance writers . . . rendering personal services as "employees." . . . An employee . . . shall be any writer . . . as to whom the company has the right by contract to direct the performance of personal services in making revisions.[*]

The clause, or variations of it, became standard in collective bargaining agreements covering freelance writers.

The Authors League of America approved the contract but deplored the trend. It represented, said Elmer Rice, member of the ALA council, "the industrialization of the writer." It led in 1953 to a split in the world of American writers. In an amicable divorce, the Radio Writers Guild and Screen Writers Guild severed their ties to the league and merged to form a new, independent Writers Guild of America representing writers in film, radio, and television—the "industrialized" media. The Authors League of America continued to represent writers of books and plays who wished to continue working as independent contractors, looking to copyright law as their bastion. Members of the Writers Guild of America looked— for better or worse—to labor law.

For some writers it was an uncomfortable transition. Some had long argued "We're not a *union*, we're a *guild.*" The word *guild* had a pleasantly medieval, artisanal, pre-industrial sound. They shied away from the rough-and-tumble that the word *union* seemed to evoke. But for others the association with *workers* had its own romantic as well as pragmatic appeal, which the rising unionism of the New Deal era fostered. Considering the big-business structure of the new media, the writers saw no other possible choice.

I served as first president of the eastern region of the Writers Guild of America and later as national chairman. As a writer of books, I also remained a member of the Authors League of America.

The role of the Hummerts in the RWG struggle with sponsors was

---

[*] See Erik Barnouw, "A Business Portfolio," in *The Television Writer* (New York, Hill & Wang, 1962): 161–70, for the history and ramifications of this clause.

hardly mentioned in the press. But J. R. Mandelbaum liked to take bows. He was proud of the many strike antagonists he had brought together over the years in fruitful harmony, and he counted the sponsors and writers among them. The Hummerts were content to stay out of the spotlight, and continued to prosper for a few more years. The rise of television eventually ended their saga. When Frank Hummert died, it took *Variety* two weeks to find out about it.

TALLULAH BANKHEAD

"This woman did not fly to extremes;
she lived there."
—Quentin Crisp

Now the talk was all television. As Eisenhower entered the White House,
all signs pointed to an imminent television boom. The allotting of tele-
vision channels, halted for four years by the Korean War, had been re-
sumed. Television sets again rolled off assembly lines. Networks, ad-
vertising agencies, and independent producers were in high gear with
television plans. At New York studios, ventures in every genre from quiz
show to grand opera were in progress, creating an air of excitement. New
York had been program headquarters for network radio and was like-
wise expected to dominate network television. The assumption was that
in television, as in radio, most programs would be produced "live." Both
David Sarnoff of RCA and William Paley of CBS were reportedly deter-
mined to maintain the "live" policy.

Hollywood was boycotting the whole to-do, but its unemployed artists
and technicians were worried. Many were streaming to New York to get
in on the action. Radio people, too, were worried. Comedian Fred Allen
observed that sponsors were abandoning radio "like the bones at a barbe-
cue." A number of radio successes—Amos 'n' Andy, The Aldrich Family,
The Goldbergs, Meet the Press, My Friend Irma, Information Please, Sus-
pense, You Bet Your Life, and variety shows headed by Arthur Godfrey
and Kate Smith—had successfully made the switch to television. In mid-
1953 the Theatre Guild and its sponsor, U.S. Steel, decided their moment
had likewise come. They would start in the fall.

People closely identified with radio—as I was at this time—felt edgy.
The new television bureaucracy liked to say, "This is different, this is
visual." Radio people had a sense of being elbowed aside. So a phone call

*from the Theatre Guild—about television—was very welcome, especially
when it involved Tallulah Bankhead.*

The call came in November, from Armina Marshall, Theatre Guild part-
ner. She was excited. Tallulah Bankhead had agreed to appear in the
Theatre Guild television series. She would play Hedda in Ibsen's *Hedda
Gabler.* The Theatre Guild wanted me to do the script. I was delighted.

It was Tallulah who had stipulated *Hedda Gabler.* It had something to
do with fulfilling a destiny. Thirty years earlier, during one of her first
Broadway appearances, the critic John Mason Brown had said she would
some day be the ultimate Hedda Gabler. The fact that he had heaped scorn
on another of her performances—as Cleopatra in Shakespeare's *Antony
and Cleopatra*—seemed to give special significance to his Hedda Gabler
pronouncement. For three decades the prediction had haunted her like
the words of some Greek oracle. People kept asking, "When are you going
to do *Hedda Gabler?*" It seemed high time.

January 5, 1954, was the date set for the broadcast. I would have to work
fast: the first reading was to be on December 22. Armina mentioned that
Tallulah had a Westchester estate—a luxurious retreat in Bedford Hills,
Westchester County—but would be at a New York hotel for a few days
during which she wanted to talk with me about the adaptation. Would
I please phone her immediately at the hotel and arrange a meeting? Armina gave me the details.

Before I could make the call, Armina called again. "Tallulah may want
you to explain what the play means. You'd better be prepared for that."
Armina seemed to feel that Tallulah was quite worried about this. I was
not surprised: I remembered *Hedda Gabler* as very elusive, which seemed
to contribute to its continuing fascination. I did not relish the idea of
explaining it. The following day, at the Columbia Faculty Club, I felt for-
tunate to encounter Maurice Valency, who taught a course in modern
drama. It was he who had so successfully adapted Dürrenmatt's *The Visit*
for Lunt and Fontanne. I told him of my impending visit to Tallulah. What
should I tell her about Hedda? Valency seemed amused and said simply,
"I think she wanted to be a boy." That seemed a reasonable interpretation,
but I was not sure it would help the actress.

Tallulah had recently published a memoir from which I learned that
she once had a fling at astrology and a horoscope reading by the famous

Evangeline Adams. She paid fifty dollars for it. (She could have got it for a Forhan's toothpaste carton if she had listened to our Erwin, Wasey broadcasts of Evangeline Adams.) Tallulah was especially beguiled by a passage from Evangeline Adams's book *Astrology: Your Place in the Sun.*

> Ibsen drew a perfect picture of the Scorpio woman in *Hedda Gabler.* The suddenness, violences and exaggerations of her frenzies are totally incomprehensible, not only to her easy-going husband but to the clever man of the world who thinks he has outgeneraled and mastered her. In speech Scorpios are fluent, frank and vehement. They are good conversationalists, insist on being the center of attraction in whatever gatherings they find themselves. In love Scorpio produces the most intensely passionate people of any sign of the zodiac. They are admired and feared.

Tallulah was delighted with all this, but she herself was an Aquarian, and Aquarians were described by Evangeline Adams as "calm, serene, and temperate." Tallulah felt she must be an Aquarian in a Scorpio skin. Anyway, she relished the passage. In her memoir she observes: "Quite a rip, that Norwegian! Between us, I think Hedda would be my cup of tea." *

I arrived at the hotel suite at the appointed hour, early Friday evening, and found myself in events both baffling and fascinating. I was admitted by a calm black lady who remained unruffled throughout events that followed. She appeared to be Tallulah's secretary and factotum. Tallulah was busy upbraiding two young men in salty language, but suspended this activity long enough to welcome me ceremoniously, deposit me in a corner, order champagne for me, and explain what was going on. These two young gentlemen, she said, needed to be enlightened on the vile deeds done to her by their boss, Henry Luce, via the pages of *Time.* She had almost finished with this necessary task. In a few moments she would be ready for *our* important business.

John Emery, the one man Tallulah married, once made the following comment: "Tallulah is the only woman I ever knew who could carry on a conversation, listen to the radio, read a book and do her hair at the same time." † This was the kind of performance I was now privileged to watch.

I sensed that her ceremonious treatment of me was meant to show

---

* Tallulah Bankhead, *Tallulah: my autobiography* (New York: Harper, 1952), p. 37.

† *Tallulah*, p. 226.

Tallulah Bankhead:
Aquarian or Scorpion?
(Billy Rose Theatre
Collection, New York
Public Library for the
Performing Arts—Astor,
Lenox and Tilden
Foundations)

the *Time* reporters that people of probity could expect to be treated with utmost respect. The reporters, far from being discomfited by her tongue-lashing (aimed less at them than at their boss), were obviously enjoying it hugely. Why, I wondered, had *two* reporters turned up for this interview, or whatever it was? Perhaps they knew they could expect a good show. And it was a good show, during which Tallulah occasionally turned to me to provide an illuminating footnote.

When the reporters finally left (assuring her of fair treatment), I assumed it would be time for *Hedda Gabler* talk, but apparently not yet. The secretary came in with a huge checkbook, one with many checks on each page. Tallulah explained to me that one more chore would have to be disposed of before we could get to work. A car would be coming later to take her back to Bedford Hills. Before that, checks would have to be signed. My champagne glass was replenished. Then Tallulah and the secretary settled together on the couch, with the book before them.

I recalled that a few years earlier, a Tallulah Bankhead maid had been indicted and jailed for kiting a series of Bankhead checks and pocketing awesome sums of money. In the present regime there seemed no hint of such irregularities. But the procedure was astonishing just the same. Tallulah would look at each check and let out an appropriate response—

grunt, moan, bellow, or roar—which would be followed by a quiet, brief explanation from the secretary. Tallulah seemed to be nearsighted and bent closely over each check before reacting. "Flowers! Twelve hundred dollars for flowers!" The secretary mentioned a number of actors and actresses who were hospitalized; Tallulah had wanted flowers delivered to them. Tallulah signed the check. Other items were similarly taken care of: landscaping for the Bedford grounds, wine, liquor, limousines, Screen Actors Guild and Actors Equity dues, charity donations. It was a panorama of Bankhead life. The secretary smiled at some of the outbursts. Each explanation was followed by a quick, scrawled signature by Tallulah. There seemed to be complete rapport between the two. The explosions were just part of the ritual.

Watching them, I thought about Hedda Gabler. She was described by Ibsen as twenty-nine years old, beautiful, and patrician, daughter of the renowned General Gabler. She was socially adept and could be charming and amusing. But she was also cold: behind the charm we are made to sense a ruthless, egocentric woman at work, meddling in and destroying the lives around her. It struck me that in this final respect, Tallulah was quite different. She could excoriate people in a way that gave only pleasure. Was John Mason Brown really right about her being the ideal Hedda?

The checkbook ceremony was finally over, and the secretary withdrew. Tallulah noted that the limousine would arrive in fifteen minutes, so not much time was left. But no matter: very little needed to be discussed. She asked how many acts there would be. I explained that Theatre Guild broadcasts generally included fifty-four minutes of drama, separated by U.S. Steel commercials into three acts. Ibsen's four acts would somehow have to become three. Fine, she said. In one of them she would like to wear an evening dress "to show my nice shoulders." She lightly touched her shoulders to clarify the point. I felt this could be arranged. In that case she had only one other demand. "I need at least two minutes for a costume-change; so I should probably have a portable dressing room right on stage, so I can make a quick entrance afterwards." I was sure this could be done and promised to discuss it with the Theatre Guild.

I had stored in my mind a few sage observations on Hedda, but sensed they would not be needed. Whatever her worries had been, they had not been interpretive problems. After all, she had lived with Hedda for decades, awaiting this historic moment.

Tallulah observed that the impending broadcast was crazy. "Hedda is supposed to be twenty-nine. So I should have done her twenty years ago." She laughed her throaty yet velvety laugh, and said she'd been through worse problems than that. When she played Cleopatra, John Mason Brown had written: "Tallulah barged down the Nile as Cleopatra and sank."

It occurred to her suddenly that she should give me her unlisted phone number. If there should be problems to discuss, I could call her in Bedford Hills. I jotted the number in an obscure corner of my diary: Pound Ridge 4–5122. I felt a solemn sense of responsibility. No one, I was determined, would extort that number from me. My feeling of special privilege was destined to have a disconcerting denouement. When I spoke to her two weeks later at the first reading, she seemed quite unaware of ever having met me. "Who are you?"

When I explained, she said, "Ah yes! The collaborator!"

The adaptation had involved problems new to me. A number of writers had translated *Hedda Gabler* from the Norwegian. The earliest translation appeared to be the well-known version by Edmund Gosse and William Archer, on which the copyright had by now expired. I was told I could use any part of this that I wished, but I found it stodgy and humorless, doing Ibsen an injustice. The better translations were all covered by copyright. The Theatre Guild had selected that of Noel Langley as preferable to others and had purchased the right to use it in our program. I could use any lines from this or the Gosse-Archer version or improvise variations of my own, provided I did not infringe on other translations.

A line in Ibsen's Act III posed special difficulty. Judge Brack is pursuing his design to seduce Hedda. He has already suggested that he would like to be considered a special friend of the family with the right to come and go—while also enjoying certain special privileges vis-à-vis the lady of the house. These triangular arrangements, the judge suggests, can relieve tedium. After all, her husband, the very scholarly George Tesman, is totally wrapped up in his research on the Middle Ages. In the course of all this Hedda says (in the Gosse-Archer version): "So you want to be the one cock in the basket—that is your aim?" Brack, lowering his voice, says, "Yes, that is my aim." Gosse and Archer explain, in a footnote, that the absurd sentence allotted to Hedda is "a proverbial saying." Since it would be incomprehensible in performance, I tried alternatives. Langley's line seemed, in this instance, no more satisfactory. During rehearsal I was discussing this with the director Alex Siegel, in the presence of

Tallulah and of Luther Adler, who was playing Judge Brack. Tallulah suddenly volunteered, "I know what she could say! Let's have her say, 'So you want to be the cock-of-the-walk, Judge Brack!'"

"Splendid," said Alex Siegel, and I agreed. It seemed to us all to have the right overtones. Siegel later said to me, "You know what's good about it? It's cock talk." The suggested line went into the script.

By the time of the first camera rehearsal, problems of this sort were forgotten. Siegel worried about something quite different. On the monitor Tallulah looked beautiful—almost twenty-nine-ish—from some angles; but a slight change of angle would suddenly show lines and pouches, hinting of middle age. Siegel became obsessed with camera angles and their associated lights and shadows. The set consisted of living room and adjoining master bedroom, hallways, solarium, and garden, so arranged that four cameras could prowl around the periphery and photograph characters from diverse angles. In the scene in which Hedda burns Eilert Lovborg's manuscript, apparently destroying several lives, Siegel planned to shoot her through the fireplace. For other special moments he liked to have a living room painting mounted on hinges so that it could be swiveled out of the way, allowing a camera to shoot through the wall for a brief instant. Preparing for the telecast, Siegel studied all angles— and their effects—with greatest care. Each cameraman then went into the telecast with a card mounted on his camera showing in exact order the shots he would be responsible for. He had to be in the right position, with the right lens in place, when the cue came. At that moment his camera light would go on. Over earphones he would get continual supplementary instructions from Siegel.

During the telecast I watched from the control room. I listened to Tallulah, watched her movements. She seemed to be remembering every move. She seemed to handle some scenes splendidly. But in the control room her performance was totally obliterated by the rituals of live production. Siegel watched his four camera monitors like a hawk. A steady stream of instructions went out to the cameramen. "Ready two. Take two. Four, get ready now. Closer, damn it! Three, can you avoid that vase? Ready, one! Take one! Take three. Hey, she looks great on that one. Two, can you soften that focus a little? Okay, fine. Take two!" Siegel kept picking the strategic moments for his switches. On the master monitor, shot replaced shot in rapid succession. In the control room a Hollywood visitor whispered, almost despairingly, "How can you shoot and edit at the same time?"

To any film aficionado, the procedure was preposterous. Editing was supposed to be a time for patient work, trial and error, the experimental joining of shot to shot, the study of alternatives. It was in the cutting room that films were finally made. A disastrous performance was sometimes saved in the cutting room. Here, in live television, performance and rescue operation proceeded in lockstep. It was a procedure so irrational that it seemed unlikely to survive as a dramatic technique. How could it compete with film?

Through the control room hubbub, we sensed that *Hedda Gabler* was continuing through its foreordained stages. It reaches its dramatic end. The people in the living room are seen to react in sudden horror to the sound of a shot from the adjoining bedroom. At that instant Siegel says, "Take four!" This shows us Hedda, having just shot herself in the temple with one of her father's pistols, falling back on the huge bed. Meanwhile camera four and its cameraman, riding on a boom, rise high above the scene. Rushing in from the other room, the other characters are seen on the fringes of the picture. In their midst lies Hedda. Behind her, on the wall, the portrait of the distinguished General Gabler comes into the frame.

Review comments ran the gamut. Harriet Van Horne, writing in the New York *World Telegram*, on the following day, called it "an all but impeccable production of Ibsen's *Hedda Gabler*." Of Tallulah she wrote: "She looked lovely on all cameras. With her upswept hair . . . and off-shoulder gowns" she was hardly recognizable as the "Tallu who too often appeared as a cruel caricature of herself." Here was "a vehicle worthy of her talents." At the opposite extreme was Philip Hamburger of *The New Yorker*, who had seen Alla Nazimova in the role decades ago. Apparently she had forever defined Hedda for him. He saw Tallulah's Hedda as "the sort of girl the celebrated Mae West once delighted in interpreting—all waving hips, bouncing framework, and ninety-proof larynx . . . a messy, shrill, and meaningless hour." The mess had been put together by "a man called Barnouw." *

Still another kind of reaction came a day or two later. I was at home

---

* *The New Yorker*, Jan. 23, 1954.

in Larchmont when the doorbell rang. At the door was a gentleman who asked if I was Erik Barnouw. I said I was. So he handed me an envelope and left. It bore the name of a law firm. I gathered he was a process server and that I was being sued. I was at first baffled, then terrified. Examining the document, I gathered that it was a plagiarism suit by a writer who, years earlier, had translated *Hedda Gabler* and had sent the manuscript to Tallulah Bankhead, in England at the time. She had kept it for a substantial period and finally returned it. This had now been plagiarized, said the document, as proved by the line, "So you want to be the cock-of-the-walk, Judge Brack?"

I headed for New York and the office of my friend William Fitelson, the Theatre Guild attorney, who had been through months of effort in connection with Arnold Bennett's *The Great Adventure*. I confronted him now with a different legal problem, which I explained as well as I could. He looked at the document and said, "I'll take care of this. Forget it." That is the last I heard of it.

I was immensely relieved. As I left, I reflected that it had been an interesting month. My show with the tempestuous Tallulah—on live television—and my first lawsuit. And John Mason Brown had at last been exorcised.

DR. L. E. SMITH

*"What then did you expect when you unbound
the gag that muted those black mouths?"*
—Jean-Paul Sartre

Robert Hudson, a long-time educational broadcasting leader, came to
us at the Center for Mass Communication with a proposal for a television series—better yet, a filmed series. He had become vice president
of a setup to be known as NET—National Educational Television—that
would, it was hoped, infuse life into an almost stillborn educational
television movement. In 1952 the FCC had set aside channels for 242
noncommercial television stations across the country. The move elicited
much enthusiasm but few applicants. The financial hurdles were staggering. No funds came with the channels. By 1954 only a handful of educational stations had managed to make a start and to survive precariously,
producing mainly lectures, interviews, and roundtables. NET, financed
by the Ford Foundation, was meant to change the picture with injections
of more ambitious fare. It would be a "program service" to the stations.
Hudson's query to me: Would I be interested in writing and supervising
a series of films on constitutional law—documentaries perhaps? (I knew
absolutely nothing about constitutional law. But then, I had known nothing about advertising, or radio, or syphilis. Was one supposed to know
such things in advance?) Hudson said he could offer us eighteen thousand dollars per half-hour program, which he described as the largest
budget yet earmarked for an NET-funded series. Documentarists at this
time considered one thousand dollars per minute the rock-bottom cost
for documentary production, so the plan seemed quixotic, risky, perhaps
impossible. Yet I jumped at it. I felt that film was the key to a meaningful
future for educational television—as well as for our teaching program at
Columbia. It had begun as a "radio" section, which became "radio and
television" thanks to early help from NBC. Now I wanted to add "film."

No one else at Columbia seemed to claim jurisdiction over this splendid medium.

NET approached the legal project warily. The American Bar Association (ABA) had long opposed any intrusion of audiovisual media into legal affairs. Its Canon 35 held that cameras and camera personnel should be barred from the courtroom as a threat to its integrity. This was not a legal ban but a policy backed by much of the profession. It made for caution. Hudson negotiated a visit for himself and me to U.S. Supreme Court Justice Felix Frankfurter to seek his advice. In his chambers the justice lectured us for an hour on the "awesome" responsibility we were undertaking. He urged that Professor Herbert Wechsler of Columbia University, professor of constitutional law and a former U.S. assistant attorney general, be asked to serve as final arbiter on all content matters. We found Wechsler willing to work with us. During the following months he drafted a forty-page memorandum on major issues and cases we should deal with—whatever the form we decided to adopt. It became my bible for the next four years.

Leafing through a Houston, Texas, phone directory in the New York Public Library I found, to my astonishment and delight, that both L. E. Smith, dentist, and Richard R. Grovey, barber, were listed. Could this Smith possibly be the Lonnie Smith of *Smith v Allwright* (321 US 669), a pivotal case decided by the U.S. Supreme Court in 1944? And could Grovey be the Grovey of *Grovey v Townsend* (295 US 45), decided by the Supreme Court in 1935? Phone calls to Houston revealed that they were, in fact, the people we hoped they were.

These two men had figured, years apart, in efforts to terminate the Southern "white primary," one of the devices by which blacks had been kept politically powerless even though the Fifteenth Amendment had theoretically given them full voting rights in 1870. The two legal struggles, both initiated in Houston, had eventually achieved victory in one of the grand chapters of the civil rights movement. We knew the names of some of the lawyers involved; some of these likewise appeared in the Houston phone book. Might they perhaps help us recreate their victory on film—on location, with original participants appearing as themselves? This we hoped.

Our budget had pushed us in this direction. We could not afford to hire actors nor to rent studios. Historic personages appearing "as themselves" in documentaries were generally not paid, although they might be reimbursed for expenses. Might not this on-location procedure also yield a special authenticity? With this in mind, I had recruited Stefan Sharff, a Polish-born cameraman-editor-director-producer who relished on-location work and hated large film crews. He preferred to work alone. He had studied law in Poland and was excited by our subject. I had seen some of his films and admired their sense of time and place. Our plan was that I would write and supervise; Sharff would do virtually everything else: shoot, direct, edit. Guided by the Wechsler memo, we studied cases stemming from Houston, San Francisco, Asheville, Statesboro, and New York on voting rights, labor unions, censorship, military power, and other issues and got ready for action. Dorothy Oshlag, late of Time, Inc., took over as CMC manager and became our indispensable coordinator and backup on all problems and crises.

For many years he had been outraged by the "white primary" system. Early in 1957 I flew to Houston to reconnoiter. I first visited Richard Grovey, a small, wizened, enchanting dynamo. His tiny barbershop reflected a subsistence livelihood. The letters of "Grovey's Barbershop" painted on the window must have been painted by himself. In smaller letters he announced that he was also a notary public and that he prepared income taxes. The interior, though cramped, seemed to be a gathering place. There was always a group, talking—often talking politics. Grovey, while barbering, was discussion leader posing provocative questions. He had always taken an active role in neighborhood issues and sometimes reached beyond them. I learned to my amazement that on his modest income he had put a daughter through UCLA law school.

For many years he had been outraged by the "white primary" system. Blacks were allowed to vote in the general election, never in the primary. But the primary in Texas, as in many Southern states—virtually "one-party" states controlled by Democrats—settled most issues. The vote in the main election, for candidates chosen via the racist primary system, seemed almost meaningless to blacks. Grovey finally decided to do something about it and began gathering funds for a legal tussle. Speaking at a church in Beaumont he raised $44; in Texarkana, $52. At a recreation center in San Antonio he raised $206. He took his young son with him to a YMCA in Dallas, where they garnered $208. Finally he was ready. In July 1934 he went to the county clerk's office in Houston to ask for an absentee ballot to vote in the primary. Mr. Townsend, county clerk—who knew Grovey well—refused with a smile, adding, "If they were all like you, Grovey, we wouldn't mind." Grovey said, "They are all like me." But Townsend shook his head, refusing to budge. So Grovey filed suit in the Justice Court, claiming that Texas had deprived him of his rights as a citizen. He asked damages of ten dollars.

To many it seemed an absurd charade. Ten dollars—was that the value of citizenship? Why not the usual million or two? But Grovey and his lawyer had a canny plan. The smallness of the damage claim meant that the case could not be reviewed in any other court in Texas. But because a federal issue was involved, they could appeal directly to the U.S. Supreme Court. To their amazement the Court agreed to hear the case. Argument took place in March 1935, and the Court arrived at a decision with remarkable speed. On April 1 Justice Roberts, speaking for a unanimous Court, said:

> The Democratic Party . . . as a voluntary political association . . . has the power to determine who shall be eligible to participate in the party's primaries.

It was a party matter, said the Court, not a government matter. It was private, not public business. The decision went against Grovey 9-0.

It was worse than a defeat. For blacks—in Houston and throughout the South—it meant that the outrageous system had been affirmed at the highest level of government. It was a disaster. Sooner or later, someone would have to try again.

Five years later, in July 1940, the black dentist L. E. Smith took the same walk that Grovey had taken, again requesting an absentee ballot for the primary. This time the case had wider backing, including that of the NAACP, the National Association for the Advancement of Colored People. What happened at the county clerk's office was well documented. Smith brought two witnesses, one a photographer. The court record included ample testimony on what was said. The brief confrontation would be a key element in our film, placed at or near the opening. The Grovey material would come later, to emphasize the crucial nature of the Smith venture and its legal maneuvers.

Grovey promptly agreed to be in our film, both in a barbershop discussion and reenactment of some of his fund-raising trips. These would give a sense of the black communities in this Texas area. Throughout our series, which we had decided to call *Decision: The Constitution in Action,* we were finding losers even more ready than winners to help in reenactment. Perhaps it seemed a chance to fight a battle over again, to reaffirm the justice of one's cause. Winners were sometimes more cautious. They had won—why do it again? Wasn't there a risk? The educational importance of the effort generally won them over. Smith, after discussion with his Houston lawyer, agreed.

The lawyer was Carter Wesley, who had become editor-publisher of a Houston newspaper addressing black interests. He too proved ready to take part and suggested that Thurgood Marshall, longtime NAACP attorney, who had given strategic advice in a crucial phone call, might be willing to help reenact it. He proved ready to do so. The Marshall-Wesley phone colloquy, shot in New York and Houston, became a climactic moment in the film.

With Wesley I discussed another problem—one that worried me. Mr. Allwright, the county clerk who had refused to give Smith a ballot, had died. To reenact the confrontation, we needed a substitute. The content was not an issue; the dialogue was in the court record. But I dared not do the casting, sensing that my Northern prejudices would be at work. I preferred that someone else designate an appropriate person. Surely there were others who had handled this apparently ritualistic refusal? Who might help us find such a person?

Wesley smiled appreciatively, and made an answer that astounded me. "Why not ask our Democratic Party headquarters? They'll find you someone." I was incredulous, but Wesley explained. "Ever since we won the Smith case, Houston has had a large black vote. The first thing a Houston politician now does, when he's been nominated, is head for the Negro districts to campaign. We hold the balance of power."

Next morning I duly announced myself at Democratic Party headquarters. Although Wesley inspired confidence, I could hardly believe what I was doing. I explained that I was from Columbia University, making a film about a Democratic Party matter. That got me to the office of a man who appeared to be in charge.

Again I explained: Columbia University—educational television—constitutional law—crucial modern cases—cases studied by every law student. "We are including a case of 1944—a Houston case—*Smith v Allwright*. You remember that case?"

He answered in a soft, crooning Texas melody, drawing out the words. "Ye-es, I remember that case."

"We want to reenact the part where Dr. Smith asks for a ballot and

Allwright says no. Mr. Allwright is dead. We know what he said—it's all written down here." I handed him a typed copy of the brief dialogue. "But we need someone else to say it, the way he would have done it. I thought you might help us find someone. Maybe someone who had done this occasionally. Could you find us someone?"

He assumed a benign look. "Sure I could. And if I can't, I'll do it mahself." It occurred to me that he would be perfect. But in the end, he found someone even better.

I could hardly believe my good fortune. In three days, I had accomplished everything I had hoped to in Houston. I flew back to New York, went over the details with Sharff, finished writing the script, and submitted it to Wechsler. Wechsler was a stickler for details; he allowed no compromise. Any phrase that wasn't quite right had to be changed. Some scripts went through three or four versions—but quickly.

A few weeks later Sharff and I flew back to Houston together. He was delighted with the people and locations. There were a few problems to resolve. The Smith-Allwright confrontation had taken place in the "old County Courthouse"—since then replaced by the "new County Courthouse," which seemed too glittery for us to use. The old one had become an office building. We decided to use the exterior of the grand old courthouse and reproduce the interior somewhere—anywhere.

By this time we had decided to open the film in Smith's office, in a black district near the old county courthouse. Smith would be explaining to a female patient, in an improvisation, that he couldn't quite finish the work that day. He had to go to the courthouse on an important matter. (A bit of half-suppressed pride here.) Then we would see him closing his office and walking the few blocks to the courthouse, meeting his friend the photographer and another witness. The three would climb the steps together. CUT TO INTERIOR.

For the scene inside we arranged to borrow the studio of a black photographer. We would only need a counter, easily improvised. On one side, Smith and his group; on the other, "Allwright" and an assistant clerk.

Our various interiors—barbershop, Smith's office, clerk's office—would need strong lighting, for which Sharff had brought equipment. He now decided, as a matter of prudence, to ask the local electrical union to furnish an electrician. We would of course pay union scale. A local electrician would know local requirements and problems, which would be helpful. But Sharff's caution did not really stem from such technical matters, which he could have handled himself. Houston was a strong union town. Our outdoor shooting would attract attention, perhaps from union organizers. The major film unions generally ignored small documentary operations like ours, though not always. The film medium had a long history of persuasion based on rough stuff. It seemed best to take the initiative of asking for a union electrician, at union scale. So Sharff went off to visit the union.

Rejoining me later at our motel, he looked shaken. The union's reaction had been totally unexpected. The representative had listened to Sharff's request, then replied with contempt and indignation. "Who the fuck do you think we are? We're not going to put a man on a nigger picture!"

Sharff had fortunately not revealed our planned locations nor our shooting schedule. But he immediately began to revise the schedule. He had planned to do exterior work first, weather permitting. Now it would be done last. Meanwhile we would be as invisible as possible. He had nightmare visions of mysterious power failures or shooting sessions plagued by a chorus of horn blowing.

The very last sequence to be shot would be Smith's walk to the courthouse and up the courthouse steps. It would be done at 4:30 A.M. on our final day. Later that morning we would be on our way home.

The sudden change of schedule, and awareness of the racial nastiness behind it, put a new tension into our work. This was unnerving, but perhaps to the good. It was no longer a mere exercise in repeating events long past. When I first saw Sharff's footage of Smith approaching the counter, asking for a ballot, I sensed that Smith was experiencing once more the tensions of a more poisonous time. The fear was there. Perspiration stood on his forehead.

ASST. CLERK: Yes?

DR. SMITH: I'd like an absentee ballot—for the primary.

ASST. CLERK: (wary) You'd better talk to the chief clerk. (Clerk steps up to the counter. Assistant watches.)

CLERK: Yes?

DR. SMITH: I'd like an absentee ballot, please. For the primary.

CLERK: (smooth as silk) I can't give you that. But you come in November, to the general election. You can vote in the general election.

DR. SMITH: But I'd like to vote in the primary—help choose my congressman.

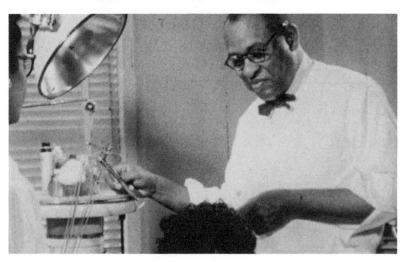

CLERK: (kindly) You *know* I can't give you a ballot for the primary.

DR. SMITH: Why not? I'd like to help choose my congressman.

CLERK: (shaking his head) It's an all-white primary. The party convention decided that, unanimously. The U.S. Supreme Court upheld it. I have nothing to do with it. I do as I'm told.

DR. SMITH: I'd still like to vote in the primary. (The photographer snaps his picture).

Smith's haunted look stays with me to this day. Meanwhile his lawyers had skillfully put the spotlight on a strictly legalistic issue, in no sense racial. The clerk who was claiming to uphold a party decision was not a party spokesman, but a public official. Four years later—April 3, 1944—the U.S. Supreme Court, reviewing *Smith v Allwright*, took note of this. Chief Justice Harlan Fisk Stone, speaking for a 5–3 majority of the Court, said:

> The state makes the action of the party the action of the state. . . . When convinced of former error, this Court has never felt constrained to follow precedent.

Smith won his case.

In 1957, as we were busy editing our reenactment, Smith became an election commissioner in Houston. Sharff returned to Houston for a shot showing Smith smiling broadly, supervising at the polls. It appears in our film with the final ritual words used in each of the *Decision* films:

> Our forefathers lived in an agricultural era, very different from our day. The system they established has been through many changes, via amendment, legislation, and litigation—all avenues of peaceful change in a system based on law.

A letter from the NAACP informed us that the film was shown at its annual membership meeting on February 18, 1959, and "enthusiastically received."

Issue: The White Primary. (top) April 1935: In Houston, Texas, Richard Grovey tastes bitter U.S. Supreme Court defeat, 9–0. (middle) March 1944: Thurgood Marshall leads the NAACP legal team up the court steps for the "Smith case." (bottom) Dr. Lonnie Smith of *Smith v Allwright* savors victory in the U.S. Supreme Court, 5–3. (Three frames from "The Constitution and the Right to Vote" in the *Decision* series)

Seventeen years later, when I became a Fellow of the Woodrow Wilson International Center for Scholars, at the Smithsonian, I was asked to show a few of my films. Among them I showed *The Constitution and the Right to Vote*—to the delight of a young black who had just become assistant librarian of the center and who handled the projector. Having shown the film, he told the assembled fellows that he was from Houston and had gone to college on a Lonnie Smith Memorial Fellowship, established in honor of the dentist whose walk to the courthouse had consigned the white primary to the garbage dump of history.

BUD LEYRA

"Laws, like houses, lean on one another."
—*Edmund Burke*

In *1958, when we had completed six films for* Decision: The Constitution in Action, *Hudson asked Wechsler whether NET might now assume that the most important judicial issues of the time had been treated. Not so, thought Wechsler. One remaining issue especially characterized the period. To ignore it would be a serious omission. In a number of recent cases, a conviction had been overturned on appeal because of the unlawful procedure of police, prosecution, or judiciary. In these cases, the Supreme Court had decided that protecting the integrity of the legal system was even more crucial than the outcome of any particular case. As an especially dramatic, even bizarre example, Wechsler cited* Leyra v Denno, 347 US 556 (1954), *in which the accused, Camilo "Bud" Leyra, was convicted by three different juries of killing his father and mother. He spent five years in the death house at Sing Sing awaiting his turn in the electric chair, but finally went free—on the issue of "fair procedure." Wechsler urged us to look into the case.*

The extension of the series suited me well. The film series was indirectly strengthening our teaching program. Students sometimes served as interns on the film projects. Sharff had become an adjunct professor, teaching courses on film editing and production. In the general studies catalogue I simply changed the title of our division to Film, Radio, and Television. No one protested. Our documentary film offering became increasingly important to me. Several of the Decision *films were shown at the annual Robert Flaherty Seminars, which had since 1955 grown important in the independent film field. Dorothy Oshlag became a central figure in them as well as at the Center for Mass Communication. We got to work avidly on our final* Decision *film.*

I went first to see Frederick W. Scholem, Leyra's attorney, at his midtown offices. Rough-hewn and blunt, he seemed more like a policeman than a lawyer. But his direct manner put me at ease. When I told him we were planning a film on the Leyra case, he said "Fine." When I asked if he would be willing to take part, as himself, he said "Of course."

But the case offered problems we had not previously faced. It had burst into public attention in 1950 via a garish *Daily News* front page—"Find Aged Pair Hacked to Death"—showing the murdered old couple lying in blood on the floor of their Brooklyn apartment.* Bud Leyra, their son, was in a group that had discovered them. What he did and said on that occasion was the subject of much later testimony. I contemplated some reenactment of the episode—silent, with passages of the voice-over testimony. But could one possibly ask Leyra to reenact such an occasion? I had no idea where Leyra was or what had become of him, but felt that as a matter of taste we should, in this case, consider a look-alike. I hated to do this for the central figure in a case. But Scholem agreed, and said he would help us find an appropriate person.

He said he had entered the case as a public defender, appointed at public expense because Leyra could not afford counsel. Public funds were available for an original trial, not for appeals. But Scholem said he had become so enraged over the handling of the case by the Brooklyn police, the prosecution, and even the trial judge, that he had decided to finance the appeals himself. At one point the judge, according to Scholem, had told him in chambers, "Fred, you'd better plead him guilty. They've found the blood-stained clothing, you know." No blood-stained clothing was ever presented in evidence. This typified the mendacity that Scholem felt had characterized the proceedings. Eventually the case and its remarkable outcome represented Scholem's niche in legal history and went far to explain his readiness to take part in the film.

After brief discussion I arranged to return the following week with Stefan Sharff, to consider our plans further—particularly the problem of finding "a Leyra." Newsreel footage was available depicting Leyra's final release from prison, accompanied by Scholem and associate counsel Osmond K. Fraenkel; this, and front-page photos from the *Daily News*, would be usable if a look-alike could be found for the dramatized sequences.

* *Daily News*, January 11, 1950, p. 1.

I learned from the case record that Leyra had once been a professional musician and said he had played in Paul Whiteman's orchestra. During the Depression he fell on difficult times and became a bartender, for a while at the Stork Club. At the time of the "Leyra case" he was a bartender in the Greenwich Village section of Manhattan. Estranged from his wife, who lived in New Jersey, he shared a Greenwich Village apartment with a young woman who had a job in a Brooklyn pencil factory. Bud's bartending was mainly an evening activity; in the daytime he worked with his father in a small business making and selling typewriter ribbons, operated from a loft in the Manhattan financial district. The business was in trouble and this brought on frequent arguments with his father. According to the prosecution version of the case, a violent quarrel and his mother's efforts to halt it had led to the murders. In the old couple's Brooklyn apartment three used teacups were noted at the breakfast table, suggesting there had been a trusted morning visitor. Leyra, after three days of grilling, was charged and brought to trial. The evidence presented was enough to convince the jury—and later two other juries—of his guilt. During his five years on death row, 1950–55, a number of prisoners had passed his cell on their way to the chair, including Julius and Ethel Rosenberg.

When Sharff and I arrived the following week for our planning session, Scholem had a surprise announcement. He had felt obliged to inform Leyra of our film plans and had phoned him in Las Vegas. Leyra had become a bartender there, was prospering, and had even remarried. The moment he learned of the film plans, Leyra had resolved to get a leave of absence and head for New York—in order to help, he said. In fact, said Scholem, looking at his watch, Leyra should already have landed at LaGuardia airport. Ten minutes later Leyra walked in the door and Scholem introduced him—a stocky figure neatly dressed in a dark suit. A whiff of perfume had preceded him into the room. We stood around rather awkwardly.

According to my recollection, the conversation proceeded along these lines: I said, "Mr. Leyra, I guess you've heard—we're going to make a film about 'the Leyra case.'"

"Yes—great. Whatever I can do to help—"

"We're going to dramatize various scenes. You mean you—would consider playing yourself?"

"Whatever I can do to help."

"Perhaps you should first read this script I've written—before you decide. Why don't you take this with you? We can meet again tomorrow, if that's convenient, and we'll talk it over."

"Whatever you say. Anything I can do to help."

All this went on in a quiet, businesslike manner, but I was uneasy. In writing my draft, I had resolved that audiences must understand why three juries had found Leyra guilty, as well as why three appellate courts had voided the convictions. The most damaging facts against Leyra, as well as against the prosecution, were included in my draft. How would Leyra react to all this? Would he be indignant? If so, what could be done about it? And what form might his anger take?

When we met again, he was as calm as before. He pointed out a small technical error in the script, easily corrected—one that Scholem should have noticed but hadn't. I began to learn that Leyra knew his case at least as well as his lawyer did. Leyra explained: he had had five years to study it. He also said he was ready to take part. Both he and Scholem signed the sweeping release forms that NET had provided for our use. Neither had any objection to the choice of sequences.

When I told Wechsler of these developments, he was astounded. After reading the script, and approving it, he commented, "Either on the theory that he's guilty—or on the theory that he's innocent—I can't understand him deciding to do it." Puzzles like this confronted us throughout the series.

I was still uneasy. Conflicting impulses are a part of any autobiographical venture. Deciding to reveal means a chance to amend—to make things a bit better than they were. In inviting people to portray themselves we knew we were giving them a degree of control. We gained authenticity, but with risks. We had accepted the risks because key scenes were based on a legal record. We would allow no deviation from this record.

Even so I was worried, and so was Sharff. Would Leyra, at some crucial moment, draw back from the record? This fear began to control our shooting schedule. Weeks of work might be wasted—and funds lost—if we learned too late that he would pull back from some central event. We therefore decided to begin work with the sequence most damaging to Leyra. It was, in fact, damaging to both sides.

When the Brooklyn police began to suspect Leyra, they questioned him for three days and nights with only an hour and a half of sleep during the entire period. There was also an interval during which he was allowed to attend his parents' funeral—under police guard, although he was not yet technically under arrest. Except for these intervals, the interrogation was continued day and night by relays of questioners. They hammered at him with questions about the day of the murder. He told them that on that morning he had suddenly remembered that it was his wife's birthday and had decided to visit her in New Jersey, buying a box of candy on the way. Investigation confirmed all this. But what had he done before the New Jersey trip? The woman with whom he shared an apartment said she had gotten up early that morning, to go to work; he was still sleeping. When she saw him later that day, he was wearing a suit she didn't remember having seen before. It looked "brand new," she said. He also had a new raincoat. Leyra told the police he had bought a new raincoat because it was raining.

They continued the questions without productive results. Leyra meanwhile began to complain of unendurable sinus pains. Finally the police told him they had sent for a doctor to take care of his sinuses. A doctor arrived and took him into a room alone. The doctor, it later turned out, was a psychiatrist with a reputation for hypnotism. He had been offered a bonus if he could elicit a confession from Leyra. The session was overheard by police in an adjoining room.

The doctor told Leyra he would try to help him. He held his hand on Leyra's forehead and talked quietly to "ease" Leyra's "mental tension." After a time, the police heard Leyra giving information he had not given before. They heard him say that on the morning of the murder he had gone to Brooklyn and had tea with his parents. There had been a violent quarrel with his father—about the business. His father, in a fury, had left to buy a morning newspaper, planning to return immediately. The mother had pleaded with Bud not to resume the argument. But Bud had likewise been furious. The psychiatrist kept urging him to tell what happened after that. Leyra went on haltingly, dazedly. He couldn't remember, he said. Then suddenly he asked to "speak with the captain" and was rushed back to the police; questioning continued.

On the basis of the revelations a "confession" was typed up by the police—which, however, Leyra never signed. It said that Leyra had committed the murder in a fit of anger. It mentioned a hammer as the murder weapon. It said that Leyra had disposed of the hammer in a passing garbage truck and had gone to Manhattan, changed his clothing, and later given his blood-stained garments to a man on the street who looked down on his luck. Then he went to New Jersey.

Leyra was formally charged. In jail he had his first meeting with the lawyer assigned to him, Frederick Scholem. During the trial Scholem began to suspect that the session with the psychiatrist had been recorded with one of the recently invented wire or tape recorders. After legal sparring this was established as a fact. The court ordered the recording produced. A complete transcript was read into the record and became a two-edged sword. Its contents assured Leyra's conviction, but it also showed that the doctor had led the questioning throughout. The quarrel, the hammer, and other details had been introduced not by Leyra but by the psychiatrist-hypnotist. The session included such passages as:

> DOCTOR: Then you hit your mother, didn't you? With what did you hit—with a hammer? Your thoughts are coming back to you. What did you use to hit your mother with?
> LEYRA: I loved my mother.
> DOCTOR: I know you did. You lost your temper. Don't be afraid. A lot of people do things that they are not responsible for while in a fit of temper. You see?
> LEYRA: My mother was the only thing in the world.
> DOCTOR: That's right. What did you hit her with?

Minutes later:

> DOCTOR: Speak up now. Speak up. See, I can make you talk very truly. I can give you an injection now. It's much better if you tell it to me this way. Come on now, speak up.
> LEYRA: I can't, doctor.
> DOCTOR: What kind of a hammer was it?
> LEYRA: A big hammer.
> DOCTOR: Was it a carpenter's hammer?
> LEYRA: It was a big hammer.
> DOCTOR: A big hammer. You picked it up and then what? Don't be afraid. Say it.

Still later:

> DOCTOR: What did you do with the hammer—you swung it?
> LEYRA: I must have, Doc. Nobody else could have done it.

DOCTOR: Nobody else could have, you say? You must have swung it?

LEYRA: I must have.

DOCTOR: And your mother fell down.

Still later:

DOCTOR: Everything is clear up to the point where you held the hammer in your hand?

LEYRA: That's right but why can't I remember from there on?

DOCTOR: If you will just stop for a moment, you will remember. And your thoughts will come into you.

LEYRA: Doctor, I am exhausted, so please be patient.

DOCTOR: I am patient.

LEYRA: I appreciate that.

DOCTOR: These people are going to throw the book at you unless you can show that in a fit of temper you got so angry that you did it. Otherwise they toss premeditation in and it's premeditation. See? . . . Take your time. Just relax. Want some more coffee?

LEYRA: I would like to speak with the captain.

The session lasted an hour and a half. Long passages from it were incorporated in the 1954 U.S. Supreme Court decision, and formed the basis for its dictum describing the session as "mental coercion." Extorted confessions are barred as evidence by the laws of every state. Thus the Court ruled:

We hold that use of confessions extracted in such a manner, from a lone defendant unprotected by counsel, is not consistent with due process of law as required by our constitution.[*]

Sharff and I decided that the psychiatrist session must be the first item on our production schedule. We would begin with a straight-through *audio* enactment—a reading. We would not photograph this but merely record it on audiotape. The Brooklyn police had declined to make the original recording available to us, but we could duplicate it punctiliously from the court transcript.

With this audio recording in hand, we would then *film* the colloquy with sound, shooting short passages at a time to ease the memorization

[*]Leyra v Denno, 347 US 556 (1959).

problem. We would also film (without sound) shots of policemen listening in an "adjoining room," bent over a tape recorder. If Leyra should resist or flounder in our filming of any key passage, we could in those cases cut to an "adjoining room" shot, using it with a passage from the audiotape.

The NET attorney worried constantly about the entire project. Fears were eased when Leyra agreed to take part and he and Scholem signed our sweeping release forms. But now worries centered on the psychiatrist. The film could not possibly aid his professional reputation, and it seemed unthinkable that he would want to participate. We were urged not to ask him: a substitute *must* be used, and we must not use the psychiatrist's name. Although "publication of a fair and true report of any judicial proceeding" is protected from suit under New York State civil rights law, the attorney was still nervous about the impersonation aspect. In a long memorandum he pointed out that if our substitute resembled the psychiatrist, the psychiatrist could assert that his "likeness" was used without his consent—a possible violation of privacy rights. On the other hand, if there was no resemblance, he could complain that we had given a false, unfavorable impression of him. The memorandum continued:

> To meet this problem, I suggest that the psychiatrist and the suspect be shown as seated facing each other during the questioning and that the camera positions be such that it is the suspect's face which is seen at all times. These may be close-ups or medium shots over the psychiatrist's shoulder so that for part of the time the back of the questioner is in the foreground. Then, if the questions are asked in a quiet, even, almost mechanical manner (as they probably were asked) this aspect of the production would in my opinion be justifiable.

Stefan Sharff, our director-cameraman, was delighted with this legal excursion into film technique. It was precisely how he had planned to shoot the sequence in the first place. A Columbia University speech instructor was enlisted as our "psychiatrist." Our audiotape session went with extraordinary precision, without any hesitation by Leyra. Then came the filming. Again, Leyra never drew back. The same was true of all subsequent sequences.

Between shots, as lights were shifted and camera adjustments made, Leyra would sit quietly in a corner. Sharff at one time congratulated him on his patience. Leyra replied, "I've had to learn to be patient."

Leyra wanted to see the film. He had sent for his new wife to join him in New York. After the shooting they remained in the city, staying with friends in Astoria. Sharff and I meanwhile worked on the editing and narration. Gradually the film–*The Constitution and Fair Procedure*–took shape.

In spite of the smooth progress, I felt decidedly nervous about Leyra seeing the assembled film. I was sure it would lead most viewers to assume his guilt. Yet we felt it essential to show him the film before releasing it.

I confided my anxieties to Scholem, who at once suggested a procedure. The people involved in the film should be invited to see it together in our small screening room. "You sit on one side of Bud," said Scholem, "and I'll sit on the other. As soon as it's over I'll jump up and say, 'It's great!' We'll get a sort of bandwagon going."

We adopted this embarrassing scenario. Leyra brought his new wife, a pert red-headed lady who went by the name of Rusty. Bud and Rusty sat between Scholem and me.

Throughout the film I tried to sense any unusual motion or action by Leyra. I noticed none. At the end Scholem duly jumped up. "It's wonderful! It's really good!" Leyra got up slowly, and nodded. "It's very good." Then Rusty said, "Yes, it's very good." There were handshakes and words of congratulation all around. We promised Leyra a print of the film. He and Rusty returned soon afterwards to Las Vegas.

A member of our group once asked Scholem whether he thought Leyra was guilty or innocent. Scholem had a formula answer: "I didn't care whether he was guilty or innocent. If they can do that to a guilty man, they can do it to an innocent man." This seemed an effective formula. I began to use it.

The series *Decision: The Constitution in Action* won the Sylvania Award as the best educational television series of 1959, as well as the Gavel Award of the American Bar Association. To accept the gavel I had to travel to Miami for an award ceremony at the annual ABA banquet, attended by lawyers and judges en masse. I rented a white tuxedo jacket. Several gavels were bestowed, including one to Henry Luce. We prize-winners sat together at a table below the dais. Each of us in turn stood in a spotlight while cameras clicked and ABA President Ross Malone read a nice paragraph of praise. Recipients were all instructed: "No response, please!" Mr. Luce had to discard his speech, and so did I.

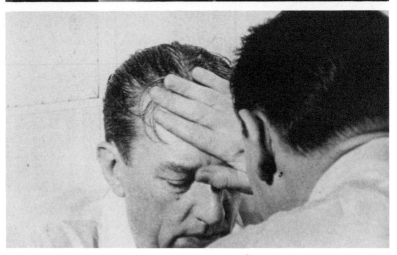

A word of explanation is needed concerning the two awards. For these, prints of the films were submitted to award committees. People who saw the series on the air must have been infinitesimal in number. The public television system, at the time the series was released, had no outlets in New York, Washington, or Los Angeles. The two dozen stations struggling to survive generally had ratings of "L.T."—meaning "less than" one percent of the available audience. The films were seen mainly via showings at conferences and film societies.

I myself showed it many times at such sessions. When I did, I was always haunted by Leyra's glazed-eye look in the interrogation scene, as he seemed truly to slip into a hypnotic trance. The psychiatrist kept at him to finish the story of the fatal morning, and Leyra could only say, ". . . why can't I remember from there on?" I wondered how far this was from a possible truth—that the final moments of the morning were no longer available to his conscious mind, that they had somehow been sealed off, like a tubercular scar in the lung, firmly walled off from surrounding tissues.

Leyra, when leaving New York, told us he would be interested in further television ventures. A number of Sing Sing dwellers had, on the night before their execution, spent the night in the cell next to his and done a lot of talking. Julius Rosenberg was one of them. Another was Harry Stein, who told of having been involved in the disappearance of Judge Crater, a famous unsolved mystery of 1930. Stein had supplied many details, which Leyra said he clearly remembered. He said he would be glad to talk about all that. Some people thought Leyra was lying. I wasn't sure.

I heard no news of Leyra for more than a year. Then came a long, neatly typed letter from Las Vegas.

> Dear Erik:
>
> I'll bet you will be surprised to hear from me—hope it is a pleasant surprise.
>
> The past fourteen months have been wonderful for us, and we have

Issue: Procedures. (top) January 11, 1950: New York's *Daily News* proclaims the Leyra case. (middle) Public defender Frederick W. Scholem is assigned to defend Leyra. (bottom) Psychiatrist-hypnotist is hired by the prosecution to extract a confession. (Three frames from "The Constitution and Fair Procedure" in the *Decision* series) enjoyed every moment. This place is fabulous. We now have a lovely home which is furnished in the best of taste and quality. We have an Oldsmobile at present, but if our good fortune continues we expect to have a pink Cadillac in the near future. I trust that dame fortune has smiled on you and yours.

Leyra mentioned that he and Rusty had bought twenty acres at Mountain Springs, Nevada, which had turned out to be rich in copper,

> . . . the best prospect in the eleven western states. I am about to lease the property to a responsible group of Texas mining operators on a royalty basis. It looks as if we have hit pay dirt and that we have it made.

He concluded with an invitation.

> I hereby extend an open invitation to you and Stefan Sharff to visit with us at any time that would be convenient to your respective schedules. We have all modern conveniences for your comfort and it would be a pleasure to have you as our guests.*

A few months later I heard from him again. He wanted me to help him write his memoirs. I explained that I was about to leave for India on a research venture and would be away for at least a year. A few years later, after my return, I learned that he had died.

Looking back, I could not suppress a curious respect for Bud Leyra. His case had absorbed me deeply. It belonged to a moment in judicial history when concern for fair procedure burned with a special brightness. I hoped it would again.

As for educational television, it seemed a precarious creature. Survival appeared to depend on the Ford Foundation's periodic injections. How long would they continue? Would the educational channels continue to be a sort of electronic tin cup? Much idealism was focused on them. But for most television entrepreneurs, channels were simply new gold mines. The FCC, created to regulate them, seemed intent on propelling the rush. Its revolving door was a busy one.

---

* Letter dated August 30, 1960.

M. G. RAMACHANDRAN

"As far as the film-making process is concerned,
stars are essentially worthless—and
absolutely necessary."
—*William Goldman*

India had been on my mind for some years. When the unknown Satyajit
Ray of Calcutta won a top award at the 1956 Cannes Film Festival for his
Pather Panchali *(song of the road) there was astonishment among U.S.*
cineastes. "India? I didn't know they made films." From UNESCO's sta-
tistical reports I learned that India, like Japan, was making more films
than the United States (which barely nosed out Hong Kong). Thus three
of the four most active film-producing nations were in Asia. Why was
I so oblivious to all this? When Ray came to the United States for the
U.S. premiere of Pather Panchali, *I was invited to meet him at a week-*
end gathering in Vermont at the home of Frances Flaherty, widow of
Robert Flaherty. All present were stunned by Ray and his film. The occa-
sion turned into a feverish seminar on the nature of film and its current
state—which evolved into the annual Flaherty Film Seminars.

In the fall of 1959 an Indian student, S. Krishnaswamy of Madras, en-
rolled in my course for credit toward a master's degree. His term paper
on the turbulent Indian film industry fascinated me, and I peppered
him with questions. I gathered that its productions ranged from a Ray-
inspired "new wave" to colossal musicals in a dozen languages, domi-
nated by stars who had developed an extraordinary grip over the public.
In 1963 the industry planned to celebrate its fiftieth anniversary of feature
film production. I had a sabbatical leave due in 1961-62 and began to
think about a year in India, with family. The Japanese Film, *by Joseph L.*
Anderson and Donald Richie, was published in 1959 to wide applause.
Shouldn't Indian film be next?

Applying for a Fulbright research grant, I cautiously listed my topic
as "the role of the mass media in a developing country"—which sounded

highly respectable and won approval. But on my mind was a book of film history. I suggested to Columbia University Press that it would be splendid if in 1963 we came out with the first book on Indian films, to coincide with their fiftieth anniversary. A contract was drawn up. S. Krishnaswamy—whom everyone called "Babu"—asked if he might be my research assistant. I said no, it would be better if we became collaborators. A U.S.-Indian venture would be less presumptuous than a solo expedition by a professor plunging into new territory. The Columbia University Press contract was signed by both. We agreed to meet in Madras in September 1961 to begin our work. Babu Krishnaswamy, M.A. degree in hand, left for India to prepare the way.

Five Barnouws—Dotty and I plus Jeff (21), Suzy (16), and Karen (10), born in 1951—went to India on the Greek freighter *Hellenic Splendor*, which took two months for the trip, with stops at Gibraltar, Crete, Alexandria, Port Sudan, Jeddah, Karachi, and Bombay. A fantastic educational journey for all of us. Our cabin was air-conditioned and had a desk. In intervals between ports I managed to write a short book titled *The Television Writer* and shipped it off to New York.* In the fall we finally settled in an apartment in New Delhi, after which I flew south to join Babu.

On the morning of October 16, as I stepped off the plane in Madras, I noticed a crowd at the airport. It did not occur to me that it might have a connection with my arrival. As I was greeted by Babu, others clustered around. A man stepped forward to place a garland of wet flowers over my head. In the blazing heat it felt pleasant. He explained that he represented the South Indian Film Journalists Association, who were planning a "function" that evening at 6 P.M. and hoped I would be their guest. I said I would be delighted. As Babu relieved me of the wet flowers, another man stepped forward, explaining that he represented the South Indian Cine Technicians Association, and bestowed another wet garland on my shoulders. They were planning a function for later that week; would I be their guest? I accepted with delight. He was followed by a lady from Nrithyodaya, a Madras dance and music center, which was planning a tea. Still others were waiting in line. Babu showed me a schedule he had drawn up. It began:

*Erik Barnouw, *The Television Writer* (New York, Hill and Wang, 1962).

Arrival 10:15 A.M. Reception and garlanding by various organizations.

So began a dizzying day—and a dizzying year. For the next few months
it was meetings, interviews, "functions," screenings, lunches, studio visits, festivals—along with reading sessions at libraries and newspaper archives. We zigzagged across the map: Bombay (India's Hollywood, headquarters for filmmaking in the languages of northern India, particularly
Hindi); Calcutta (home of Satyajit Ray and several avant-garde followers,
producing mainly in the language of Bengal, in northeast India); Madras
(film center rivaling Bombay in volume of production, making films in
Tamil and other languages of the southern regions); New Delhi (home
of government ministries); and various lesser centers. We talked with
producers, financiers, directors, writers, actors, cameramen, composers,
choreographers, designers, exhibitors, censors, critics, fan clubs. In major
centers we talked with industry officials, who all seemed amazed that
Columbia University, a citadel of learning halfway around the globe, had
planned a book on fifty years of Indian film production—and that a professor had come such a distance to work on it. Their surprise was shared
by many. No Indian scholar had apparently considered such a notion.
Thanks to them, Babu and I plowed untilled soil.

Our itinerary was a triumph of planning. Babu turned out to be an
organizing genius. He was helped by the fact that his father, K. Subrahmanyam (it is common in South India for father and son to be known by
different names) had been a South Indian film pioneer, known throughout India, and he had helped Babu identify fellow pioneers we should seek
out. Subrahmanyam had originally been a lawyer but had felt drawn to
the nascent cinema. In the 1920s, as Gandhi emerged as a unifying force
in the independence movement, Subrahmanyam had produced films with
a pro-Gandhi slant, often echoing Gandhi's condemnations of the caste
system—though Subrahmanyam himself was of Brahmin caste. His activities had earned him the suspicions of the British as well as the enmity
of more tradition-bound Brahmins. That Indian films had, from earliest
years, involved such political aspects surprised and delighted me. It was
an angle I was intent on pursuing.

While Babu and I were in a remote part of India, the elderly Subrahmanyam traveled to New Delhi to attend an international film festival

and phoned Dotty to ask if he might escort her to it. She was astonished and gratified. Prime Minister Jawaharlal Nehru, arriving for a ceremonial opening, walked down the aisle and stopped when he saw Subrahmanyam. "Subrahmanyam! Are you still busy with films? You ought to be in politics." They chatted briefly. Thus Dotty met Nehru, I didn't.

Babu and I were spending a week with Satyajit Ray on location in Darjeeling, high in the Himalayas, where he was shooting *Kanchanjanga*. A towering figure, he was always impressive, but directed quietly. At times he would take an actor or actress aside, away from others, to discuss some nuance of interpretation. He seemed determined never to humiliate an actor. In the evenings, at the Mount Everest Hotel, Babu and I had a chance to talk with him at length about his life. He had grown up in Calcutta, then the capital of British India, so his schooling had inevitably featured British and European achievements. At the University of Calcutta he studied economics. But then he went to study with Rabindranath Tagore at Santiniketan ("the abode of peace"), a school started by Tagore. Here the emphasis was on the arts and development from within. Tagore, a Nobel Prize winner in literature, was becoming an influence on all the arts of India. In the 1920s, after the Amritsar massacre, he shed his English title (which had made him Sir Rabindranath) and became an icon of the independence movement. Ray, like Tagore, became a practitioner in all the arts, composing, illustrating books, designing posters. When he finally focused on film, his filmmaking became for him a discovery of India. Every film became a story of Indian people in a particular period, at a particular place, under particular circumstances. There were no villains. ("Villains are boring.") Most stories were laid in Bengal, but the precision of the relationships made them universal, and they struck a chord of recognition throughout the world. Ray said he hesitated to deal with unfamiliar locales and cultures. Artists who did so, he felt, were inevitably prisoners of stereotypes and preconceptions. Besides, Bengal was inexhaustible. One could find a world in Bengal.

Babu and I, admiring Ray, had to face the fact that very different forces dominated the Indian film world. Its popular epics, saturated with song and dance, seemed to take place in a vacuum. Many dealt with mythical kingdoms populated by tyrants and heroes. They were played by actors whose images confronted us from huge painted posters in every city, from calendars on shop walls and magazines by the hundreds. Their voices drifted across every street from radios and phonograph records. The first

Satyajit Ray of Calcutta. (Rosalind Solomon)

Indian sound films, premiered in 1931, had been musicals with many songs and dances. They followed a dramatic tradition that dated from ancient times. Though Islamic taboos had frowned on drama, and during the Mughal era had banned it from the halls of kings, it had always continued in the villages. Through the centuries itinerant players had carried their song-and-dance drama throughout India. Indian sound film at its birth had seized on this tradition, tapping an inexhaustible river of music. The first sound films were so successful that it took more than twenty years before any producer dared to produce a film without songs or dances. Meanwhile the music evolved, acquiring African, Latin, and American rhythms and instrumentation. It was decried by purists as "hybrid" music but had become the music of India's masses, played at weddings, funerals, and public events. Most songs were associated with stars. At public appearances, stars sang their songs.

What were we to make of India's epic music drama and its stars who, since independence, had evolved into a new species of maharajah? We sought out stars of earlier days, many of whom were hard to find. We found some living in squalor, others in luxury; most were virtually forgotten. All were delighted to talk into our tape recorders about the birth and rise of their industry. Meanwhile new stars were followed by vast throngs whenever they appeared in public.

Among current stars, I was determined to meet M. G. Ramachandran, known as MGR. The reigning star of Tamil films, he was "the idol of the masses" and called the "Indian Reagan." After more than a hundred successes, combating tyrants in never-never-land, he had decided to enter Madras politics. As with Reagan, his screen image seemed at once to infuse his political persona. He seemed sure of election. To some observers, all this was absurd. His pronouncements were considered simplistic. Asked about his political views, he said he believed in "the best of capitalism combined with the best of communism." He seldom went beyond this, and wasn't asked to. His campaign appearances were more like movie premieres than political rallies. They were variety shows with guest stars: movie singers, dancers, and comedians. Film songs rang through the air.

The party he adopted, founded by the screenwriter C. N. Annadurai, was the Dravida Munnetra Kazhagam, or DMK. Its name identified it as part of the so-called Dravidian movement. The four languages of South India—Tamil, Telegu, Malayalam, and Kannada—were descended from ancient Dravidian roots, having no relation to Sanskrit, from which most languages of northern India had descended. Among these northern languages, by far the most widely spoken was Hindi, the language of almost 200 million people. Another 100 million spoke languages related to Hindi, with common Sanskrit roots, and could learn Hindi without great difficulty. For all these reasons the Indian republic's founding fathers had decreed, in 1947, that Hindi should eventually be the national tongue; it was so designated in the constitution. But the starting date for the official debut of Hindi as the official language was postponed to give time for a learning process. Hindi became compulsory in schools.

But resistance developed, especially among those who spoke Tamil, the parent of the Dravidian languages. To the Tamils, Hindi seemed as strange as Chinese. That a Dravidian party, focusing on this issue, should be started by a screenwriter had a certain logic. Film people saw it not only as a political issue but as a defense of their market—against the widely distributed Hindi films, already dominant in much of India.

MGR's people assured Babu that he would find time to see us. Meanwhile it seemed best to see as many MGR films as we could and to learn more about the DMK. The party had had a curious growth, which often seemed more filmic than Dravidian. The DMK had adopted the rising sun as its symbol; black and red were its colors. The party founder, C. N. Annadurai, was widely known as "Anna," meaning older brother. These symbols were occasionally injected into films. When they occurred, the faithful cheered and applauded, setting off a game that became contagious. It led to such sequences as:

MAN 1: The night is dark.
MAN 2: Don't worry. The rising sun will soon bring light and good fortune.
(AUDIENCE: WILD CHEERS AND APPLAUSE)

Or:

HE: Believe me, Sister!
SHE: I do, Anna, I do! The whole land believes in you, and will follow you.
(AUDIENCE: WILD CHEERS AND APPLAUSE)

In the casual selection of a sari:

SHE: I always like a black sari, with a red border.
(AUDIENCE: WILD CHEERS AND APPLAUSE)

Two people lost in a forest:

MAN 1: Should we turn north?
MAN 2: No, never! South is much better.
(AUDIENCE: WILD CHEERS AND APPLAUSE)

While this was started by party faithful, others soon joined in. Producers having no connection with the party began to introduce the symbols, which seemed to trigger automatic applause, and applause was welcome. Ramachandran, long regarded as nonpolitical, was thought by some to have merely jumped on the bandwagon in adopting the DMK. He did attend its rallies, especially when releasing a new film. He always got a tumultuous reception. His songs rang through the air. DMK rallies seemed essentially movie events.

This had caused a venerable Madras politician, long identified with the Congress Party that had led India to independence, to ask, "How can there be government by actors?" For "actors" he used the most invidious term available—*koothadi*, or "mountebank." The DMK became accustomed to such ridicule.

People in India often asked me, with a puzzled, troubled look, why on earth I was studying Indian films. Why not Bharata Natyam dancing, or Indian classical music, or the cave temples of the seventh century with their magnificent sculptures and wall paintings—all honored subjects for scholars? But films? It was as though we were focusing on—and abetting—some national disgrace. I found the question hard to answer to their satisfaction. But in our book I knew we would have to answer it.

A recent Ramachandran film, *Nadodi Mannan* (the vagabond king), featured spectacular swordplay, an MGR specialty for which he was compared to Douglas Fairbanks. In a promotional ceremony for *Nadodi Mannan*, an MGR fan club—there were hundreds of them—presented him with a silver sword. The event was featured in fan magazines as indicating the fans' devotion to him. The same magazines told us that the sword had been provided by the financial backer of the film, who had chosen a fan club to present it. This did not seem to dim the wonder of the event.

In several films MGR played brothers—sometimes separated brothers eventually reunited as they expose official corruption and bring down a tyrant. The formula gave MGR a chance to rescue himself. MGR heroes had no vices. They went out of their way to be kind to widows and children. They were helpful in a disaster. But when confronted by corruption, they were furious and implacable in combat.

We noted that fans, fan magazines, and even critics generally referred to stars as "film heroes" and "film heroines" rather than as actors. An actor, having won "film hero" or "film heroine" status, hardly dared to accept roles that blurred the image. Thus actors *became* stereotypes, requiring scripts built around the stereotypes. The critic Satish Bahadur, founder of the Agra Film Society, observed that the dramaturgy dominating the industry was "firmly interlocked in the stable equilibrium of a vicious circle." *

* Satish Bahadur, *The Context of Indian Film Culture.* Study Material Series No. 2, National Film Archive, Pune, 1978.

Word came at last that MGR would see us. He received us in courtly manner. He was built on the generous proportions favored among Indian stars, especially in the south. His office was decorated with innumerable plaques and cups; he took time to explain some of them. He was like an athlete exhibiting his trophies. From a wall he brought down the silver sword presented in recognition of *Nadodi Mannan.* Settling down, he talked easily about his life.

His father had been principal of a school in Sri Lanka—at the time, Ceylon—where MGR was born. But his father died when MGR was three, causing the family to move to Madras, where he said they lived in poverty. Two sisters and a brother died. At six MGR joined a dramatic troupe, the Madurai Original Boys Company, who trained him in dancing and swordplay. His film career began when he was in his teens. He became a star in his twenties. Since then he had played some hundred hero roles. There were theaters that had, for several years, played only MGR films.

We asked about his interest in politics. How committed was he to a political career? We pointed out that his films were often compared to those of Douglas Fairbanks. Because they seemed escapist to most people, we had not suspected him of political interest.

Escapist? MGR protested. His films were certainly not escapist, he said. He recognized the link to Fairbanks. But "Fairbanks, great as he was, is now forgotten." An acting career, said MGR, must now have a political dimension, and he himself had found that in the Dravidian movement. The roles he played, like the folk hero in *Nadodi Mannan,* battling a royal usurper, meant something. To his followers it represented their own struggle against the north, controlled by Hindi-speaking bureaucrats. Already in New Delhi, government positions went mainly to those who spoke Hindi. Their policies favored the north. Under the Congress Party the south was becoming a sort of colony. The establishment in New Delhi, led by old Brahmins, had turned into a kind of royalty. They were the usurpers who must be overthrown. MGR's followers understood all that. In *Nadodi Mannan,* the opening song made it clear: "Oh divine Tamil . . . who reflect the glories of ancient Dravidians!"

We were surprised by these words. Such ideas did not find expression in film journals. We had not anticipated a rationale of this sort from the "idol of the masses." Yet the fact was that the DMK—that fan club in politics, that absurdity, that band of *koothadi*—was transforming Indian politics. It had already taken control of the Madras city government and

Film hero to Chief Minister: M. G. Ramachandran of Tamilnadu. (*Nadodi Mannan*, MGR Pictures)

put scores of film people into state legislatures, Soon afterwards it sent the party founder, screenwriter Annadurai, brother of the lowly, to the parliament in New Delhi, to breathe defiance in the stronghold of the enemy. An astounding political turn appeared in the making.

We so described it in our book *Indian Film*, published in 1963 in the United States by Columbia University Press and in India by Orient Longmans. Amid the fiftieth anniversary celebrations the book appeared to have considerable impact. In 1964 the government established in Pune (previously known as Poona), a National Film Archive, a first effort to preserve India's cinema heritage. Adjoining it, on a tract of land that had once housed a silent film studio, rose the Film Institute of India, training a new generation of filmmakers—from other Third World countries as well as from India. Various states established film subsidies for promising work. So much was happening that it soon seemed to me essential to return to India to prepare, again with Krishnaswamy, an updated edition of *Indian Film*. This would finally be achieved during my retirement years, in a 1980 Oxford University Press edition. In this we were able to report that the new wave set in motion by Satyajit Ray was producing a surge of fine work by such directors as Shyam Benegal, Girish Karnad, Mrinal Sen, M. S. Sathyu, Basu Chatterji, B. V. Karanth, and others. We also re-

Film deity to Chief Minister: N. T. Rama Rao of Andhra Pradesh.
(Gamma-Liaison/Pablo Bartholomew)

ported that the dominant cinema of the stars was in no sense jolted by
this phenomenon, but careened onward on its own course. In the south
the rise of the "Indian Reagan" remained an ongoing saga.

   In many Ramachandran films the villain had been played by the actor
M. R. Radha. Between the villain-actor and the hero-actor some ani-
mosity developed. On a day in 1967 Radha paid Ramachandran a visit.
Two shots were fired. Both men were found wounded. Each said the other
had fired first; no one believed the villain. He was indicted, convicted,
and jailed. MGR languished in a hospital. He was at the time a candidate
for the state legislature, and the campaign went on. Campaign posters
showed MGR with his head swathed in bandages. Huge crowds kept vigil.
His survival seemed to confirm his more-than-human status. He was
elected in an unprecedented landslide. In 1977 he became chief minister
of the state of Madras—which had meanwhile been renamed Tamilnadu.
He was to remain its chief minister for more than a decade, a power in
national politics. When he died in 1988, at least ten followers were said
to have committed suicide.

   My Indian venture of 1961–62 had turned out to be an educational experience beyond any other. I had learned a lot about India and about

film—but both still posed more mysteries than certainties. I noted that the MGR phenomenon soon reenacted itself in other states of India. The actor N. T. Rama Rao often played gods in India's mythological films. He became so identified with these roles that Indian religious calendars depicted gods as looking precisely like N. T. Rama Rao. In 1984 he ran for chief minister of Andhra Pradesh, the state adjoining Tamilnadu. In his campaign he said little. Dressed in ochre robes, he squatted like a benevolent deity on the roof of his Chevrolet van, moving slowly through the gathering crowds as he signaled his blessing. He was triumphantly elected. The need to believe seemed to be overwhelming.

In India's elections, a huge proportion of eligible voters participated. It had become known as the world's largest democracy. But in an era so dominated by images of film and television, I found myself less and less sure what "democracy" meant. Could democracy survive the new-age democratic procedures?

Show-business styles of journalism were widely blamed for distorting our view of the world and its disputes. But was fiction, especially "escapist" fiction (so omnipresent, and now starting in everyone's infancy), perhaps a more powerful force in structuring our "reality"? If so, what did this mean for "democracy"?

CLIFFORD J. DURR

"Secrecy is the badge of fraud."
—Sir John Chadwick

Shortly before our departure for India a phone call came from Oxford University Press. Its editor, Sheldon Meyer, whom I did not know, asked me to lunch at the Princeton Club, and during lunch posed an astounding question. Would I be interested in a commission to write a three-volume history of American broadcasting—radio and television? I was dumbfounded. I could hardly have made such a suggestion. It would have felt like the ultimate in arrogance. Yet here it was. Meyer explained that a three-volume study of British broadcasting had been commissioned in Britain with historian Asa Briggs as writer; Oxford University Press headquarters had urged that its New York branch start a parallel U.S. project. I explained about the India book, projected for a 1963 appearance. No matter, said Meyer; Oxford could plan accordingly. The first volume might come out in 1966, the second in 1968, the third in 1970. A week or so later—shortly before our departure for India—a contract was signed and an advance paid.

In India the new task was constantly in the back of my mind. I had seemingly segued into a new life: media chronicler. India became a kind of rehearsal. Then, from the moment we got back, the new project began to organize my life—and family life. Every family trip meant detours to visit historic radio stations or to interview early broadcasters. I discovered a treasure trove on my own campus. Historian Alan Nevins, who in 1948 had created at Columbia the first of all oral history projects, had included among its interviewees many pioneers of wireless and radio, which he considered major twentieth-century forces. Many of the interviewees were long dead, but neatly typed transcripts of the tapes were in the library's Special Collections Reading Room, seemingly waiting for me, each suggesting wide vistas for further exploration. I became in-satiably curious about the evolution of this industry into which I had blundered with so little thought. And it became fascinating—sometimes disturbing—to see from the vantage of others events through which I had lived. I had been on the fringes of the blacklist madness. Now I visited some—writers, directors, performers, and others—who had lived at the heart of it. One of my interviewees helped especially to give the story historic context. He was Clifford Durr of Alabama, former member of the Federal Communications Commission.

A mild-mannered man, a former Rhodes scholar, Durr had been a storm center at the FCC. Dissenting from crucial decisions, he was able to ex-plain his views with utmost clarity. Hearing him speak at a dinner, I was awed by the quiet eloquence.

During the Radio Writers Guild days I once dropped in, hesitantly, at his FCC office and was surprised to find him delighted at my intrusion. A parade of station managers came to see him, he said, all wanting things. It was a pleasure to talk with someone from the world of programming. Why didn't writers and directors ever drop by? FCC commissioners needed educating.

His seven years (one term) at the FCC, 1941–48, culminated in the feverish postwar years when television station licenses of huge poten-tial value were doled out. This involved Durr in a tense dispute with the FBI and won him the unforgiving enmity of its director, J. Edgar Hoover. Durr, to the surprise of many, returned after his term to his native Ala-bama to practice law in Montgomery. In the following years his name seldom appeared in the broadcasting trade press. He seemed to have van-ished. But as I worked on my trilogy, I felt it increasingly important to consult Durr.

While he was visiting a daughter in New Haven, Connecticut, I was able to have a long talk with him in a villa near the Yale campus. It was a warm day in May 1965. My first volume was already due, yet I had months of work before me. I expected each day an ultimatum from Sheldon Meyer. (When I finally phoned him, a few months late, to say that *A Tower in Babel*, first volume of the trilogy, was ready for delivery, he seemed surprised. "So soon?" I became known at Oxford Press as the writer who hands things in on time.) In my questions to Durr I zeroed in on his FCC disputes. The granting of television licenses, halted abruptly

Eloquent dissenter: Clifford Durr of the FCC. (State Historical Society of Wisconsin)

by World War II, was restarted in a charged atmosphere. In the battle for lucrative channels, the stakes were raised by other issues. Concerning various applicants the FCC began to receive, from J. Edgar Hoover, unsolicited memoranda marked "confidential." Assessing a group of applicants for a California license, Hoover wrote:

> I thought you would be interested in knowing that an examination of this list reflects that the majority of these individuals are members of the Communist Party or have affiliated themselves sympathetically with the activities of the communist movement.

The FCC, at Durr's urging, asked Hoover for particulars and pointed out that rejected applicants were by law entitled to a public hearing. Could the FBI supply information that could be publicly presented as evidence? Hoover replied that this would be impossible; FBI sources had to be kept confidential.

The FCC has its own investigators and sent one of them to California. He reported that it was impossible to determine who was a communist and who was not, but that the people referred to by Hoover were, on the whole, well regarded. Their main political activity had revolved around efforts to reelect President Franklin D. Roosevelt. The FCC, having no basis for an unfavorable action that could be defended in court, refrained from acting. The applicants had no knowledge of charges against them. All they knew was that action seemed indefinitely—mysteriously—delayed. Durr felt this was, in effect, "to deny the application by not acting on it." At a meeting of broadcasters in Chicago he discussed this situation, resulting in a column by Marquis Childs in the *Washington Post* and making the issue public, to the fury of Hoover.

Hoover asked the FCC if he should assume the commission was not interested in FBI data. The query produced a crisis atmosphere at the FCC as it convened to consider a reply. Durr used the occasion to summarize what he felt was Hoover's contribution to their deliberations. He felt it was of little help to the commission to be informed that an applicant was, in 1944, at the height of the war, reported by an unidentified source as being in contact with another unidentified individual "who was *suspected of possible* pro-Russian activity"; or that the applicant was reported by an unidentified informant to have been a visitor in the residence of another individual who was reported by another unidentified source to have been identified by still another unidentified source with "communistic" activities; or that "according to an unknown outside source" the name of the applicant "appears" as a member of a committee of an organization of artists and professional people which was active in support of the Democratic presidential nominee in the 1944 presidential elections; or that another unidentified source had described that organization "as a communist infiltrated and/or influenced organization"; or that a local Democratic committee had been reported by an unidentified informant "to be under the influence of the communist element"; or that according to a newspaper account of a speech delivered by Republican vice presidential candidate Bricker in the 1944 campaign, the speaker charged that the Democratic Party had become the "Hillman-Browder communistic party" and that the applicant had left his job with the government to support the campaign of President Roosevelt, the founder of this "communistic party"; or that the applicant had been reported by an unidentified source to have been a member of the committee to greet the late president of a large labor union . . .*

* Minutes, FCC, December 1, 1947, qtd. in Erik Barnouw, *The Golden Web* (New York: Oxford University Press, 1968), pp. 246–247.

All this was what Director Hoover called "unevaluated data." To Durr it was stuff that could not possibly be a basis for decision. The other commissioners were more cautious. They seemed terrified of giving further offense to Hoover, who was said to have secret files on innumerable people in government. According to rumor, he occasionally dropped hints to high officials regarding scurrilous allegations about them that had been fed to him—which, he assured them, were fortunately in good hands and would not be allowed to get out. Such rumors created caution in dealing with Hoover. Durr's fellow commissioners drafted a conciliatory reply, assuring Hoover that they welcomed his continuing advice. It was a repudiation of Durr.

The tide was, in any case, against Durr. The year 1947 was dominated by a monomania: the search for subversives, pursued via mutual espionage and denunciation. In Congress it seemed to take precedence over all other matters. President Harry Truman was ceaselessly badgered about alleged "traitors" in government agencies. Finally, in a desperate attempt to stem the flood and get on with the work of government, he announced Executive Order No. 9835, a "loyalty-security program" under which, at huge expense, 2 million federal employees would be checked by "loyalty review boards." Derogatory information from the FBI or other sources would be carefully and discreetly weighed. As a guide, Attorney General Tom Clark (later a U.S. Supreme Court justice), prepared a list of organizations he deemed subversive. Membership in any of them could, under rules of the program, be considered significant.

Among those who spoke out in protest was Commissioner Durr, who pressed the issue in a number of forums. He told a meeting of the American Political Science Association:

> We are going to elevate to a new level of dignity informers, stool pigeons and gossips, a class which since the days of Leviticus we have been taught to regard with suspicion and scorn. We are going to fight communism by employing the methods upon which we profess to base our abhorrence of communism.

He told a group of churchmen:

> Can we safely vest, in our secret police, jurisdiction over the "association" and "sympathetic affiliation" and thoughts of men, and be sure that we are safe? Can men fairly be tried when their right to

face their accusers, and to be fully advised of the nature and cause of the charge against them, depends on the "discretion" of those who accuse them?

The loyalty-security program applied only to government employees, but Durr asked:

will the example of government stop with government itself? Once it has been established and accepted, can its influence be kept from spreading to industry, to the press, to our schools and universities, and even to our churches? *

From the vantage of later years, those 1947 words were a prediction of astounding accuracy. Even as Durr spoke, a House committee on un-American activities was preparing a glittering show trial before television cameras on "communism in the film industry." Screenwriters were the first targets. Chairman J. Parnell Thomas promised evidence on "communistic films," but no such evidence followed. Hollywood officialdom at first seemed to rally in defense, but soon instituted a blacklist regime. Joining the bandwagon were a number of film union officers, including Ronald Reagan, newly elected president of the Screen Actors Guild, who (as FBI informant T-10) was feeding the FBI information on people he regarded with suspicion.

To broadcasters all this seemed—briefly—a Hollywood phenomenon not affecting them. Their newscasts helped publicize and magnify the phenomenon. It gave television one of its first major spectacles. In its zeal the broadcasting industry seemed to be proclaiming its own lily-white purity. But in New York, three entrepreneurs calling themselves American Business Consultants, fresh from years as FBI agents, were pioneering a lucrative private enterprise. Offering their services to networks, advertising agencies, and sponsors as "security" specialists, they provided allegations on writers, directors, and performers who should be shunned for patriotic and business reasons. The trio's Madison Avenue office featured a large framed photo of J. Edgar Hoover. The climax of their activity came in June 1950, when they published *Red Channels*.

I well remember the day—it happened to be my forty-second birthday—when I came on this 215-page book in a Doubleday bookshop. Its paper cover showed a red hand closing on a microphone. The introduc-

* Barnouw, *The Golden Web*, p. 248.

Witches' brew, 1950.
(State Historical Society
of Wisconsin)

tion said: "the Cominform and the Communist Party USA now rely more on radio and TV than on the press and motion pictures as 'belts' to transmit pro-Sovietism to the American public." Setting the stage with such words, *Red Channels* listed 151 people—alphabetically arranged for easy reference, with "citations"—described as the infiltrators carrying out this mission. The book cost one dollar. I promptly bought a copy. It is well I did. A day later all copies had disappeared from New York bookstores— many apparently into the desks of broadcasting executives, to become their secret "security" manual.

Glancing over the list of 151 people made my knees tremble. While many were unknown to me, many were also my associates of the past two decades, people I had worked with closely day by day: directors, writers, musicians. Many were people I especially admired. The list included one government official—Clifford Durr.

Here were the brilliant Norman Corwin and numerous artists he had introduced to CBS audiences on his *Pursuit of Happiness* series (on which I had served as writer-editor): Burl Ives, John Latouche, Burgess Meredith, Earl Robinson, Pete Seeger, Josh White; others who had figured importantly in Corwin's later specials: Martin Gabel, Joe Julian, Lynn Murray. Here too were such CBS figures as Orson Welles of the *Mercury Theater on the Air*, Robert Lewis Shayon of *CBS Was There*, William N. Robson of *Columbia Workshop*, True Boardman of *The Silver Theater*, William L. Shirer of CBS News, and galaxies of other talents: Leonard Bernstein, Abe Burrows, Marc Connelly, Aaron Copland, Jose Ferrer, Ruth Gordon, Morton Gould, Nat Hiken, Judy Holliday, Lena Horne, Henry Morgan, Zero Mostel, Dorothy Parker, Irwin Shaw. Even Gypsy Rose Lee. Here also were writers I had featured in my script anthology, *Radio Drama in Action:* Langston Hughes, Millard Lampell, Arthur Laurents, Alan Lomax, Peter Lyon, Arthur Miller, Norman Rosten.

I looked for my name. It was not there. This brought a strange swirl of feelings. Relief. Also questions. What had I failed to do that these others— well known and not so well known—*had* done? I felt a sense of guilt, like that mentioned by soldiers who survive their friends in a war. Then came a further question. I thought I had known these people, some of them very well. Did I *really* know them? Were there things about them I did *not* know that had landed them in this strange volume? To find myself asking such questions, even to myself, was chilling. The poison was spreading, as Durr had predicted.

At home I studied the "citations"—lists of memberships, meetings attended, petitions signed, speeches made. These made clear what these men and women had been concerned with over the years. They had opposed Franco, combated segregation, campaigned against poll taxes and other voting barriers, condemned censorship and blacklists, worked against nazism and fascism, assailed the House committee on un-American activities, criticized the FBI, hoped for peace, and favored efforts toward better U.S.-Soviet relations. These were the liberal impulses of two decades. None were statutory crimes, although J. Edgar Hoover seemed to proceed as though they were. Even membership in the Communist Party was not a crime; the party was listed on official ballots. Were these a kind of entrapment? Some blacklisters were urging that the party be outlawed, so that communists "and their ilk" could more properly be expelled from the media. Meanwhile it would apparently be done by invective. John Keenan, one of the *Red Channels* impresarios, said he did not know which listees might be party members; most, he thought, probably were not. But that made no difference. His organization considered "fronters," "dupes," "stooges," "appeasers," and "fellow travelers" all part of "communism" and tools of a foreign power. So they should be ostracized, barred from the media "to the extent possible by law." The important thing was to "base your whole policy on a firmly moral foundation."

He conceded that some might have been unjustly listed, so his group had set up a clearance procedure. Applicants would have a chance to bare their souls and denounce the nation's enemies. One listee told a reporter he would have nothing to do with people "playing god."

I realized that circumstances had sheltered me. The witch-hunt had begun at a time when my work became focused on university projects that had often kept me traveling; I had moved away from the eye of the storm. Meanwhile the insanity had not only persisted but spread. Senator McCarthy had entered the fray and outdid all others in proclamations of treason. He stormed the country, waving sheafs of paper he called "documentation"—allegedly lists of "traitors" in the state department, army, Voice of America, and elsewhere. He dominated newspaper headlines. Politicians kowtowed to him. Even Eisenhower, campaigning for the presidency, sought to placate him. The whole hubbub became known as McCarthyism. New groups entered the picture, outdoing each other. A group called AWARE offered ever longer rosters of subversive artists and invented a new gambit: it enlisted the support of grocery chains. Sponsors not shunning "commie" artists were threatened with boycotts; they risked losing their places on supermarket shelves. Obeisance to blacklists acquired a financial (i.e., respectable) rationale.

Looking back with Clifford Durr from the vantage of 1965, I could see how the evolving phenomenon had shaped the psyche of the postwar decades. To me it seemed especially ironic—and tragic—that CBS, where I had worked in happier days, had become a special target for blacklisters. CBS had been the center of the radio renascence of the 1930s. It had invigorated a sterile medium with the drama of ideas. It had made its mark by welcoming to the airwaves the ferment of the Depression. In so doing it had apparently made itself a happy hunting ground for the list-bearers. CBS had reacted to this as Truman had done—and as Hollywood had done—with a purge of its own. CBS instituted its own loyalty oath. It became blacklist headquarters.

An academic, Frank N. Stanton, had moved into the CBS presidency in the late 1940s. With a Ph.D. from Ohio State, a specialist in social psychology, he seemed especially qualified to understand the madness with which he was dealing. Instead he became a skillful coordinator of suppression policies. CBS founder and chairman William Paley was known to set policy, but Paley always had a No. 2 man to execute policy. For some years Stanton, with a well-publicized six-figure salary, did the executing. He was an acknowledged audience research genius. His polls became powerful administrative instruments. Stanton knew how to frame poll questions that would elicit the answers that CBS felt it needed.

In 1954 the CBS veteran Edward R. Murrow decided on a cautious move against the high-riding McCarthy. Over a period of months researchers for the *See It Now* series, produced by Murrow with Fred W. Friendly, gathered film footage of the senator's appearances around the country. This compilation showed clearly his self-contradictions, irresponsibility, and utter mendacity. Commentary was scarcely needed to make the point. The compilation was scheduled for a March 9 broadcast. Paley and Stanton were unhappy over this, and refused to let CBS publicize the broadcast; Murrow and Friendly dug into their own pockets for a *New York Times* advertisement announcing their "Report on Senator Joseph McCarthy." Murrow, on the air, offered McCarthy a later *See It Now* period to reply—a somewhat ironic offer, since McCarthy would, in effect, be answering himself. But McCarthy, accepting the proffered period, ignored Murrow's exposé and used the time for a virulent attack on Murrow:

> Now, ordinarily I would not take time out from important work at hand to answer Murrow. However, in this case I felt justified in doing so because Murrow is a symbol, the leader and cleverest of the jackal pack which is always found at the throat of anyone who dares to expose individual communists and traitors. . . .*

The McCarthy reply won a wide audience. A few days later Stanton asked Fred Friendly to come to his office, and showed him the results of a poll he had instituted, to which he apparently attached great importance. The figures showed that 59 percent of those questioned about the McCarthy rebuttal had seen it or had heard about it. Of these, 33 percent believed McCarthy had raised doubts about Murrow, or proved him pro-communist. Stanton seemed greatly disturbed by these findings and expected Friendly to feel likewise. But Friendly reacted differently. He

*CBS-TV, April 6, 1954.

suggested that if the figures had been even more favorable to McCarthy, they would have demonstrated even more compellingly the need for Murrow's television scrutiny of McCarthy. It was a reaction that Stanton was unlikely to appreciate.

My interviews gave me further glimpses of Stanton in action. William N. Robson had been responsible for some of CBS's most splendid moments. As longtime producer of the network's *Columbia Workshop* series, he had won numerous awards. After the Detroit race riots of 1943 he had written and produced *Open Letter on Race Hatred*, narrated by Wendell Willkie, which *Time* magazine called "one of the most eloquent and outspoken programs in radio history."* During World War II Robson produced *The Man Behind the Gun*, one of the most honored of war series. After the war he was in Hollywood directing a CBS mystery series, *Sure As Fate*, when *Red Channels* appeared. Robson was promptly notified that he was relieved of his duties. His CBS salary ceased. He learned that his *Red Channels* entry included four "citations": (1) In 1942 he had been a sponsor of an Artists Front to Win the War organized at a meeting in Carnegie Hall; (2) in December 1946 he had made a speech in Los Angeles protesting encroachments on freedom of expression; (3) in 1948 he had signed with other artists a "We Are for Wallace" advertisement in the *New York Times*; and (4) he was listed as an "associate" on the masthead of the *Hollywood Quarterly*, a scholarly journal of film, radio, and television published by the University of California Press. Robson could not believe that these four items meant the end of his years at CBS. He got in touch with Stanton, who at first seemed to reassure him. But soon thereafter all communication with the CBS leaders was cut off. His phone calls to Paley and Stanton were not put through. His calls were not returned. His messages were ignored. His earnings plummeted. He barely survived.

There was one slip-up. In 1954 the Anti-Defamation League of B'nai B'rith was awarded an hour on CBS for a broadcast celebrating its fortieth anniversary and engaged Robson to write the script. When CBS learned of this it protested: "We don't use him." But Robson had written the ADL's thirtieth anniversary program, with distinction, so the ADL insisted on keeping him. CBS gave in, but Robson's name was omitted from the on-

* See Erik Barnouw (ed.), *Radio Drama in Action* (New York: Rinehart & Company, 1945), pp. 59–77.

air credits. The anniversary celebration involved a reception at which Stanton unexpectedly found himself facing Robson. "Bill, like old times!"

When Robson later recalled this episode, during my interview with him, he could hardly contain his fury. He paced the room, trembling with rage. "The bastards! Bastards!" *

The blacklisting of Robson had a postscript. In 1961, when Edward R. Murrow left CBS to accept an appointment from President Kennedy to head the U.S. Information Agency, he phoned his one-time CBS colleague William Robson and asked if he would like to join the Voice of America as a writer. Robson said, "You're crazy—I'm on the list. They'll never clear me." Murrow said, "Let me try." So a standard "full field investigation" was ordered, in which the FBI found no obstacle to Robson's employment at the Voice of America. He remained there until retirement on his seventieth birthday.

The blacklist affected decades of American life. It created a dangerous era of silence. Ideology disappeared from daily talk. Safer subjects were sports, business, and the bottom line. The caution even penetrated to Oxford University Press. I wanted, in *The Golden Web*, the second volume of the trilogy, to publish the names of the 151 people in *Red Channels* and to say it was a roll of honor. The lawyer who reviewed the manuscript vetoed the idea: too risky to publish the list. Even in 1968, many might not like it known they were listed and would sue for damage to their careers. I argued. Two earlier books on the blacklists, by John Cogley and Merle Miller, included interviews with listees but called them "actor D. L.," "director S. N.," "producer Z. A." This seemed to me to give them a sinister aura. In hiding behind initials—fictive initials at that—what were these people hiding? In proposing to publish the full *Red Channels* list, calling it a roll of honor, I felt the list itself would justify the term. Oxford University Press finally overrode its lawyer but demanded that I assume financial liability. I did—after transferring our home to my wife. But no listee ever complained. A few thanked me warmly. Among them was William Robson. For years, he said, his children had known that some cloud hung over his career, which he somehow could never discuss. Finally he bought each one a set of the three-volume history, saying: "Read this. It will tell you what Daddy did in the war."

---

* W. N. Robson, *Reminiscences* Columbia University Oral History Project, 1966, pp. 25-26.

Clifford Durr, the FCC's fine dissenter, holds for me a special place in the roll of honor. Many people assume that President Truman did not offer Durr a second term on the FCC, but I learned this was not so. Truman strongly urged Durr to accept a second seven-year term, but Durr declined because of his strong feelings about the "loyalty review." If he stayed, he would share responsibility for the inquisition. He decided to practice law—and somewhat later, to do so in Montgomery, Alabama, the town that had been his boyhood home. It was also where he and his wife had begun their married life. And here the Durr law office was opened in 1961. It began a new and extraordinary chapter in their lives.

I knew nothing of it when I interviewed him in 1965. I was intent on data for my trilogy. The Montgomery story became known to me later, mainly through an unforgettable memoir by Durr's widow, Virginia Durr, titled *Outside the Magic Circle.**

When they resettled in Montgomery, they were anxious to play a role in the world in which they had grown up. In earlier days he had taught Sunday school in the Presbyterian Church. He took up where he had left off and soon had an eager following. Virginia Durr was an Alabama belle in the old tradition, raised to be always gay and pleasing but at all costs to preserve her purity for a Prince Charming who would surely appear. He had appeared, in the form of a young Rhodes scholar. It was considered a splendid match, but she had no inkling of how he would change her life. Her sister Josephine was likewise felt to have done well: she had married Hugo Black, a young lawyer who became a U.S. senator from Alabama and later a Supreme Court justice. The Durrs, returning to Montgomery, were at first welcomed into the old social circles.

But the old circles were not the same, nor were the Durrs. The 1950s were the time of *Brown v Board of Education,* of the rise of militant White Citizens Councils, of the bus boycott—all of which polarized Montgomery. The Durr law office was for a time busy with wills and real estate transactions, but more and more often they were handling civil rights cases, police brutality cases, and cases involving young blacks who usually couldn't pay a fee. Durr took the cases anyway, and soon became known as the lawyer who represented blacks, often against the Montgomery establishment. When Rosa Parks was arrested and jailed for refusing to move to the back of the bus, it was Clifford and Virginia Durr

*V. F. Durr, *Outside the Magic Circle* (New York: Simon & Schuster, 1985).

who visited the jail and bailed her out and then arranged for the NAACP's national office to pursue the case—on constitutional grounds. Other civil rights cases followed in rapid succession. Martin Luther King and Coretta King became their friends. When the Selma-Montgomery march brought an influx of supporters to Montgomery, dozens of them bedded down in the Durr home. It became a stopping place for civil rights workers.

This was an exhilarating time for the Durrs, but it exacted a toll. At school the Durrs' youngest daughter was told her father was a "nigger lover." More often he was called a communist. So was Justice Hugo Black, for his Supreme Court vote in *Brown v Board of Education*. These families found themselves ostracized by people who had been their childhood friends. The poison spread, as Durr had predicted. One Sunday, as he arrived for his Sunday school class, there was no one there. It had spread, as he had said it would, "even to our churches."

Fortunately, the polarization was not always on racial lines. During the bus boycott, when many domestic servants walked miles to and from work, in support of the boycott, some white women were moved to offer them rides. Virginia Durr frequently gave lifts to domestics walking home or to work, and so did other women. Police harassment did not stop them. The mayor of Montgomery addressed a strong plea to white women of Montgomery: if they would refrain from giving lifts, the boycott would quickly collapse and everything would be back to normal. His plea was ignored.

The trend may have spurred other trends. The rise of the blacks, thought Virginia Durr, had given long-range impetus to the women's movement.

For Durr's law office the years were catastrophic. It was always busy, but incoming funds were a trickle. Durr fought one case to the Supreme Court for a twenty-five-dollar fee. Virginia, the Alabama belle, became his secretary, typing briefs and letters in the office when not taking care of their home. She relished the struggle, but it couldn't go on forever. Sometimes, instead of collecting fees, they were loaning money to their clients to keep them going.

By the time the trilogy was in print—*A Tower in Babel, The Golden Web,* and *The Image Empire,* comprising my "History of Broadcasting in the United States"—Durr had closed his office and retired. His wife bought him a set of the books. The following year, while Dotty and I were in Cairo (on a round-the-world research trip for my next project), I received a three-page, single-spaced letter from Durr, commenting on the books. I treasured his words of enthusiasm and agreement. There were also sardonic comments that I found especially striking. He wrote: "I like especially the way you deal with *Dr.* Frank Stanton. He goes down in my book as the first of the academic call girls."

One of Durr's grandfathers had been a slave owner, and Durr's own background was, as his wife put it, "Southern through and through." He went through deep changes, as did she. Yet throughout the final, contentious Alabama years, Durr was seldom heard to criticize his Montgomery neighbors. He said he would have been like them if he had stayed in Montgomery. He had had a chance to see other worlds. If he had not, he would have lived among the same pressures that had shaped their lives. Changes, he said, were sure to come slowly.

Blacks sometimes thanked him profusely for what he had done for them. But any imputation of nobility was rebuffed by Durr. He would say: "Look here, I'm not a damn bit interested in your legal and constitutional rights as Negroes, but I am interested in your legal and constitutional rights as people because I happen to be people myself." Legal rights, he said, have to protect everybody "or in time they won't protect any of us." *

Clifford Durr, returning to Montgomery, was not well treated by his home town. During these years he often received offers from the North, usually from universities. Apparently he never considered accepting one. He often said how good it felt to be back in Alabama. He sometimes said it on waking in the morning. Alabama was his territory. It was where he had to be. There he died in 1975.

---

* Quoted, in V. F. Durr, *Outside the Magic Circle,* p. 306.

THE KAUFMAN BROTHERS

"The photographic image . . . is a
message without a code."
—Roland Barthes

While The Image Empire, *final book of the trilogy, was still on the presses, Sheldon Meyer asked what I would like to do next. It was now my turn to make a preposterous suggestion. I said I would like to write a history of the documentary film, as internationally as possible, but not until I could somehow go around the world and visit film archives. Several dozen countries, including new nations, had started film archives since World War II, many to document their own history and heritage. Filmmaking was erupting worldwide, spurred by the rise of safety film, 16mm film, 8mm film, television, and later video. Documentary was prominent in this explosion. The Flaherty Seminars, in which I had been active from their early days, had reflected and abetted this trend. The main book on documentary history, Paul Rotha's* Documentary Film *(1938), had virtually confined itself to Britain, Russia, and the United States. That seemed a bit too Eurocentric even then. Now was the time for a wider look. Fine, said Sheldon. Would a target date several years off—such as 1974— be feasible? It hardly seemed feasible, but a contract was signed and an advance paid.*

Astonishingly, pieces began to fall into place. The 1971 Bancroft Prize in American History awarded to The Image Empire—*four thousand dollars, tax exempt—was the catalyst. Our three children were at college or ready to go, so our ten-room suburban house wasn't really needed, and we rented it. It became the residence of Malawi's United Nations representative. The JDR III Fund, dedicated to promoting Asian arts, provided round-the-world air transport for Dotty and me and living expenses during any time we would spend in Asia. Targeting twenty-odd film producing nations, I began writing to film archives, documentary studios, and writers associations, explaining the project. A zigzag round-the-world itinerary began to take shape. In January 1972 we were off.*

Japan, Korea, Hong Kong, India, Lebanon, Egypt, Yugoslavia, the USSR, Poland, East Germany—then the more familiar domains of Western Europe. Our three-week limit for any one country proved ideal: long enough for interviews with major documentarists, film viewing at archives, and gala receptions—yet not long enough, it seemed, to wear out our welcome. Cooperation was overwhelming. The prospect of an Oxford history of the documentary and the hope for recognition in it opened many doors.

In each country we tended to focus on its national output, but unexpected treasures turned up. Yugoslavia was a delight. In three weeks we saw a hundred of its short documentaries, which were regularly winning top awards at European festivals. Made by cooperatives in Yugoslavia's diverse republics, they were apparently free to criticize and satirize their government. The critical films were called "black films," a term said to have originated in Poland during its "springtime thaw" in the 1950s, after the death of Stalin. The term had spread—along with the thaw— to Czechoslovakia, Hungary, and especially Yugoslavia, where controls were already more relaxed. Clampdowns had followed in Hungary and Czechoslovakia but not—at least so far—in Yugoslavia. Shortly before we left there the archivist, with a touch of flamboyance, said, "Mr. Barnouw, I believe you have seen all the Yugoslavian documentaries you need to see. But before you go—if you like—I can show you some Hungarian documentaries they will not show you in Hungary, and some Czechoslovakian documentaries they will not show you in Czechoslovakia." So that is how Dotty and I spent our last two days in Yugoslavia. Later in Poland, one of its leading documentarists, Jerzy Bossak, said, "There are some works of mine I would like you to see that won awards during our springtime thaw. You won't be able to see them here—not now, anyway—but you can see them at the Belgian archive." He proved right; that is where we saw them. Meanwhile, in East Germany, after we had screened a number of East German films, its scholarly archivist said, "Have you read about those Cuban documentaries that were seized by the U.S. customs to prevent a showing near Columbia University?" I had indeed read about the seizure in the European *Herald-Tribune*. He said, "We have them here, if you'd like to see them." So in East Berlin we spent many hours on Cuban films. Later, in Sweden, where antipathy to the continuing U.S. war in Vietnam ran high, we found a huge collection of Vietcong and North Vietnamese films, which U.S. customs officials were keeping out of the United States on "national security" grounds. We spent two days on those at a Stockholm archive called Film Centrum. Each archivist seemed to take pleasure in documenting foolish censorship policies—focusing on the foolishness of others, no doubt for reasons of prudence. We became very fond of archivists. Keeping in touch with each other, working out exchanges, they seemed to care little about ideological tempests high above them. Their concern was to preserve the historic record—for generations that might, perhaps, have the sense to learn from it.

We anticipated our Soviet stay nervously. We had written to its film archive, its main documentary studio, and its writers association. For four months no reply came from any of these. From most countries replies had come quickly; the smaller the country, the more immediate the reply, assuring cooperation. Finally, in Belgrade, last stop before Moscow, a letter from the USSR awaited us. It was as though our three letters had finally converged at some higher point of authority, where a decision could be made. We were assured of cooperation and given a phone number to call on arrival. From then on, Moscow astonished us with its helpfulness. We wondered briefly whether this had something to do with the simultaneous arrival of President Richard Nixon for a summit conference with Leonid Brezhnev. We hoped not. We explained on several occasions, perhaps a bit too emphatically, that we were not part of "the Nixon party."

The designated phone number reached one Bella Epstein, a dynamic lady, a zealous film devotee. She was one of the coordinators of the Moscow Film Festivals, held in alternate years. This was not a festival year, so she had been instructed to look after us and seemed very happy about it. She directed us to Domkino, the House of Film. There she explained in a rapid stream of Russian-accented English, "This is the headquarters of the Association of Film Makers of the USSR. There are four screening rooms here—of various sizes. One is reserved for you each morning during your visit. My task is to get you the films you want to see, and arrange appointments. I did not know whether you knew Russian; I assumed you did not, so I have arranged for a high school English teacher, Sonya Berkovskaya, to be released from her teaching duties while you are here, to be with you each day."

Astonishingly, this routine began promptly the following morning with films from a wish list I had sent with my letters—films I had read about but had not been able to see in the United States. Heading the list were films of Vertov (Denis Kaufman) and his brother Mikhail Kaufman, Vertov's main cameraman and the central character in their most famous film, *The Man With the Movie Camera*, which was available in the United States and was shown annually at Columbia. Many of their other films had not been available, including some episodes of their *Kino Pravda* newsreels of 1922–25 and films made by Mikhail Kaufman without Vertov.

I discussed with Bella my special interest in the Kaufman brothers. The eldest, Denis—who had renamed himself Dziga Vertov during the 1917 revolution (both names suggested a rapid whirling motion, perhaps symbolizing a spinning film reel, or revolution itself)—was known in Russia as "father of the documentary," as Robert Flaherty was known among us as "father of the documentary." Their careers had striking parallels. Each had taken up film during the 1910s. After a brief period of prominence in the early 1920s, each had worked for the rest of his life on the fringes of his nation's film industry, which preferred dream films. Both continued their missionary struggle for a new kind of film not built on studio artifice. Both hated large production units. Each worked closely with a wife and a brother, adding others as needed. Both died in the early 1950s. Each was survived by the wife and brother who had been his chief collaborators, who then carried on the struggle. The genre they had created lived on and grew in importance. Flaherty's work inspired a generation of non-studio films of the sort shown at the annual Flaherty Seminars, including ethnographic films. And Vertov's *Kino Pravda* (*Film Truth*) was said to have inspired *The March of Time* as well as the cinema verite movement named after the Vertov newsreel.

I had become well acquainted with Frances Flaherty, Robert's widow, and with David Flaherty, his brother, and had learned a good deal about early documentary history from them. I hoped in Moscow to learn about Vertov's career and impact. If Mikhail Kaufman and Elizaveta Svilova, Vertov's widow, were alive, I hoped to interview them. And there was something else. In 1954 one Boris Kaufman, a war refugee from France, had scored an impressive success in the United States as cameraman for *On the Waterfront* and later for other films including *Baby Doll* and *Twelve Angry Men*. He too was said to be a brother of Vertov. Was this true? Some doubted it. In France Boris Kaufman had worked with the French director Jean Vigo on *A Propos de Nice*, one of the "city films" of the 1920s. In a monograph on Vigo the film historian Sales Gomes described Boris Kaufman as "a cameraman of Russian origin" and then speculated:

> Boris is often confused with Mikhail Kaufman, Dziga Vertov's brother and cameraman on the most important of the *Kino Pravda* films. Boris is perhaps the third Kaufman brother, the youngest, but it is also possible that Vigo and Boris deliberately created a myth.*

I told Bella I hoped to sort all this out. She said she could tell me nothing about Boris and did not know Svilova's whereabouts. But she knew that Mikhail Kaufman was alive. For years he, like Vertov, had lived under a cloud of official disfavor. But a rehabilitation seemed to be in process, and it was now possible to mention both of them and even to speak well of them. Bella was clearly an admirer of Mikhail and seemed anxious to arrange an interview. She said she would do her best.

Each morning at the screening room a pile of film cans awaited us, brought overnight from the archive outside Moscow. Bella kept saying, "Mr. Privato is being an angel." At the screenings the young Sonya Berkovskaya, our attractive red-headed schoolteacher, sat between Dotty and me and did simultaneous translation—as she did regularly for the Moscow festivals. She astonished us with her easy, idiomatic English and uncanny word choice, all sounding more American than English. She said she had never been outside the Soviet Union; American recordings and films must have been important in her training. She and Dotty became warm friends; she invited Dotty to the cramped flat she shared with her mother. One day she surprised us by saying, "I noticed you reading the *Herald-Tribune*. Would you save me Art Buchwald's column? I like to use it with my students." This suggested a sophisticated grasp of American politics as well as of idioms. Buchwald's favorite target of the moment was Richard Nixon, whose career of deceit was beginning to unravel at the Watergate hearings. The current summit with Brezhnev had been instituted—many were certain—as a distraction from those hearings.

At some time during each morning Bella was likely to pop into the screening room with an excited announcement such as "We're lunching

*P. E. Gomes Sales, *Jean Vigo* (Berkeley: University of California Press, 1971).

with Grigori Chukrai!" or "We will meet with Roman Karmen!" On the third morning she was more excited than usual. Mikhail Kaufman would come for an interview that afternoon.

This began a strange, memorable sequence. We conversed in a quiet Domkino lounge, drinking tea. On this occasion Bella herself did the translating. I had my tape recorder running. She treated Mikhail Kaufman with deep respect, as some patriarchal leader. He had a courtly manner. In his mid-seventies, he seemed in good health but spoke slowly, with a quiet, resonant voice. Short questions often elicited long, thoughtful answers, which Bella obviously hesitated to interrupt. So our exchanges took time. Having begun with pleasantries and the pouring of tea, we finally seemed ready for the interview. But Kaufman surprised me with an urgent question of his own. The following discussion, stretched out via Bella's translations, unwound slowly.

"Mr. Kaufman says he is worried about Boris. Do you know whether Boris is all right? He has not heard from Boris for several months."

"I don't know Boris. I know nothing about him. You mean they write to each other?"

"Mr. Kaufman says he writes to Boris often, and Boris writes to him."

"You mean regularly?"

"He says they write regularly."

"Do letters go through without difficulty?"

After Bella relayed this question, he considered before replying. Then Bella reported: "Mr. Kaufman thinks they are often read by others. There are delays. Usually the letters arrive."

"When did he and Boris last see each other?"

"1917."

"All this time, letters have gone back and forth?"

"Yes."

"What could they write about?"

Hearing this question translated, Mikhail Kaufman smiled reminiscently. "I taught him cinematography by mail."

A saga gradually emerged. The Kaufman family originally came from Bialystok, in the Polish part of the czarist empire. The parents were both librarians. When the Great War—World War I—erupted in 1914, they decided to take their sons eastward to what seemed the comparative safety of Moscow. Denis pursued advanced studies. But in 1917 he and Mikhail were quickly caught up in the excitement of the revolution. Denis volunteered to the cinema committee and became Dziga Vertov. During the years of foreign intervention and civil war, 1917–20, he helped to make agitprop films to further the Soviet cause. The parents meanwhile decided to take the much younger Boris back to Poland, away from the turmoil. When peace came to Europe, they sent him on to France for his education. In the young Soviet Union Vertov had become a writer of zealous manifestos, calling on film artists to play a formative role in shaping the new order—not with dream films but with films of "Soviet actuality." The idea won support from a high source: Lenin. In 1922 Vertov, now joined by Mikhail, was able to launch a new kind of newsreel, *Kino Pravda*, with Mikhail as chief cameraman and Svilova as film editor.

Mikhail, with my tape recorder running, recalled this period through a mist of nostalgia. They worked ceaselessly. Vertov would outline larger strategies, then send Mikhail and other cameramen out into the world to record events of the hour: the moment when a Moscow trolley, long out of operation in torn-up streets, began running again; army tanks, used as tractors, leveling an area for an airport; a hospital trying to salvage, with minimal means, child drifters surviving in rubble. *Kino Pravda* cameramen abhorred staged action: they caught moments in marketplaces, factories, schools, taverns, streets—glimpses of order emerging from chaos. Mikhail recalled that he never thought of it as work: it seemed a life necessity, like eating or breathing. When he approached exhaustion and was ordered by Vertov into the country for a rest, he found himself unable to enjoy the beauty around him. "When I could not see it with the help of my camera, it was not beauty for me."

At Svilova's editing tables, under Vertov's supervision, accumulating footage was also made into feature-length documentaries, like *One Sixth of the World*, which was widely shown abroad. It celebrated the Soviet domain for its sweep and ethnic diversity. Boris saw it and other Vertov works in Paris.

After the death of the elder Kaufmans, Mikhail felt a special responsibility for the faraway Boris. He wrote him regularly, telling about the film work. Boris was drawn into similar work, making film studies of the Seine and the Champs Elysées. His cinematography impressed the director Jean Vigo, who enlisted him for *A Propos de Nice*, which became a Vigo-Kaufman coproduction. While it established Boris as a documentary producer, it was his camera work that became the key to much of his later career, in France and elsewhere. When World War II broke out, Boris became a war refugee once again and embarked for Canada, where he found work as a cameraman for the National Film Board of Canada, organized by John Grierson. Later Boris entered the United States, became a citizen, and began a U.S. film career.

It seemed extraordinary to me that the mail link had persisted through war and cold war. Had Mikhail and Boris ever talked by phone? No, Mikhail told us. I promised to inquire about Boris, and I secretly resolved that I would some day seek him out, interview him, and let him hear once more his brother's voice.

Mikhail wanted us especially to see two of his own films, made after the conclusion of the *Kino Pravda* series. One was *Moscow*, made with Ilya Kopalin in 1927, one of the earliest of the international wave of "city films." The other was *In Spring*, made in 1939, a feature-length film shown abroad but always in such mutilated form that he wanted us to see the original. He explained that it depicted the violence of spring storms and floods, and the havoc they left, and then the glory of new birth. Mikhail used all this as a metaphor for revolution, which was likewise shown to be violent in the cleaning out of the old—the entrenched bureaucracies and hierarchies—but was also essential in setting the stage for rebirth. The difficulty was, said Mikhail, that foreign distributors had removed all the symbolic context and presented the work as a glorious nature film. It had won a vogue under that guise. Bella promised to screen both *Moscow* and *In Spring* for us.

I sent an overnight cable to Stefan Sharff at Columbia, inquiring about Boris. It seemed to me likely that Sharff, being Polish and a cameraman, would know Boris Kaufman or at least know where to find him. A reply came promptly. At the next meeting with Mikhail, over a long lunch, I was able to tell him that Boris was fine but worried because he had not heard from Mikhail for several months. It seemed to be a time of mail delays. Was there some special reason? The Brezhnev-Nixon summit? We would never know.

Dotty and I assumed from the beginning of our visit that the task assigned to Bella—and perhaps to Sonya—was not only to serve us but to watch us and probably to report on our activities. This did not trouble us. During a week's research and interviews in Hollywood at the Universal Pictures lot, the same procedure had been followed: a charming young woman assigned by management was our constant guide and intermediary. The same procedure had been followed at CBS News in New York, during research at the huge block of offices and studios on West Fifty-Seventh Street. It seemed a sensible merging of "public relations" and "security" functions. But it created cautious relationships. We enjoyed the company of Bella and Sonya but stuck to the business at hand. We avoided politics. For this reason, one Moscow moment stands out in my recollection. Dotty and I were lunching with Bella and Sonya. Bella, glancing at a newspaper, commented that she regretted the imminent retirement of Kosygin. She had trusted him. Then she added, "Brezhnev—I wouldn't trust him any more than I would trust Nixon." There were seconds of total silence after this comment. Dotty or I might well have responded, "Amen!" But we didn't. After a few moments, we simply passed on to other matters.

Bella's comment, its background and its intent, might be analyzed forever. So might our silence. But the moment passed. We sensed we were among congenial souls but had reached a line we dared not cross. Afterwards we felt relieved, yet had our regrets. For several years thereafter, we exchanged New Year greeting cards with Bella and Sonya—hoping, perhaps, it would give us absolution for our silence.

Mikhail gave me photos reproduced from his family album. There was one I found especially haunting. It was from the Bialystok days and showed the three brothers together. The two older boys were in school uniforms. Boris looked childlike beside them. The photo eventually appeared in my book *Documentary: A History of the Non-Fiction Film.*

Back at Columbia, I learned that Boris Kaufman lived on Ninth Street in downtown New York. His wife answered my phone call. I said I was anxious to interview Boris and mentioned that I had been in Moscow and seen Mikhail and wanted to tell Boris about it. Could she suggest a time when an interview might be convenient? She seemed on guard. It was as though she felt I might be a KGB agent, planning something devious or dangerous. She promised to call back but no call came. A few days later I tried again and once more found her edgy and evasive. On my third try, Boris answered the phone. He too seemed wary but I persisted, and he finally set a time for a visit. This took place in his living room, with Mrs. Kaufman watching from an adjoining room through the open door. I set up my recorder. Boris was brief in reply to my questions, but we managed to clarify several points in his career. In the United States his

---

* Erik Barnouw, *Documentary* (New York: Oxford University Press, 1974), p. 75.

Kaufman brothers: Boris, Mikhail, and Denis (a.k.a. Dziga Vertov) as pre-World War I students in Bialystok, Poland. (Mikhail Kaufman album)

main achievements had been as cinematographer for feature films. He became a specialist in features shot on location, like *On the Waterfront,* which Hollywood tended to call "documentaries." In a sense they did represent, for Boris, a continuation of his documentary beginnings. One comment in the interview, concerning Mikhail, especially fascinated me. Boris said, "Mikhail taught me cinematography by mail."

After the interview I brought out my cassette of the Mikhail interview. I asked Boris if he would like to hear his brother's voice; without waiting for a reply I started the record. Boris looked uneasy, but soon a change came over him. He listened with growing intensity, sometimes with astonishment. As Mikhail talked about his work and the mysteries of the film medium, Boris exclaimed, "Our ideas are so similar! So similar!" It was clearly an emotional experience. Later I sent Boris a copy of the photo from Mikhail's album. He wrote back: "Thank you very much for the photo of the three of us. I didn't have it but somehow remember it. It's not easy to face oneself through time, telescoping into the past. It brings back images, sounds, even odors." I had said I found the photo "haunting." He agreed that it evoked a feeling of expectation—of a potential "never fully realized." *

To me the unfolding of the Kaufman story had been a wondrous saga.

*Letter dated January 28, 1975.

I mentioned it to friends at the Museum of Modern Art, who at once conceived the idea of a MOMA exhibition of Films of the Kaufman Brothers—by Vertov with Mikhail (*Kino Pravda, The Man With the Movie Camera, One Sixth of the World*); by Mikhail alone (*In Spring, Moscow*); and by Boris in France, Canada, and the United States (*A Propos de Nice, On the Waterfront*). It seemed a fine idea for a major series. Weeks later I asked how the plan was progressing, and learned that it had been quickly abandoned. Boris had said, "No! Absolutely not!" He was very decisive about it. "I have nothing to do with all that!" he said. It seemed to me, sadly, that I was hearing a kind of loyalty oath.

It was a disappointment, but a minor one in a fabulous year. I had seen eight hundred films and learned a lot about archives and archivists. I had no inkling that I would soon be an archivist myself. My next project propelled me further in that direction.

AKIRA IWASAKI

*"To the living we owe respect, but to
the dead we owe only the truth."*
—*Voltaire*

*Books and teaching left little time for filmmaking, but in 1968 a film
project suddenly riveted my attention and would not let go. The catalyst was a clipping from an English-language Japanese newspaper,* Asahi
Evening News, *sent to me by a friend and supporter of the Flaherty Seminars, Mrs. Lucy Lemann. She was also a supporter of the World Law Fund
and had received the clipping from a Japanese associate of the fund, Professor Yoshikazu Sakamoto of the University of Tokyo. The news item,
dated January 26, 1968, reported that film footage shot in Hiroshima and
Nagasaki in 1945 by Japanese cameramen—and subsequently seized and
impounded by the United States—had finally been returned to Japan by
the U.S. government. The Japanese government was said to be planning
a television showing "after certain scenes showing victims' disfiguring
burns are deleted." With the clipping Mrs. Lemann sent a short note:
"Don't you want to do something about this?" Indeed I did.*

*I had never heard of such footage. It had never occurred to me that any-
thing of this sort existed. According to Professor Sakamoto the Japanese
government had negotiated with the U.S. Department of State, but the
Department of Defense was thought to have the footage. I assumed that
the material received by Japan was a copy of the 1945 original, which
must have been on perishable nitrate film. Somewhat impulsively I wrote
a letter on Columbia stationery signed as "Chairman, Film, Radio, Television" addressed to "The Honorable Clark M. Clifford, Secretary of Defense," with a notation that copies should go to Secretary of State Dean
Rusk and to Dr. Grayson Kirk, president of Columbia University. I felt
a bit flamboyant about all this but sensed I had little to lose. The letter
asked whether Columbia's Center for Mass Communication, a division*

of Columbia University Press producing and distributing documentary
films and recordings, might have the privilege of releasing in the United
States the footage recently made available in Japan. A note from Presi-
dent Kirk assured us he supported our proposal. Soon afterwards came
a letter from the defense department—one that electrified us. Signed by
Deputy Assistant Secretary of Defense Daniel Z. Henkin, it said that the
film in question had been transferred to the National Archives and that
we could have access to it there.

So it was that a few days later I sat with several CMC associates,
plus Mrs. Lemann, in the auditorium of the National Archives looking at
some two hours and forty minutes of black-and-white film of the Hiro-
shima and Nagasaki havoc—historic testimony suppressed for almost
a quarter of a century. We found ourselves in a strange and improb-
able world.

The material we saw had been organized in sequences, which included
"effects on wood," "effects on concrete," "effects on internal organs,"
and so forth, as though scientific questions had determined the shooting. Other sequences showed grotesque destruction of buildings and
bridges. There were also a few sequences of people at improvised treatment shelters—"human-effects footage," we found ourselves calling it.
The archivist on duty showed us "shot lists" in which the locale of
every shot was identified and the day of photography indicated. Nippon
Eiga Sha, the Japanese government newsreel, was listed as the production unit. No individual filmmakers were identified. Every page of the
lists was stamped S E C R E T, but this stamp had been penciled out
and a new stamp substituted: "Not to be released without approval of
the D.O.D." This apparent declassification was not dated. We inquired
whether all this, film and paper records, could be reproduced and were
assured that this had been authorized. Mrs. Lemann promptly offered to
pay for reproduction of all footage and shot lists (she had her checkbook
with her), so an order was placed. A month later the material arrived at
our offices and we began a long process of studying, cataloguing, arranging and rearranging. Barbara Van Dyke, a long-time Flaherty Seminar
colleague, joined the CMC staff as associate producer for the project. Two
graduate students of the department, Geoffrey Bartz and Paul Ronder, did
the editing. Ronder eventually wrote and spoke the narration, along with
his Japanese girlfriend, Kazuko Oshima. So far as we knew, we alone were

working with this footage. Had some automatic declassification schedule made it available? Perhaps we were merely the first to have asked for it. Not questioning our good fortune, we worked as rapidly as we could.

It took longer than we expected. The paucity of "human-effects footage" troubled us, so Barbara Van Dyke wrote to Donald Richie in Tokyo, film critic of the *Japan Times* and coauthor of *The Japanese Film*, asking if he knew of other such material. He suggested names of people who might prove helpful, but none of these leads yielded further film. In the end we clustered most of our crucial human footage near the end. Leading up to it we focused on desolation, which had an eloquence of its own. Words of a Hiroshima girl who had survived on the fringes of the blast, read by Kazuko Oshima (who had been in Japan during the war), accompanied traveling shots that moved through rubble and twisted ruins:

GIRL: I remember—I remember—a big light comes. I never see so strong. I do not know what is happening. My friend, she and I are always together, but I could not find her. So dark it gets, so red like fire. All is smoking dark red. I cannot see anyone. Many people run, I just follow. Pretty soon like fog, red fog, then gray—people down all around me. Many people look so awful. Skin come off. Just awful. Makes me so scared, so afraid. I never knew such hurt on people. Not human. I think, if I am in hell, it is like this—no faces, no eyes, red and burned all things. Like women's hair, dusty and smoking with burning. Many people go into the river. I watch them. Many people are drinking water, but they fall in and die, and they float away. Voices cry, calling names. I cannot hear because so many voices cry, all calling names . . . *

Our first assembly of footage ran forty minutes. We all felt it was too long. The editors reduced it to thirty; I wanted it still shorter. As we kept reducing it for sharper impact, narrative words drafted by Ronder became constantly more terse and meaningful. The final version of our film, sixteen minutes long, began:

NARRATOR: On the clear bright morning of August 6th, 1945, an atomic bomb was dropped on Hiroshima, Japan. The pilots of the United States Air Force's 509th Composite Group could see flowers in the gardens below. . . .

*New York Times, August 6, 1958.

"August 6. . . . The temperature at the center of the fireball was as hot as the surface of the sun. Near the center, people become nothing." (*Hiroshima-Nagasaki, August 1945*)

The bomb exploded within a hundred feet of the target. The fireball was 18,000 feet across. The temperature at the center of the fireball was as hot as the surface of the sun. Near the center people became nothing. Near the center there was no sound. . . .

At this point viewers saw the center of Hiroshima as found by the Nippon Eiga Sha cameramen.

In January 1970 the CMC film *Hiroshima-Nagasaki, August 1945* was finally ready for a preview screening at the Museum of Modern Art. The large auditorium was crammed with invitees. Our invitation had mentioned footage "withheld" for almost a quarter of a century. As the film ended, the audience sat in total silence for what felt like several minutes. What did this mean? A few hours later the UPI ticker carried a long dispatch that treated the screening as a historic event. It mentioned the CMC print price: ninety-six dollars. From all over the country checks and orders began arriving from universities, libraries, schools, churches, and others. By the end of the year almost a thousand prints had been

"August 6. . . . The flash of the bomb made permanent shadows, burned into wood, etched into stone. Leaves, flowers, and men disappeared but their shadows remained. . . ." (*Hiroshima-Nagasaki, August 1945*)

sold. Meanwhile the Public Broadcasting System contracted to telecast the film on the twenty-fifth anniversary of the Hiroshima bomb. Our film was well on its way.

Reviews poured in, in some cases extravagant. The *Boston Globe* called it the century's "most important documentary film" and excoriated the commercial networks for not carrying it.* The networks had ignored our invitation to the preview screening.

But another commercial network—a foreign one—*had* attended, and this led to an event that seemed almost bizarre. In the auditorium, a moment after the screening, I was approached by a Japanese gentleman who said he represented Tokyo Television, one of Japan's commercial systems. He wanted to buy rights for two Japan-wide telecasts. I expressed puzzlement. Didn't the Japanese government have the footage? Hadn't it announced plans for a television screening over its noncommercial system? The Tokyo Television man nodded but persisted. So an agreement was

*Boston Globe, April 5, 1970.

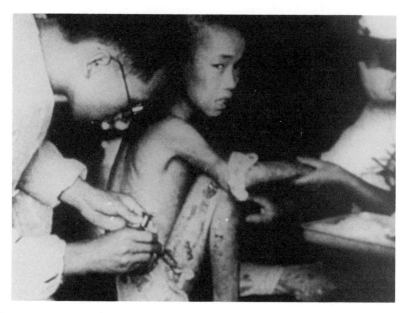

"At the hospitals, between three and ten thousand people came each day for help, and each day two thousand of them died." (*Hiroshima-Nagasaki, August 1945*)

concluded and payment made. Soon afterwards we began to receive from Professor Sakamoto in Tokyo translations of scores of newspaper reports concerning our film—responses to the two Tokyo Television telecasts. These were both months before the U.S. television premiere. What had happened to the announced Japanese government showing remained, for the moment, a mystery to us.

Along with reviews came letters, including one that caused a special stir at CMC. It was from one Akira Iwasaki, who identified himself as the executive producer of the film that had provided our raw material. He explained that he had had the astonishing experience of seeing, on Tokyo Television, footage he knew so well but had not seen for twenty-five years. He had even been asked to review our film for a large-circulation Japanese magazine, and had done so, praising the film warmly. "I knew every cut of it . . . yet I was speechless." He thanked us for the way we had handled his long-lost footage. He said he had been deeply moved.*

This was my introduction to the amazing Akira Iwasaki. Actually his

*Asahi-Graph, April 3, 1970.

name was already in our files. He had been mentioned by critic Donald Richie as one of those who might know of additional footage, and Iwasaki had received one of Barbara Van Dyke's letters of inquiry. But he had not answered. Now suddenly he became a living presence. His words were enormously gratifying. Yet his emergence gave me a strange feeling. The credits for our film read:

Produced by Erik Barnouw
Associate Producer, Barbara M. Van Dyke
Written by Paul Ronder
Edited by Paul Ronder and Geoffrey Bartz
Musical Effects by Linea Johnson and Terrill Schukraft
Narrated by Paul Ronder and Kazuko Oshima
Special Acknowledgements: Harold M. Agnew, Henry F. Graff,
    Albert W. Hilberg, Lucy B. Lemann, Shigeko Niimoto

As producer, I had assigned these credits. Knowing so little about the 1945 events, I had not dwelt on what names might be missing. Now we knew that one Akira Iwasaki (among others) had set the stage for us— anonymously. He had said nothing about this. He had expressed only gratitude. We were awed by this.

I wrote to Iwasaki, and we began a correspondence that lasted till the day of his death. I resolved to meet him. Two years later, during the round-the-world research for *Documentary: A History of the Non-Fiction Film*, I met him in Tokyo—a thin, wiry figure, quiet in manner. He spoke good English. One could not help noticing a long scar that ran from his hair-line to his chin, barely missing one of his eyes. He proved enormously helpful in introducing me to Japanese documentarists, who treated him with great respect. We recorded a brief interview. I gave him a copy of my book *The Image Empire*, final volume of the broadcasting trilogy. He later decided to translate *The Image Empire* into Japanese and arranged for its publication. In 1978 when I again had occasion to visit Japan, this time as chief of the newly formed Motion Picture, Broadcasting, and Recorded Sound Division of the Library of Congress, I again met with Iwasaki and interviewed him at greater length. He said he was writing a memoir titled *Occupied Screen* on his film experiences during the American occupa-tion and would send me a copy. Since it would deal in part with the atom bomb film, he thought it would be of special interest to me and he hoped I might find a student to translate some of it. Fortunately, *Japan Quar-*

Akira Iwasaki with the author, Tokyo 1972.

terly published a segment in English soon after publication; I later found a translator for other passages.* The more I learned about Iwasaki, the more fascinated I became with his strange career. Its dramatic ups and downs and its sudden (sometimes calamitous) reversals of fortune were extraordinary. And I was struck by the fact that so many of these were related to events in other parts of the world, including the United States.

Senryo Sareta Sukurin (Occupied Screen). A copy is in the Asian collection, Library of Congress. *Japan Quarterly* (Tokyo, Asahi Shinbun) published an excerpt in its July-August issue, 1978.

His life—the more I learned of it—seemed another way of looking back at years through which I had lived.

Iwasaki graduated in 1927 from the University of Tokyo, where he studied literature and became a film devotee. It was a beginning not unlike mine. His film interests soon led to a role as film critic. He also became a member of Prokino (short for Proletarian Film League), a counterpart to the Workers Film and Photo League in the United States and similar groups in Britain and elsewhere—all aspects of the "united front" against fascism, Marxism, and, in Japan, militarist imperialism. Iwasaki became the head of Prokino. I was familiar with the Film and Photo League movement in the United States. My friend Willard Van Dyke (husband of Barbara) had been active in the New York League, as had Ralph Steiner, Thomas Brandon, Leo Seltzer, Margaret Bourke-White, and others I had known. All these groups despised the newsreels of the time for steadily disregarding strikes and hunger marches and concentrating instead on such events as battleship launchings serviced by beauty queens. The agonies of the Depression were virtually taboo in the newsreels. In answer, all film and photo leagues started their own newsreels, produced on a shoestring but shown in labor unions, political meetings, and occasionally fringe theaters. Iwasaki himself produced many newsreel sequences during the 1930s and meanwhile wrote books about film as well as a stream of articles of social criticism. His books during the 1930s included *History of Film (Geibunshoin*, 1930), *Film and Capitalism (Ohraisha*, 1931), *Film Art (Kyowashoin*, 1936), *Cinematography (Mikasahobo*, 1936), *Film Aesthetics (Seibido*, 1937), and *Film and Reality (Shunyodo*, 1939).

In the mid-1930s the government began a rapid series of moves to bring all media under tight control. All Japan's newsreels—originally subsidiaries of the major Japanese studios—were consolidated into one government newsreel, Nippon Eiga Sha, popularly known as Nichi-ei. As Japanese armies struck in various directions to create a Greater East Asia Co-prosperity Sphere, Nichi-ei became a propaganda organ of imperial headquarters; theaters were required to book (and pay for) its releases, offered under such titles as *Rising Sun News* and *Banzai News*. Prokino was declared illegal and dissolved. When a new cinema law was decreed, modeled after those of Joseph Goebbels in Germany, few dared protest, but Iwasaki did so in the course of his writings on the film world. According to a postwar account in *Japan Quarterly*, "he alone opposed the cinema law that put movie production under state control."* His name appeared on a government list of authors whose works it would be "imprudent to publish." In 1939 he was arrested under the Peace Preservation Law and taken to a place known as the "pig box," the subterranean Ikebukuro police prison. After some months he was tried, convicted, and moved to Sugamo Prison, considered a place where Class A war criminals were kept—in some cases to be executed. But some two years later he was returned to his home in Setagaya-ku, a Tokyo suburb, to live under surveillance. An inspector regularly checked on his activities. All his books had been confiscated. Forbidden to write, he lived quietly with his wife Iku and their daughter Atsuko, tended his vegetable garden, and maintained cautious but friendly relationships with his neighbors, even taking part in communal defense measures. He occasionally—again, cautiously—saw old friends from the film world, but assumed that arena was now closed to him. Books could be borrowed from the library but were checked for anything "red"—anything touching on politics.

It seemed to him a good time to learn something about mathematics and science, subjects he had avoided in school. In a book on physics he came across a paragraph he could not forget. Discussing the energy in the nucleus of an atom, it suggested that an entire battleship might one day be blown to bits by "a bomb the size of a matchbox." This imagined bomb was called a "uranium bomb." He was reminded of this when he heard, early in August 1945, an Imperial Headquarters radio bulletin that a "new style bomb" had been used against Hiroshima and was being investigated. A few days later the same phrase was used for a bomb dropped on Nagasaki, with damage described as "comparatively insignificant." Despite the downplaying, there seemed reason for alarm, because the bulletins were followed by government advice and reassurance. Air raid shelters were said to offer complete protection against the new bomb, but it was a good idea to have "a layer of wood covering the opening." White undergarments were also recommended as good protection. The advice resembled the absurd reassurance propagated in the postwar years by U.S. agencies.

In *Occupied Screen* Iwasaki described August 14, 1945, as a stiflingly hot day in Setagaya-ku. No breeze stirred; there was even a lull in the

---

Japan Quarterly, July–August, 1978, introduction to *Occupied Screen* except.

enemy air raids. It was Iwasaki's turn to head the neighborhood association, so he had to go to the office of the town council to deal with rationing. Burdened with emergency gear, including the helmet and puttees of his national civilian uniform, he needed strong determination to drag himself through the heat. On the way he met the wife of a neighbor who worked for Nippon Optics. Since this was a military supplier, the family was rumored to get extra rations, yet her face was as sunk as his own, and her pants had holes in the knees. When she saw him she exclaimed, as he later recalled in his memoir, "Mr. Iwasaki! Did you hear on the radio? It seems there will be a broadcast of highest importance, tomorrow at noon!"

"I heard."

"What can it be—this broadcast of highest importance?"

"I wonder. I don't know, but—" After a moment Iwasaki was surprised to hear himself saying, "It could mean the war will be over."

At this her face lit up radiantly. Overflowing with joy she said, "That must mean that the Americans have unconditionally surrendered!"

Discussing this later, Iwasaki assured me her reaction was not strange. All media had constantly proclaimed the imminence and inevitability of victory. Against this background, words that came from the radio the next day must have been both puzzling and shocking. What was heard was the emperor's voice, infinitely fragile, announcing that certain decisions had been made. There was mention of a "cruel bomb," which had turned the war "not necessarily to Japan's advantage." Therefore:

> We have resolved to pave the way for a grand peace for all the generations to come by enduring the unendurable and suffering the insufferable.

It seemed to mean a surrender. Listeners were told to "follow the direction of the allied joint proclamation." This apparently meant the Potsdam Declaration, which most Japanese had never heard of.

Reactions ranged from suicides—some in front of the emperor's palace —to anger and relief. There was widespread uncertainty and turmoil. Among employees at Nichi-ei, the government newsreel, the revelation that the organization had played a major role in years of deception brought dismay and bitterness. Its wartime managers, ardent purveyors of the glorious war bulletins, were virtually hounded from office by the employees themselves. Some thought the organization might be saved from extinction by drastic reorganization from within, totally changing policy and leadership. Iwasaki, to his astonishment, found a delegation of Nichi-ei staff members visiting him, urging him to take on the role of production head, supervising both newsreels and documentaries. It was a measure of the sudden decline of the military. Iwasaki was overwhelmed. He had ceased to think of himself as a filmmaker and doubted his capacity for this new task. But the historic nature of the moment—and the urgency of the appeal made to him—swept him forward. He realized that Nichi-ei activities had already come to an abrupt halt. But one project on its agenda seemed to him of utmost importance: a documentary on the "new style bomb" and what it had done at Hiroshima and Nagasaki.

There was difference of opinion on what sort of film it should be: a protest film? a scientific film? a requiem? Certainly it was clear that the project could not wait. When the Ministry of Education came forward to offer sponsorship of the project, the question was automatically settled. It would be a scientific report, guided by the ministry's consultants, on the impact of the bomb on soil, vegetation, metals, concrete, and living creatures. The focus would put much of the photography near the epicenters of the bombings, with their wastelands of ruin. Effects on human survivors could be studied mainly on the fringes, where improvised hospitals continued to struggle with insoluble catastrophe. Appropriate consultants, cameramen, and other technicians were quickly chosen. No one resisted, though some assumed it might be a death warrant. The location budget provided: "33 people × 20 days . . . . ¥27,000."

It was clear that each participant must take provisions for the full period. Each carried a knapsack. It took time to assemble needed supplies. Film was scarce; only black-and-white film was available, mostly "short ends"—bits left over from other projects and spliced together. Because of the breakdown of transportation, it also took time to reach the locations. The delays may have saved lives. But in September crews were in operation in both Hiroshima and Nagasaki. Production coordinator was Ryuichi Kano, well known to Iwasaki from earlier days. As footage began arriving at Nichi-ei headquarters, Kano and Iwasaki together viewed and studied the rushes. Iwasaki later recalled: "Every frame burned into my brain."

In mid-September the U.S. Occupation began to take control in Tokyo, but for weeks remained unaware of the documentary activity elsewhere. On 22 September film industry executives were summoned by GHQ (the term would soon be part of the Japanese language) and briefed on what would be expected of them. In accordance with the Potsdam Declaration, Japan was to be transformed into a democratic nation that would never again disturb the peace of the world. This would require, in the film industry, an uprooting of all feudalistic, militaristic, imperialistic tendencies. Personnel and content would be affected. Executives received a list of themes to be stressed in the future, such as democratic rights, including the right to form labor unions. A few days later, to initiate and emphasize the transformation, GHQ staged a bonfire of 256 films of recent years considered feudal and imperialistic.

Late in October occupation officials spotted Nichi-ei cameraman Toshio Sekuguchi photographing in the ruins of Nagasaki and promptly arrested him. News of the arrest was conveyed to GHQ in Tokyo, with the result that Iwasaki was summoned and questioned.

"Who authorized the filming of an atomic documentary?"

Iwasaki explained that Nichi-ei, a newsreel and documentary agency, had the task of recording and reporting significant events. The event here concerned was of historic importance.

"Fine. From now on, in the name of the army occupying Japan, the filming is suspended."

Iwasaki did not protest, but asked questions. In view of the plans for reeducating Japan and establishing democratic practices, would it not be well to clarify the issue for him and his staff? If this was a subject *not* to be filmed, should there not be a written directive, if only for future guidance? A written directive from GHQ seemed essential.

Various functionaries became involved; the issue seemed to be regarded as potentially troublesome. Reporters from many countries were converging on Tokyo and were difficult to control. In the end, a compromise was proposed. Nichi-ei personnel were to continue the photography under U.S. supervision. They were then to proceed with cataloguing and editing the accumulating thousands of feet of film—a task almost impossible for anyone not familiar with its content. This too would be done under U.S. supervision. Iwasaki welcomed the plan. The shooting would at least continue. He realized that the film they would edit under U.S. supervision might differ from the sort of film he and Kano would want to make; he assumed that the U.S. version would focus on the military value of the atomic bombs. But after completing the U.S. version, he assumed he and others would be able to prepare a Japanese version, such as he already envisioned. With this in mind Iwasaki had the Nichi-ei laboratory during the following weeks make a duplicate set of all footage.

GHQ, during these early interactions with the Japanese, was compiling files on everyone with whom it was dealing and discovered that Iwasaki had long-standing antifeudal, antimilitarist, anti-imperialist credentials—something not easily found in Tokyo at this time. This helped to resolve a pending GHQ policy decision. Occupation officials had assumed that an essential step under the Potsdam agenda would be the creation of a totally new newsreel organization. Now it seemed that a revamped Nichi-ei under someone like Iwasaki (working under U.S. supervision) might have advantages. It would seem less authoritarian. It would conform to ideas of the U.S. joint chiefs of staff, who had recommended exercise of controls through existing Japanese agencies whenever feasible. The chiefs had even suggested that enlightened dissenters jailed during the war might be sought out as administrators. This was the course now adopted. It centered on Iwasaki.

Events moved rapidly. On December 29, 1945, a reborn Nichi-ei was proclaimed in a ceremony attended by U.S. Occupation officials, Nichi-ei staff, and press. A manifesto was read. Drafted by Iwasaki on the basis of the Potsdam Declaration, reviewed and approved by GHQ, it was read by Iwasaki, who would now be working under GHQ mandate toward the democratization of Japan. Still haggard from incarceration, Iwasaki stood before the assemblage and read:

> Nippon Eiga Sha, on this occasion of setting out on a new beginning, hereby declares:
> 1. That it will participate in the building of a peaceful Japan, democratically reeducating its people through the use of film.
> 2. That it will, through the building of an advanced film culture, work to bring Japan into full membership in the world community.
> 3. That the focus of its films will be the mass of the working people.
> 4. That the objective of its films will be the realization of social justice.
> 5. That its administration will emphasize a democratized management structure recognizing the rights and responsibilities of each and every employee.

Discussing this statement years later, Iwasaki seemed abashed by the idealism of the words. Yet the Potsdam Declaration and U.S. governmental pronouncements based on it had offered precedents for such sweeping statements. And the distrust that clouded the name of Nichi-ei at the end of the war seemed to call for an "immense gesture," signaling a total break with the past. Nichi-ei, previously a national corporation, had by now been privatized to become a joint stock company, Nichi-ei, Ltd. Its first newsreel appeared on January 1, 1946.

Iwasaki was becoming well acquainted with GHQ personnel. He was to work directly with its Civil Information and Education Section, known as CIE, which was staffed mainly with people from U.S. universities, communication media, and social agencies. They seemed idealistic and were, without question, strongly challenged by their extraordinary mission. Iwasaki took a liking to them; he felt that most were imbued with the spirit of President Franklin D. Roosevelt's New Deal. In negotiating with them Iwasaki began to feel he himself was more feudalistic and militaristic than he had suspected. He was surprised that these young men of the CIE, though all in uniform, carried on their business on a first-name basis, as though there were no such thing as rank. Iwasaki had never felt quite so casual about rank.

He was aware that films produced by Nichi-ei under CIE aegis would have to be approved before public distribution by another GHQ unit, the Civil Censorship Division, known as CCD, staffed mainly with career military men. They clearly lived in a different world, in which orders were given and promptly obeyed. Iwasaki sensed he might have more trouble with them, although so far they had seemed reasonable enough.

Thus began a period in which Iwasaki worked "with eight faces and six arms." Like many others, he was often near exhaustion. Going home at the end of each day, by a commuter railway line still in woeful disrepair, he often sat or slumped on the station platform while awaiting his train. At home he could do little more than fall into bed. Yet he began each day with exhilaration. It was as though the old Prokino days had returned under miraculous new circumstances. There was a feeling that Japan was moving into an important new era and that to participate in it was a duty and a privilege. The idea that an individual could count for something was new to many people. "We at Nichi-ei felt that if we could participate in Japan's reform and democratization with newsreels and documentary films and if we pushed forward one inch, Japan progressed one inch."

Relations with GHQ began encouragingly. Iwasaki especially liked David Conde, an ex-journalist in charge of CIE's supervision of film and

theater. Conde and his associates, disliking the appearance of regulation and censorship, worked through "suggestions." They would say that
such and such an incident had happened—Why don't you cover it? The
Americans had at this time an information network far more extensive
than Nichi-ei's, and Nichi-ei was often grateful for their suggestions and
promptly proceeded with them. Ideas that proved of little value could
generally be sidetracked later. On events of immediate impact, Nichi-ei
was allowed to proceed on its own initiative; before release to theaters,
the required approvals would come into play. It was regulation masked
in ways satisfying to all concerned.

As newsreel production moved into high gear, the atom bomb documentary also proceeded. Iwasaki tried to keep an eye on both. He realized
that his role—especially as it related to the newsreel—was no recipe for
popularity. Ideas at odds with long-hallowed traditions were bound to
bring mixed reactions. The very first issue of the new Nichi-ei newsreel, surveying the "Whirlwind of Democratic Revolution," elicited both
enthusiasm and unease. One aspect of the whirlwind was a new wave
of unionization, proclaimed by the Potsdam Declaration as one of the
blessings of liberation. As new unions sprang up, Nichi-ei could scarcely
ignore the development, and several early sequences focused on new
unions, including a teachers union and a film studio union. These unprecedented newsreel items quickly brought charges that "reds" were
at work in Nichi-ei. Coverage of a food demonstration brought similar
charges, as did coverage of the Tokyo war crimes trial. Iwasaki, strongly
supported by Conde, felt Nichi-ei would weather such attacks.

More worrisome was the financial health of the newsreel. Iwasaki felt
that its survival would depend in the long run on the willingness of theaters to continue to book and pay for newsreels that to some seemed
"controversial" and even unpatriotic. The payments were no longer required. His task, as he saw it, was to make the newsreel so essential to an
understanding of the current world that few would dare to miss it, and
public demand would keep it going.

After consultation with CIE, Iwasaki embarked on a second documentary, based on historic footage that Nichi-ei had inherited from prewar
newsreels. It would review several decades of history, detailing how Japanese militarists and imperialists (*gunbatsu*) allied with elite business
interests (*zaibatsu*) had brought Japan to ruin and shame. Titled *The*

*Tragedy of Japan,** it would be painful in some ways, but a necessary step to a saner future. CIE was enthusiastic about the plan, which covered material similar to that brought out in the Tokyo war crimes trial. Fumio Kamei, associate of Iwasaki in the prewar Prokino, was enlisted as writer and director and worked rapidly. At the end he placed a dissolve that seemed to symbolize the transition to democracy: a shot of the emperor in glittering wartime uniform slowly dissolving to the emperor in a business suit—the garb in which he now made public appearances. The sequence delighted CIE, which quickly approved the entire film and sent it on to CCD. Iwasaki was not sure how its military personnel would react; to his delight, CCD requested only a few minor changes, then approved the film for immediate theatrical release.

It was in many ways the high point of Iwasaki's Nichi-ei career. His life now had a sense of direction. His domestic life was happy; his wife had given birth to a son, whom they named Hiroshi. Meanwhile the atom bomb film, a two-hour, forty-minute compilation that the Americans called *Effects of the Atomic Bomb,* was nearing completion. Then a devastating blow fell.

Two U.S. military personnel, armed with an official document, arrived at Iwasaki's office. As recounted by Iwasaki, they stood in front of him while he read it. He quickly realized what it was but read slowly, to give himself time to think and gather composure. The document was an order to turn over to GHQ all footage relating to the atom bomb film, including negatives, rushes, prints, and outtakes—in short, every scrap of film. Iwasaki, finishing his reading, told the two Americans he would comply with the order. Some time would be needed to organize the material, he said, so he asked that he be given till the following day to comply. They agreed.

Iwasaki conferred with Kano and two of their closest associates. The duplicate copy of the original negative footage was hurriedly packed and taken to a former Nichi-ei technician who had started his own developing laboratory. They asked him to store this for a while and to say nothing about it. The technician, Shigeru Miki, agreed and concealed the material

---

*Also translated as *The Japanese Tragedy.* However, Iwasaki in conversation with me called it *The Tragedy of Japan.*

in a space over his laboratory. He did not ask what it was. They thought he might have guessed, but nothing was said.

Next day the soldiers returned to Nichi-ei in a jeep and received from Iwasaki a number of boxes of film. He was asked to sign a document affirming that every foot of the atom bomb project had been handed over and nothing withheld. He signed "without blinking." The film, now classified S E C R E T, was soon on its way to the United States along with all paper records—which were likewise marked S E C R E T.

Nichi-ei employees were dismayed over what they saw happening. They had given months to the film, some at possible risk to their lives. Many begged Iwasaki to organize a protest to reverse the action. He could not tell them what had been done.

The four conspirators joined in a solemn oath to tell no one, under any circumstances, about their action. Uppermost in their minds was the bonfire of 256 Japanese films staged by the U.S. Occupation in its earliest days. They felt they were now averting some irreparable act of vandalism. It was a duty to humanity. They felt immensely relieved by what they had done. Some day the film would be made—their film.

Meanwhile work went on. The newsreel seemed increasingly precarious. There was talk of a possible need to transfer it to some entrepreneur prepared to take it over and infuse new capital—that is, to "privatize" it. There was indeed one ubiquitous entrepreneur, Akira Ando, who was eager to take it over. He had let it be known that he could put Nichi-ei on a profitable basis and at the same time raise everybody's salary. Some employees thought he might indeed be Nichi-ei's savior. But Iwasaki had some knowledge of Ando. He was a military contractor who, before, during, and after the war, had built airfields, roads, docks, and tunnels while expanding into innumerable other fields, including real estate, automobile tires, fleets of trucks, and service shops. Among other things he launched postwar nightclubs: a cabaret catering to GIs and an elitist club where high-level guests, American and Japanese, were treated to good food, liquor, and women—sometimes, it was said, "on the house." He was said to be on good terms with Prince Takamatsu, the emperor's brother. Iwasaki, urged by Nichi-ei employees, took three associates with him for a visit to Ando at the latter's headquarters, where they found him reclining on a polar bear skin. The group was treated to a soliloquy. Ando said he himself had had no education, but could hire as many educated men as he might wish or need. He boasted of his fine relations with the U.S. Occupation. He was devoted to democracy and would help to make it work. As for Nichi-ei's financial problems, they were nothing for him. He knew how to get things done. He never had trouble with strikes. His loyal *gumi*, who would lay down their lives for him, helped to see to that. Democracy and the imperial system, those were the things he valued. He urged the delegation to decide promptly—and wisely—about his generous offer to rescue Nichi-ei.

Iwasaki was baffled and repelled by his glimpse of Ando. He was sure that a takeover by Ando would subvert everything in Nichi-ei's mandate. But some resolution was clearly needed. A new Nichi-ei crisis brought Iwasaki to action.

The Tragedy of Japan, as approved by CIE and licensed by CCD, was beginning its distribution when a new, astonishing order came from GHQ. The approval had been rescinded. In addition, the film was to be destroyed. Within a week all prints and negatives were to be turned in for this purpose.

Iwasaki was incredulous. What was the explanation? He went from one office to another, but found no ray of hope. No one at CIE or CCD felt that anything could be done. This order had come from higher up. An American journalist known for investigative reporting, Mark Gayn of the Chicago *Daily News*, offered to look into the mystery. He learned of a small, high-level dinner held by the Japanese prime minister, Shigeru Yoshida, with several U.S. generals as guests. They had looked at some recent movie releases, including *The Tragedy of Japan*. It prompted angry mutterings and, at the final imperial dissolve—from military uniform to business suit—an explosion. "This time," someone had said, "those reds at the CIE have gone too far!" The destruction order was thought to have come from Major General Charles Willoughby, aide to MacArthur, or perhaps from MacArthur himself.

The emperor was a special issue for MacArthur. Throughout the war U.S. policy had placed Hitler, Mussolini, and Emperor Hirohito on equal footing as war criminals. The film *Prelude to War* (1942) one of the War Department's *Why We Fight* films made under Frank Capra, had shown the three side by side while a narrator told the GIs: "Take a good look at this trio. . . . If you ever meet them, don't hesitate." In 1945 Congress had passed a resolution that the emperor should be tried as a war criminal. But General MacArthur, taking command of the U.S. Occupation, had favored an opposite view: that retention of the emperor would help maintain law and order. In a long telegram to Washington he insisted that a trial of the emperor would create such a "tremendous convulsion" that an occupational force of at least "a million troops" would be needed for an indefinite number of years, backed by a huge civil service bureaucracy. MacArthur prevailed. Some felt that the idea of a still hallowed emperor, taking orders from MacArthur, had a special appeal to the general.

With only a few days to maneuver, Iwasaki entered into intense negotiations with Toho, which he considered the most responsible of the major film studios. An agreement was concluded. Toho would take over Nichi-ei, with a budget sufficient to guarantee its continuance. Toho's chain of theaters would have free use of the newsreel, and Toho could sell the service to other theaters for revenue. Thus newsreels as an institution would return to their prewar status. When the necessary signatures were in place, Iwasaki submitted his resignation. Delivery of *The Tragedy of Japan* to CCD was made on schedule. Iwasaki had been in Nichi-ei scarcely a year.

A few evenings later, as he retired for the night in Setagaya-ku, there was a knock at the door. Late-night messages had not been unusual during the feverish Nichi-ei period. He opened the door to two young men, one of whom held back in the dark. The other asked: "Are you Mr. Iwasaki?"

"Yes."

He motioned to the other, who stepped forward into the light. Iwasaki saw a flash of metal and felt an extraordinary pain rushing vertically up his face. A surge of heat went through him. He found himself lying in a pool of blood. His wife was over him screaming wildly while pressing a towel to his wound. Help came. Neighbors gathered. It seemed a miracle that he survived.

The gash on his face, just missing one eye, became a permanent scar. The attack was widely ascribed to Ando's enforcers, his *gumi*, but no arrest was ever made. During the following months McCarthyism rapidly took over the major Japanese media, mirroring events in the United States. The Japanese called it the "red purge." In the case of Iwasaki, the very things that had earlier made him the man of the hour—his record as an antifeudal, anti-imperialist dissident—now made him suspect. Iwasaki returned to writing books. Also, like others in his situation, he had a go at independent production, and in *Vacuum Zone (Sinku Chitai)* made one of the most successful of the independently produced films of this period, many of which were on antiwar themes. The film was released in 1952.

That same year brought an end to the U.S. Occupation. After the exodus of Americans, the four conspirators breathed a sigh of relief. Harsh punishment for what they had done had always seemed a possibility. They had never uttered a word to others about the hidden footage, but their determination to make the historic atom bomb film, a warning to mankind, had never left them. Now they met and conferred. Capital would be needed, and they began to sound out possible backers. But when they paid a visit to Shigero Miki's laboratory they found to their surprise that he no longer had the film. He told them Toho had in recent days heard about the footage and as the new owner of Nichi-ei and its archives had sent someone to collect the materials. Iwasaki and his colleagues decided to visit Toho. The studio had undergone a turnover in personnel and, to their dismay, seemed totally uninterested in making the footage available for an atom bomb film. Toho refused to cooperate. The problem seemed to be that Japanese features, including Toho's, were beginning to win international recognition and were finding a valuable market in the United States—sparked by an Academy Award to Kinugasa's *Gate of Hell* as best foreign film. Perhaps Toho feared that the atom bomb film would anger the United States, bring retaliation, and end the new bonanza. Appeals over the years brought no change. The studio was adamant. Fourteen years went by.

In 1967 Iwasaki and his friends were transfixed by astonishing news. Japanese newspapers carried a report that the Hiroshima and Nagasaki film confiscated in 1946 by U.S. officials would be returned to the Japanese government. The collaborators were jubilant—then alarmed over a follow-up report. According to a January 26, 1968, story in *Asahi Evening News*, the Japanese government was making plans for a public screening "after certain scenes showing victims' disfiguring burns are deleted." It also announced that there would be severe restrictions on distribution of the film, and that applications "from labor unions and political organizations will be turned down."

What did this mean? Would this historic record, after decades of suppression by the United States (as well as by the Toho studio) be sabotaged by Japan's own government? If so, why?

Surviving participants in the film's production formed a Committee of Producers of the Atomic Bomb Film. They claimed a right to participate in decisions about the film. They protested proposed cuts. They were ready, as ever, to devote themselves to a Japanese version. There were meetings, resolutions, heated letters to the press. In the end the government did precisely what it had said it would do. Its telecast showed little more than ruins and rubble. Everything the government called "medical footage" had been eliminated.

The showing touched off a new firestorm of protest in letters and editorials. Showing Hiroshima and Nagasaki ruins (not so different from Tokyo ruins) without showing the torment of the Hibakusha—the human victims of the atom bomb—was condemned as a cruel hoax, a suppression of the very meaning of the atomic attack.

Because the government said its deletions were in deference to the "human rights" of the victims, the committee sought out surviving Hibakusha appearing in the film and found twelve; all signed an appeal that the footage be included in a new showing. A number of the scientific consultants joined in the demand. The government stood its ground.

What was the motive? Had the return of the film been hedged by secret understandings? Had it all been an international public relations gesture without meaning? Did the policies represent a Japanese decision?

It was a time of intricate U.S.-Japanese relations. The Vietnam War was at its height. Airlifts of military supplies were flying to Vietnam continually via Japanese airfields. U.S. supply ships stopped at Japanese ports. The cooperation was carried on with as little fanfare as possible. Was the government afraid the footage would focus new anger on the United States—and on Japan's current assistance to it in an unpopular war? The producers, pondering such questions, continued to plead their case, but without success.

November 1969 brought a startling development from an unexpected source. Iwasaki received an airmail letter from the United States on stationery of Columbia University Press, signed by Barbara Van Dyke. She explained that she was associate producer of a film being made at Columbia from previously secret Hiroshima and Nagasaki footage released to it by the Pentagon and shot by a Japanese film unit. The Columbia group hoped to find additional human-effects footage. Could Iwasaki help them in any way? He scarcely knew how to reply. That he could do nothing was clear. And was she to be trusted? In the end he left the letter unanswered.

The year 1970 brought new developments in rapid succession. In January the principal Japanese papers carried a UPI report that a preview of

Hiroshima-Nagasaki, August 1945 had been held at the Museum of Modern Art in New York and had left a packed audience stunned. Columbia was starting distribution of the sixteen-minute film, selling 16mm prints to anyone for ninety-six dollars. The dispatch gave the address. Iwasaki at once sent an order for a print.

Meanwhile he was startled to learn that a representative of Tokyo Television had attended the Museum of Modern Art preview and had purchased rights for two Japanese telecasts. Soon afterwards Iwasaki had the strange experience of seeing on prime-time television the footage that had "burned itself" into his brain a quarter-century earlier. Stranger yet, he was asked by a major magazine to review the film's television debut.

The Tokyo telecast used the English-language narration written by Paul Ronder and spoken by him and Kazuko Oshima. Nevertheless the film won a wide Japanese audience and was at once rescheduled for a second telecast, again in prime time. According to *Mainichi Shinbun*, it "caused a sensation throughout the country." One paper thanked Columbia University for showing the Japanese people "what our own government tried to withhold from us." In Hiroshima "the viewing rate soared to four times the normal rate." The government made no comment.

The magazine that had asked for a review by Iwasaki, *Asahi-Graph*, was a large-format pictorial magazine similar to *Life*. It carried a number of stills from the film. In his review Iwasaki described his feelings after watching the first telecast.

> I was lost in thought for a long time, deeply moved by this film. . . .
> I was the producer of the original long film which offered the basic materials for this short film. . . . Yet I was speechless. . . . It was not the kind of film the Japanese thought Americans would produce. The film is an appeal or warning from man to man for peaceful reflection—to prevent the use of the bomb ever again. I like the narration, in which the emotion is well controlled and the voice is never raised. . . . That made me cry. In this part, the producers are no longer Americans. Their feelings are completely identical to our feelings.

Columbia's film included all the most crucial shots eliminated in the Japanese government showing.

In 1975 Iwasaki published *Occupied Screen: My Postwar Story* and sent me a copy. *Japan Quarterly*, in its English-language excerpt, focused on *The Tragedy of Japan* and its destruction. I found it so fascinating that I commissioned translations of other segments of the book. I was at this time with the Library of Congress and was excited to discover that its film archive, over which I had jurisdiction, included a print of *The Tragedy of Japan*. The library's Tokyo representative had managed to ship it to Washington before the destruction order. I was happy to send Iwasaki this news; he was delighted. He mentioned that he was writing a more extensive memoir. A heart attack had slowed him, but he was determined to complete the new work. I sent him a copy of the book I had completed at the Library of Congress, titled *The Magician and the Cinema*, dealing with the influence of magicians on the evolution of cinema.

His last letter to me was dated September 15, 1981:

Dear Mr. Barnouw!

Thank you very much for your new book *The Magician and the Cinema*. It is most interesting—informative and instructive. The Japanese version is absolutely needed. If I were not ill, I would do the translation. But after the second heart attack I am weakened, spending better part of time in bed. It is quite regrettable. Nevertheless, I am slowly getting better. It seems I can live on a few years more. I am looking forward to seeing you again in Japan. With best wishes to you and your family.

Akira Iwasaki

The letter came to me with the following note from his son:

Dear Sir,

I send you the last letter of my father, found on his desk the day after his death. Akira Iwasaki died on the evening of the 16th of September, as his disease had taken a sudden turn for the worse.

I herewith wish to express my deep thanks for your kindness and favors given him while in life.

Hiroshi Iwasaki

The note moved me deeply, but its last words were troublesome. *Hiroshima-Nagasaki, August 1945* had become important in my life, and I realized my debt to him in that connection. Expressions of gratitude from him and his family made me uneasy.

When the final portions of *Occupied Screen: My Postwar Story* arrived from my translator, I began to have a glimpse of how his family apparently viewed these postwar years. Iwasaki had written several dozen books, a number of which had been well received. I found eleven of them in the Asian collection of the Library of Congress. But the final focus of his career had been on the two documentaries of his Nichi-ei days. He had poured his life's blood into those, and his frustration over them had wounded him deeply. In *Occupied Screen* I was astonished to read "*Hiroshima-Nagasaki, August 1945* is all that I now possess."

I discussed the situation with Barbara Van Dyke and others involved in our film, and we decided to add to all subsequent prints a final credit: "Japanese footage shot by Nippon Eiga Sha under the supervision of Akira Iwasaki."

In the following years I was often asked to lecture on the film and the long suppression of the footage, and used the title: "How Can We Know What's Going On in the World?" The question remains difficult to answer, even amid the continuing explosion of new media. Perhaps it becomes more so.*

˙A file of letters and documents relating to *Hiroshima-Nagasaki, August 1945* is in the Barnouw file, Special Collections, Columbia University Library. Copies of the complete file are in the library of the Museum of Modern Art (New York), the Library of Congress (Washington), and the Imperial War Museum (London).

ROBERT OSBORN

"Peace is itself a war in masquerade."
—*John Dryden*

After completion of the Hiroshima film there were three years before I could choose retirement from Columbia. I still relished teaching but felt more and more like a double agent. Many of the students who came to my courses wanted to get into television; many accomplished this. But I was increasingly appalled by the industry I was helping them plunge into. Was I turning into a Jeremiah? The world of the advertiser, where I had started my journey, had won hegemony over almost all crannies of the industry, including public television, which was increasingly dependent on corporate bounty and choice of vehicles. This dependence seemed to me a threat to the independent documentary, which I felt had given television some of its finest moments. Salesmanship ("huckstering," to an earlier era) was everywhere glorified. Kindergarten children loved to "do a commercial." Statistics of the Screen Actors Guild showed that professional actors earned more from commercials than from theatrical features, television films, and the Broadway theater combined. What were we to make of this? In our world-girdling "information" services (Voice of America, Radio Liberty, Radio Free Europe, and others) salesmanship was likewise the keynote. Personnel, rationales, strategies drew heavily on the image-processing industries. In their rhetoric, "democracy" and "market forces" seemed to have become the same thing. An especially sinister achievement of advertising was its gradual takeover of our increasingly undemocratic electoral machinery, in which a campaign had become a war of "commercials" booked by advertising agencies, financed with the help of kickbacks ("campaign contributions") to receptive politicians. The impact on the composition of government agencies threatened to engulf hallowed U.S. traditions.

*Considerations of this sort clouded my future plans with ambiva-
lence. I began to think about a book on the influence of sponsors on
U.S television and life—a plan for the postretirement years. Meanwhile
my three final university years, 1970-1973, included continued activities stemming from the Hiroshima film—interviews, articles, broadcasts,
and one project that gave me special delight. It involved the artist Robert
Osborn.*

In 1970 Elodie Osborn, wife of Robert Osborn, came to me at the Center
for Mass Communication with several dozen slides of Osborn drawings
and said, "Bob liked your Hiroshima film. He wondered if you could make
a film out of these." For the next week I was glued to a slide projector,
looking at the slides again and again.

I had long been an admirer of Osborn. I knew little about his early
career. I only knew that since I had become aware of him he had made
powerful, mordant drawings of things he apparently disliked as much as
I did. In *Osborn on Leisure* and *The Vulgarians* he had heaped scorn on
the advertising industry. In recent years he had more often focused on
the violence of "civilized" society and its obsession with war and weap-
onry. He made wonderful drawings of generals who looked like weapons
and weapons that looked like generals. They had appeared in *Harper's,
Life, Look, New Republic* and sometimes on the op-ed page of the *New
York Times.* Even his Christmas cards focused on the theme, as did the
group of slides. He had used the slides to illustrate a talk at Aspen, where
various artists and writers had been asked to visualize the future. He had
called his talk *Fable Safe.*

For a week I walked around with the drawings swirling in my head.
Elodie had given me a copy of the comments he had made with the drawings; these seemed to me ineffectual. The drawings were the message.
As I pondered them, they seemed to me to represent a short history of
the arms race—infused with anger, but a special Osborn anger, joyful and
righteous. I found myself writing a ballad history of the arms race in
eleven stanzas, to be sung to Osborn's drawings. It would be a short film,
probably less than ten minutes, using Osborn's title *Fable Safe.*

I sent the script to Osborn at his home in Salisbury, Connecticut. I
told him it would be an animated film using almost all the drawings in
the slide collection—but I added that the film would require additional
drawings, as outlined in the script. Would he be willing to work in this

way? When I talked to him by phone, he seemed ready to plunge into action.

In a surprisingly short time we at CMC had a budget approved by our parent organization, Columbia University Press, and also received—a crucial step—the approval of our faculty advisory committee, which had representatives from various university departments. The budget problem had been eased when Mrs. Lucy Lemann, who had so promptly paid for the National Archives footage and thus made possible the Hiroshima film, proved ready to make a grant toward this follow-up project—enough to pay for the animation camera work, which would be done by the experimental animator Ted Nemeth.

I had no notion of what Osborn's drawings might be worth. I knew he had pictures in museums here and abroad and had published his drawings widely. Almost anything we might offer him seemed paltry. Yet the project had originated with him. So I suggested that he and I collaborate on it, with each receiving a 10 percent royalty on sales (of prints, television rights, or other rights) but taking nothing from the production budget. He accepted this. It meant that Columbia University Press's investment in the film had to cover only the sound track, which Tom Glazer would compose and sing, and the laboratory work. Glazer would register the ballad music with ASCAP and might thus draw additional revenue from telecasts. Laboratory relations would be handled by Sumner Glimcher as CMC manager. He had succeeded Dorothy Oshlag when she married attorney Paul Olson and moved to Vermont. I would be credited as writer and director. I received at this time no salary from Columbia University Press and would share financially only through the 10 percent royalty.

The Osborns were aware that the film would not use the Disney style of cel-animation, a technique that could consume over a thousand drawings for a minute of film, all processed via a profligate assembly line of designers (of key situations), inbetweeners (responsible for the linking drawings), inkers, opaquers, and others, in the course of which all semblance of individual style would be homogenized and vanish. We would, with camera movement, photograph directly from Osborn's drawings, so that Osborn's characteristic "line" would be on the screen. This was important to him. He felt his "line" was the heart of his style. In his early days, he said, he had explored various genres of drawing and painting and produced "fake Manets, Renoirs, and Cezannes"; but when he found himself drawing with a broad, flowing line, sometimes solid black but sometimes feathery when the pressure was eased, he suddenly felt he was drawing Osborns. His deepest feelings seemed to pour out through this "line." He himself marveled at how this happened.

Elodie Osborn was director of the Salisbury Film Society, where for almost thirty years residents of the northwest corner of Connecticut (Arthur Miller among them) had congregated to see and discuss unusual films. In search of material Elodie often attended the annual Flaherty Seminars, and Bob had occasionally come with her. They were quite familiar with films using "camera animation" with graphic materials.

I wrote to Osborn about the additional drawings I felt would be needed and how they would be used. New material was especially needed for the first stanza. The eleven stanzas were all four lines long, and each was followed by words delivered in a "talking blues" style, with the guitar music continuing. In the script these words appeared in parentheses. They allowed considerable improvisation by the singer. The first stanza went:

> SINGER
> This is a story of the land of the free
> And what we have done for your security.
> For the greatest thing, you must agree,
> Is that you be safe in the land of the free!
> (Safe as can be.)

What would we be looking at while hearing these words? I wrote to Osborn:

Suppose during the first line ("land of the free") we see a simple outline map of the United States. We start pulling back and see that the map is part of a globe, and that behind the globe are grouped four military leaders—almost like a basketball team that has won the championship. The globe is their basketball. They are posed as though for a college yearbook, and of course are aware of being heroes. ("What we have done for your security!") The four represent ARMY, NAVY, MARINES, AIR FORCE, as may be suggested by their uniforms or props or whatever. There might be a banner behind them, such as FREE WORLD CHAMPIONS. Having gotten the full picture, we might show closeups of each of the men separately (I love your generals), or pan across them. In this way one drawing could serve for the whole stanza.

Having written this, I felt uncomfortably brash, afraid such detailed suggestions might freeze him. I ended with a newsy paragraph as encouragement.

Glazer seems fired up and expects to have something some time next week, so we might even record the following week. Sumner has discussed the film with Jack Willis, who seems very much interested in it for *The Great American Dream Machine* on National Educational Television. We shall follow this up as soon as it seems feasible.

We soon learned that Osborn was working at a feverish pace, and he seemed to become more exhilarated as he worked. Going through the collection later at Nemeth's studio (forty-two new drawings plus forty earlier ones, all on large twenty-two-by-thirty-inch sheets of paper, allowing scope for camera movement), we kept finding little notes from Osborn:

You don't find stuff like this every day!

And:

Don't stick any pins in these drawings!

He had already asked us to insure the drawings at three hundred dollars each. Bringing the collection into the city from Connecticut by car, I had been very conscious of having $24,600 worth of art on the back seat. I wrote to Osborn the next day:

Dear Bob,

Sumner and I took the drawings to Nemeth's studio and there we opened the package and went through them together. We are simply delighted. Some of the new ones are unforgettable. Among my favorites are "Let it never be said that we . . ." and "What's happened to patriotism?" But don't let me get started on favorites.

We shall be especially rich in material for the final stanzas, but I think are covered throughout. If there are gaps I shall get in touch with you. We shall be having a work session with Nemeth next Wednesday to plan the camera action in detail.

Meanwhile we recorded the sound track. I find in my papers such notes as: "Take 3—good through *holes in the ground*." Take 7 was apparently satisfactory "through stanza 7," while Take 8 was preferred for the remaining stanzas. We assembled a composite from the many takes. From this point on the pictorial material would be edited to the pace of the recorded sound track.

Between stanzas Glazer had provided instrumental interludes, which were valuable for providing breathing moments in the very rapid progression of information. Nemeth, our animator, especially welcomed these interludes. He felt many drawings deserved to be reprised. He began to devise for each interlude a choreography of Osborn images—missiles, satellites, and generals maneuvering around each other in a sort of dance that eloquently reflected the lunacy of the arms race.

I was especially delighted with one visual sequence provided by Osborn's material: a U.S. spy satellite and a Soviet spy satellite circling the globe in opposite directions, barely missing each other in passing. We decided to reuse it as background for the credit sequence.

In the fall of 1971 we were finally ready to show *Fable Safe*, a nine-minute film, to our faculty advisory committee—with trepidation. In approving the plan at its spring meeting, the committee had been hesitant. The arms race was considered a worthy topic, but to chronicle it via Osborn drawings seemed academically unorthodox, to say the least. On the other hand, our Hiroshima film had proved so successful, in terms of finance as well as critical reception, that the committee hesitated to say no. Its solution for such dilemmas was to choose a faculty consultant as final arbiter and leave further decisions to him. Professor Henry F. Graff, a recent chairman of the history department, agreed to take on the consultant role.

The three-page *Fable Safe* script with its eleven short stanzas must have seemed to Graff a startling change from the Ph.D. dissertations piled on his desk. He read it quickly, then smiled. "Sure, why not? It's an accurate history of the arms race!"

This is what he approved and what the committee finally screened (with minor variations) at its fall meeting:

SINGER

This is a story of the land of the free
And what we have done for your security.

For the greatest thing, you must agree
Is that you be safe in the land of the free!
  (Safe as can be.)

First the A-bomb, and the H-bomb too
Seemed to promise that war was through.
Could any nation stand up to you
When you had the A- and H-bomb too?
  (Oh, but then *they* got it! Yes
  they got it. I mean, they got it!)

So we got us a missile, an ICBM,
An intercontinental atomic gem.
In forty minutes across the sea
We could really punish an enemy.
  (We could wipe him out! . . . I-C-B-M . . .
  intercontinental ballistic missiles! . . .
  But then—*they* got the same sort of thing.)

So then we showed 'em what we can do.
We got anti-missile missiles too.
If enemy missiles should come around
Our ABMs would smack 'em down!
  (And BANG, big explosion! . . . Anti-ballistic
  missiles! . . . Of course, *they* got up the
  same sort of thing—in underground silos
  too. So we stood facing each other, from
  holes in the ground! Holes in the ground,
  boys, holes in the ground! What a way to
  live—in holes in the ground!)

So then we showed that we had the means
To launch our missiles from submarines.
We sent our subs far across the sea
For retaliatory capability!
  (These, of course, wouldn't easily
  be targeted, so we maintained our
  deterrent credibility! . . . cred-i-bi-li-ty! . . .
  cred-i-bi-li-ty! . . . We could still wipe

them out! . . . Of course, they could do the
same.)

Now some people say, maybe it's great
If each can the other annihilate.
With all that power, would any state
Dare to tempt such a horrible fate?
    (Balance of terror! . . . Mutual deterrence! . . .
    Assured destruction capability on both
    sides! . . . But can we be sure they will
    stay deterred? That's the problem . . .)

So what did we do? We kept our nerve
And invented a beautiful thing called MIRV.
In every missile, not just one
But many warheads to get things done!
    (MIRV, MIRV! . . . M-I-R-V- multiple
    independent reentry vehicles—with
    each set for a separate target, and neatly
    concealed! Now we could hit tens of
    thousands of targets simultaneously with
    atomic weapons. Destruction far and
    wide! . . . Of course they could too. And
    one problem was, we couldn't tell, from our
    spy planes or our satellites, which of
    their underground missiles had these
    multiple warheads, and which didn't.
    Neither side could tell by looking . . .
    Wonder what those fellows are up to . . .)

A and H and I-C-B-M
They may spell the end for us and them.
A-B-M, M-I-R-V—
But remember, it's for security!
    (Some people don't like it. They go
    around protesting. What's happened
    to patriotism?)

So we and the enemy, day and night
We watch each other by satellite.

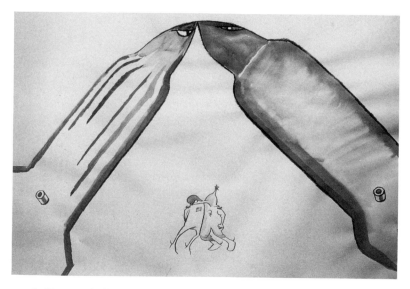

"Eyeball-to-eyeball confrontation!": Robert Osborn drawing for *Fable Safe*.

With finger on button the whole day through
We're there for the job we're ready to do—
　　(—if we must! Eyeball-to-eyeball
　　con-fron-ta-tion! It involves a lot
　　of equipment, and it costs a lot of
　　money, but we're ready to pay the price!
　　And our leaders are optimistic. It lets
　　you bargain from strength, they say.)

Now where will it end, who can tell?
And as they say, all war is hell.
Many may die—and children born
With stunted limbs and strange new forms.
　　(Radiation, you know. Strontium 90, and
　　all that. Terrible thing. Terrible . . .)

But let it never be said that we
Spared expense to keep you free.
The important thing, we did agree,

"Remember, it's for security!": Robert Osborn drawing for *Fable Safe*.

Was to keep you safe as safe could be!
(The number one priority!)

(OMINOUS CHORD ON GUITAR)

(Hey, what are those fellows up to?
What are those blips on the radar?
Canada geese? Mallard ducks? Are you
sure?? . . . Don't let those guys get the
drop on us. Are they trying for a
first-strike capability? If so, better
that we act first—right? . . . So, be
prepared!)

(SOUND EFFECTS: SERIES OF COMPUTER SOUNDS,
MISSILE LAUNCHINGS, PLANES. THEN EXPLOSION
SEQUENCE, USING HYDROGEN BOMB SOUNDS.)

In this sequence as assembled by Nemeth, the sounds were accompanied
by a fantastic kaleidoscope of Osborn images and fragments of images,
which finally ended in a scene of utter desolation. In the foreground,

some charred bodies. As this scene fades out—and just before the credit sequence—we had added a quizzical subtitle:

With only slight adjustment, this film can be made applicable to various major powers. For translation rights, apply to Center for Mass Communication.

This brought an appreciative chuckle from the committee—as it did from most subsequent audiences. I was never quite sure what the chuckle meant—perhaps relief at being rescued from the nuclear horror, or else from the film's iconoclasm. It was a gesture of evenhandedness.

The reactions expressed by the committee were enthusiastic—emphatically so. Said the cautious Mr. Charles Proffitt, president and editor of Columbia University Press: "I think this is going to be even more successful than *Hiroshima*."

A series of events seemed to confirm his prediction. The networks were alerted by a preview screening at the Museum of Modern Art, as they had been in the case of the Hiroshima film. But this time the reaction was different. NBC promptly made an offer for television rights. It wished to use the film on its recently launched "magazine" series, *First Tuesday*, a two-hour monthly event. We were delighted and sold the right to two telecasts for five thousand dollars. The payment, made immediately, meant five-hundred-dollar royalty checks for Osborn and me. The four thousand dollars retained by Columbia University Press was about what it had invested in the film. *Fable Safe* was also selected for showing at the New York Film Festival, an October event at Lincoln Center, which generally resulted in other festival screenings, in London and elsewhere. All who had been involved in the film were invited to the gala Lincoln Center showing: Lucy Lemann, Henry Graff, Tom Glazer, Ted Nemeth, Sumner Glimcher, and the Osborns. Osborn radiated delight. To his fellow workers he addressed a letter—apparently created, like many of his letters, as a work of art, using the powerful sweeping Osborn line, so that a page could scarcely hold more than a dozen words:

> Erik
> Sumner
> Ted Nemeth
> Tom Glazer, gentlemen
> I send all of you
> a full salute.

for the audience
> obviously under-
> stands what we
>> *all* were trying to say!

Nemeth you get
> full marks for
making those *stills move.*
>> Trajectory
>> paths impressed
>> me most with
>> their effective *sounds*
>> added!

Bob Osborn

Even Osborn's envelopes were executed in finest Osborn calligraphy and became collectors' items.

Two months later Dotty and I headed west on our round-the world research trip for the *Documentary* book. Months later, as we arrived in Cracow, Poland, new wonders awaited us. We learned that Glimcher had entered the film in the Cracow Film Festival, and it had been accepted. Because this festival focused on short films—especially documentaries— I had planned to attend and had paid registration fee and hotel charges long in advance. All this was now refunded to me as a contestant. I found myself loaded with wads of paper money—złotis. But this was only the beginning.

The *Fable Safe* screening was a strange experience. At the Lincoln Center screening the audience had sat hushed; one could hear a pin drop. Not so in Cracow. There were vocal reactions throughout. I got the feeling that a scattering of viewers (perhaps judges who had already seen the film) were ready to shout approval at various points, especially triggered by such phrases as "eyeball-to-eyeball confrontation!" During the final credits a drumbeat of applause was started, which culminated in a standing ovation, with loud shouts that I could not comprehend. We were sitting with a Polish documentarist, who said quietly, "Don't let this worry you. It's not anti-American; it's an anti-big-power reaction." As the audience milled about, a Russian filmmaker sitting near me (I had met him in Moscow) came up to me, shook my hand and murmured, "Thank you for that film."

Dotty and I were scheduled to leave the next day for Berlin and points west. Among the Cracow attendees was John Hanhardt, film and video curator of New York's Whitney Museum. He was planning to stay for the final award ceremonies. He said, "If you win an award, I'll accept it for you." We smiled about it.

A week later I learned from *Variety* that as director of *Fable Safe* I had won the Silver Dragon Award (second prize) and the sum of ten thousand złotis—approximately four hundred dollars, usable only in Poland. Hanhardt duly deposited the złotis in a Polish bank in my name and tucked the dragon in his suitcase. It was eighteen inches high—a white-metal dragon, reared up on its hind legs (plus tail to make a tripod) and with its jaws agape. A wonderful, fearsome animal. At each airport on the way home Hanhardt found the security machines almost screaming at his suitcase. He was promptly challenged: "What have you got in there?" Hanhardt answered as casually as he could: "A silver dragon." I did not see the dragon till I reached home. It still stands on a table near our front door. Phone messages are hooked to its handsome fangs.

In New York I asked about the NBC telecasts, but there had been no telecasts. No one knew why. We had counted on the NBC telecasts to trigger U.S. print sales. Inquiries to NBC produced no information. Almost a year had gone by since its purchase of television rights. I knew slightly one member of the *First Tuesday* staff and phoned him. When I asked about *Fable Safe,* he seemed pained. "We *almost* used it a couple of times, and then we didn't. Please don't ask me why." So I didn't until months later, when he seemed ready to explain that one high-up NBC executive had apparently felt it his patriotic duty to make sure *Fable Safe* never got on the network. But the network inaction accomplished more. Our NBC contract prevented other television showings during the NBC lien.

It was clear that changes had come over television. The "springtime thaw" of the Kennedy years (which had temporarily spurred public affairs programming) had ended during later Vietnam years. The Nixon White House fulminated against CBS over its prize-winning 1971 documentary *The Selling of the Pentagon,* an exposé of defense department activities to promote militarism in schools and business groups. The Nixon regime was also furious over network commentators, especially those who continued to question the validity of the savage and still undeclared war. President Nixon apparently deputized Vice President Spiro Agnew to bring the networks to heel. In a series of vitriolic statements—dutifully broadcast by the networks—Agnew castigated the commentators as "nattering nabobs of negativism" and pointedly reminded broadcasting companies that their very profitable operations were based on federal licenses requiring periodic renewal. Nixon seemed equally indignant at noncommercial television, as represented by National Educational Television. In 1972, after years of humdrum programming, it was winning a growing audience with such programs as *The Great American Dream Machine,* the jovial variety series that had expressed interest in *Fable Safe.* It often carried short satirical items and offered a political cabaret atmosphere that seemed to win substantial response. In 1972 Nixon replied by vetoing a two-year appropriation for public television and making it clear that he would approve no further appropriations for public television until it had totally reorganized itself to put the emphasis on "grassroots localism" instead of national program fare. The attacks put public television into prolonged crisis, in the course of which such projects as *The Great American Dream Machine* vanished. Producers of independent spirit now faced a maze of obstacles in their efforts to reach a national audience. It became clear that for *Fable Safe* a moment had come and gone, in spite of its spirited debut.

The 16mm field was at this time in a crisis of its own, threatening to our film enterprise. CMC had developed a collection of 16mm films of value to schools, colleges, libraries, and diverse associations. Now it was finding that some film users were making videotape copies of favorite films rented from CMC, apparently to save costs of further rentals. Was this permissible under the "fair use" provision of the copyright law, as claimed by zealous audiovisual directors in various school systems? Or was it "piracy"? Years might be needed to resolve this through the courts. Similar problems were rising from the organized use of photocopying to save on textbook purchases. Multiplying issues of this sort were stirring wide demands for revision of our copyright law.

What seemed to be developing was a new chapter in the rise and fall of media. The videotape recorder had at first been used mainly by networks to make copies of live telecasts, for file or rebroadcast. Then it became Hollywood's medium for home distribution of motion pictures—a new Hollywood "market." Then the advent of handheld video cameras made it suddenly an independent production medium with remarkable advantages: speed, economy, freedom from laboratory problems. It soon took over the TV newsgathering field. Best of all, in the eyes of many independent filmmakers, was the fact that video was itself a distribution system. Able to bypass gatekeepers at network or cable system, video-cassettes could go directly to homes and schools equipped with cassette players. Many observers felt that this might make video a signicant force in the battle of ideas. Yet how secure could video be in the long run, with its future already shadowed by such new wonders as the laser disc and the expanding field of laser communication via optical fiber? For many—including Columbia University Press—such uncertainties loomed large.

My Columbia retirement was scheduled for 1973, but I went on teaching while completing *Documentary* (1974) and then *Tube of Plenty* (1975), a one-volume condensation and updating of the trilogy. I received word that the Woodrow Wilson International Center for Scholars, the Smithsonian's "think tank" in Washington, would welcome me as a 1976 fellow; I proposed to devote the fellowship year to the contemplated study of our sponsorship system. Our three children—Jeffrey, Susanna, and Karen—were by now embarked on independent lives, so Dotty and I decided to sell our Larchmont house; we had the continued use of my father's Columbia University apartment, which I had been allowed to retain after his death. Retirement in Vermont had become our ultimate aim, but meanwhile we approached the coming Washington sojourn with excitement. It would be 1976, the bicentennial year.

When Columbia University Press decided to withdraw entirely from the 16mm film field, I was relieved to learn that New York's Museum of Modern Art was ready to take over the distribution—for sale and rental—of two films that were especially close to my heart: *Hiroshima-Nagasaki, August 1945* and *Fable Safe*. The MOMA film library was willing to buy remaining prints held by CMC; this triggered royalty payments to Osborn and me. Remembering his herculean labors, I was troubled by the modesty of the *Fable Safe* payment, and wrote Osborn to tell him so. He responded with another calligraphic masterpiece. "Dear Erik . . . I find that royalty checks of any kind are *always* fun to receive."

As the cold war subsided, *Fable Safe* became a museum piece. London's Imperial War Museum had a copy, and used it occasionally in its war-film screenings—because, its programmer explained, "We don't have many that are amusing."

DANIEL J. BOORSTIN

"What is past is prologue."
—Archives Building

On October 19, 1976, new copyright legislation was signed, titled:

Public Law 94-553
94th Congress

An Act

For the general revision of the Copyright Law, title 17 of the United
States Code, and for other purposes.

Among "other purposes" was a mandate: "Sec. 113. The Librarian of Congress . . . shall establish and maintain in the Library of Congress a library
to be known as the American Television and Radio Archives . . . to preserve a permanent record of the television and radio programs which are
the heritage of the people of the United States. . . ."

This happened near the end of my fellowship year. The book The Sponsor was about finished. For me it had been a fruitful year, to which the
Wilson Center had contributed a wonderful collegial atmosphere. Some
forty scholars—half foreigners, half Americans—had offices in the historic Smithsonian "castle" facing the mall. We ate our lunches together
in the center's lunchroom, either at a large table in the middle or at
small tables at the side. All fellows made their own living arrangements;
their work focused at the castle. The center had been created as a living
memorial to the international-minded Woodrow Wilson: it was to be a
sort of home away from home for selected foreign scholars doing U.S.
research, and at the same time give them contact with American scholars—who were equally benefited by it. Here, lunching at the large table,
I found myself chatting with John Gilligan, former governor of Ohio who
had narrowly missed reelection and was writing about the impact of our

broadcast media on the role of political parties; or with Estenssoro Paz, a past president of Bolivia who had led a reform regime until overthrown by a military junta and was now writing an account of his administration; or with General Andrew Goodpaster ("Andy," we called him) who had headed NATO and was now writing on "the political implications of detente." I looked forward to more such stimulating work periods, including one in India for the long-planned update of Indian Film.

An inquiry from the Library of Congress postponed this. It had set up a planning committee toward implementing the new mandate. Would I be willing to join the committee as part-time consultant? I accepted promptly. Free time, I felt, could be spent in the Houdini Collection, to put the finishing touches to The Magician and the Cinema. *Early in January 1977 a desk in the Library of Congress became my work place. The committee sessions were fascinating. There were meetings with the various Library of Congress divisions organized as Special Collections: Geography and Map Division, Manuscript Division; Prints and Photographs Division (which included a large motion picture section), and Music Division (which included a huge recorded sound section). All were scheduled to move to an enormous new building rising on Independence Avenue, to be known as the Library's Madison Building. The newly mandated Television and Radio Archives would presumably join them there. Space allocations made earlier might have to be drastically revised. Discussions on these matters, often chaired by Alan Fern, director of Special Collections, went forward quietly and doggedly.*

I was dazed by the scope and complexity of the Library of Congress. Begun modestly with Thomas Jefferson's gift of his books to assist the lawmakers, it had grown—via copyright deposits, gifts, purchases, exchanges—into an awesome treasury, not only Congress's library but the American people's library. Presiding over this media megalopolis was historian Daniel Boorstin, who since 1975 had been Librarian of Congress—a modest title for so protean a position. I had admired him ever since I first read The Image *(1961), his sparkling study from the early television years. Later, soon after completion of my three-volume history of U.S. broadcasting, a phone call from my son Jeffrey at Yale informed me that Boorstin, in a visiting lecture there, had made a glowing reference to my trilogy, calling it "masterful." Later, at the invitation of Oxford University Press, Boorstin wrote a jacket statement for my* Documen-

tary, an extraordinary send-off. So I had warm feelings for him before any close acquaintance. Now I was getting to know him. At public Library events his words were always precise, scholarly, often witty. With fellow workers he was gracious, never pompous. And he wasted no time. Early in April 1978 I was asked to be in his office for an 11:30 A.M. meeting.

I found him with Alan Fern of Special Collections. The agenda, as usual, was the new mandate. But they began talking about the Music Division. The fact that it included an enormous collection of sound recordings had long seemed logical enough, but it did raise some problems. As the collection grew, an increasing number of the recordings had nothing to do with music. Why should researchers be sent to the Music Division to study FDR's fireside chats or other historic broadcasts? At the Prints and Photographs Division a similar problem had developed. Films had been under its jurisdiction for years—as a branch of photography. The film collection had grown so rapidly that it now threatened to swamp the division's first purposes. So new decisions had been made, said Boorstin. The 700,000 or so recordings—on disk, tape, wire, wax cylinder, or whatever—would be plucked out of the Music Division, and the 252,000 reels of motion pictures would be plucked out of the Prints and Photographs Division, and both would be combined with the new mandate, creating a large new division to be known as the Motion Picture, Broadcasting and Recorded Sound Division. It would, of course, be headquartered in the new building. "Now the point is this," said Boorstin. "We want to start this new division on schedule, and open it to the public on July 31, with you as chief."

I was stunned, trying to take in all I had heard. I said, "Dan, that's crazy! I'm almost seventy years old."

Boorstin looked at me sharply and quizzically. "What's that supposed to mean?"

He too was a "retiree." I said, "Besides, I'm going to India this fall. I have a contract to update *Indian Film*. I'll be working with Krishnaswamy again."

Boorstin took this calmly. "How long will you be there?"

"Four or five months."

"That doesn't seem so insoluble. I would suggest you start here as soon as you can, work out your table of organization, choose your key people, get things running. Then we'll give you a leave of absence. You go to India, finish your work there, and after four or five months come back and take over."

His words had jolted me but were also intoxicating. I had anticipated nothing on this scale. That day and the next, long talks with Dotty settled it. I notified Boorstin I would take the plunge. Things proceeded as he had proposed. He had quietly edged me into a new career—an archival one. Vermont plans would wait. Now there were meetings, introductions, orientations—finally, a visit to the Personnel Office to fill out an application for the already accepted job. I took the oath of office. Then—the first of many surprises. The woman in charge, after administering the oath, said, "You can look at your file now, if you want to."

"File? What file?"

"Your FBI file. We have to send it back. But before we do, you're allowed to see it."

I gathered that a "full field" investigation had been made because I might be exposed to "classified" material. I had apparently passed, but was curious. From a safe the woman brought a substantial stack of documents, which I was allowed to peruse in her office. Names and sometimes whole passages had been blacked out. I saw at once that most of the papers dated from World War II and stemmed from an earlier "full field" investigation relating to my work at the Pentagon for the Armed Forces Radio Service. Like the new probe, the earlier one had been carried out during a consultancy period. Investigators apparently visited people in our Columbia University apartment building, one of whom had assured the investigator—charmingly, I thought—that I belonged to "a very good family." The investigators also visited numerous members of the Radio Writers Guild. This was during its early efforts to obtain contracts with networks, advertising agencies, and independent producers. It was a frustrating period; meetings were often contentious. I was not yet a guild officer but took part in debates—with apparently confusing results: some members told the FBI I was "liberal"; others called me "conservative." The FBI was especially interested in one member's statement: "He is very skillful at concealing his opinions, but I think he is really the leader of the radical faction of the guild." On this basis (if there were others they did not appear in the file) the FBI recommended that I *not* be hired by the War Department. But I was hired, staying through V-E Day. Some high official must have taken it on himself to decide that this FBI recommendation could be ignored—an act of courage, to judge from the ferocity of later witch-hunts. It felt creepy to learn this, considering how different my later life might have been if he had decided otherwise.

Thus began life at the Library of Congress. Dotty and I thought we had come to Washington for a year; it became five—a wondrous period. We loved our Georgetown apartment, the upper floor of a colonial brick house. The brick houses on our street reminded me of The Hague. We had a spare bedroom, so each of our children was able to stay with us, as did friends, on Washington visits. A twenty-minute drive took me past the White House to my Library of Congress reserved parking space, about which I had no guilt feelings. Life was full: Juilliard string concerts at the Library's Coolidge Auditorium, plays and concerts at Kennedy Center, occasional invitations to embassies. It was, at the same time, the most difficult and intense period of work I could remember, resembling nothing in my experience.

The announcement of my appointment began "Erik Barnouw, America's foremost broadcasting historian, has accepted an appointment to the position of chief of the Library of Congress's newly created Motion Picture, Broadcasting and Recorded Sound Division." It outlined my responsibilities: "custody, processing, preservation and servicing" of rapidly growing collections of films and recordings and "developing the newly mandated American Television and Radio Archive." Reviewing my vita, it emphasized writings and awards in media history. A heartwarming send-off. But I soon found that in any day's work, less than five minutes had anything to do with such matters. I was—there was no escaping it— a bureaucrat, an executive, an administrator, dealing with budgets, job decriptions, hirings, civil service ratings, estimated cost of equipment needs for 1979, 1980, 1981, the problem of the ninety thousand feet of nitrate films waiting to be duplicated onto safety film, the hazards posed by our duplicating arrangements, the needed revisions in the Madison Building specifications. With others I donned a hard hat to visit the evolving facilities and to bargain, blueprint in hand, over space allocations. I was not troubled by all this—it was all a new experience and seemed necessary. I had never overseen more than a dozen employees; the MBRS (the officially authorized abbreviation of our division name) would have at least sixty, working in locations still in the making. That I could cope with it at all was heartening. Contemplating myself as executive, I was amused and amazed. How long could I endure it? I was allowed to hire an

Jurisdiction: 252,000 reels. (Library of Congress)

administrative assistant and found a marvelous one. It involved a maze of procedures, but I secured Adriane Bailey, of Croatian parentage and formerly married to an American Indian. She fit none of the stereotypes of the glossy, high-powered secretary. She had a unique talent for putting people at ease. I phoned a reference, a woman at the American Anthropological Association, and asked about Ms. Bailey. The woman sighed a deep sigh, as though all the problems of the world were descending upon her. Finally she said, "When she was here, everyone was happy!"

I made another bureaucratic decision that I think had early importance. Most colleagues assumed that I would divide MBRS into sections based on media: a radio section, a film section, a television section. I decided otherwise. I would have (1) a reference section whose members—reference librarians—would advise researchers on *all* our media holdings, and help them find what they needed; (2) a cataloguing section whose members—cataloguers—would do the cataloguing for *all* MBRS media; (3) a curatorial section whose members—curators—were to become specialists in *all* our storage problems—temperature, humidity, shelving—and be alert to preservation needs; and (4) a technical services section whose members—engineers—must maintain MBRS laboratories able to duplicate, for preservation or to fill orders from library users (subject to approval of copyright owners), any holding in any format. The compelling reason for this arrangement was simple. I had learned whom I wanted as head of the laboratory services section: Robert Carneal. If each medium had been organized separately, we would have needed three Robert Carneals. I only knew of one. That settled it.

I discussed the arrangement with staff members drawn from the transferred sections. Each had been dealing with a single medium; the prospect of multimedia responsibilities was welcomed. All glimpsed a future of widening possibilities. Amid media upheavals it seemed a morale factor. As additional section heads I chose: Patrick Sheehan, reference; Harriet Harrison, cataloguing; Gerald Gibson, curatorial. As assistant chief of MBRS I chose Paul C. Spehr, who had headed the film section of Prints and Photographs. He had been at the Library for over twenty years and seemed to understand all its procedures and complexities. I was always grateful for his presence and could hardly have managed without him. He took charge when, on September 23, I left for India.

The new copyright law had wider range than its predecessors—and simpler procedures. Original works "in any tangible medium of expression now known or later developed" received copyright protection. It existed "from the time a work is created in fixed form." Ownership vested automatically in the "author." In the case of work done "for hire" the employer, as before, was "considered the author"—unless the parties "agreed otherwise." To claim copyright the creator (personal or corporate) merely placed on all published copies the copyright symbol © (or the word *copyright* or authorized abbreviation *copr*) plus the name of the claimant and first date of publication. Rules for registration and deposit of a copy or copies with the Library of Congress were eased. The Library could in some cases demand a copy or copies—an important factor for the development of its research collections. The owner too had incentives to deposit. In case of dispute, a copy on file with the government would be crucial evidence. Registration became virtually a prerequisite to infringement suits.

I spent six months in India. En route back I delivered the revised *Indian Film* to Oxford University Press in New York, then returned to my desk at the Library of Congress. I found that a flood of deposits was building our collections in all our media. All systems were working. The staff had proved itself. I felt most grateful. Big hurdles lay ahead but we moved on with confidence. In 1981 we were to move into our new quarters. With increasing frequency we made trips to the half-finished Madison premises, where new kinds of viewing facilities were being developed for the use of researchers. Before long a Library of Congress signage committee was at work determining the corridor and elevator signs that would, we hoped, guide people painlessly through the huge new building. Such problems called for endless discussion. Problems mounted, but the bureaucracy coped.

In all this busy-ness, adventure sometimes intervened. A phone call from the Canadian film archive told of odd news from Dawson City, center of the 1896 Yukon gold rush. In breaking ground for a new building, bulldozers had come up with clusters of old film cans, frozen solid in the permafrost. The films they contained were old. The bulldozers had been halted. Would the Library of Congress join the Canadian archive in examining this mystery, finding ways to salvage the films and assess their value? A slice of history began to emerge. Dawson City had been considered "an American town on Canadian soil,"* accessible mainly from the United States. During the gold rush some thirty thousand people had poured in, mainly from the United States. Most found no gold but many hung on long after the bonanza petered out. Not surprisingly a movie theater (part of another gold rush) rose to serve them. This theater was the final link of a northern circuit. Other cinemas in the circuit had instructions to forward films to the next in line, but after Dawson there was no "next," so the films piled up. There was also a swimming pool in Dawson. Both cinema and swimming pool eventually went bankrupt, and a bank took over their assets. Around 1920, when the pool site was chosen for a

---

* See *City of Gold* (1957), the celebrated historical documentary of the National Film Board of Canada.

building and "fill" was needed, the old cans were used, solving a storage problem. With a mix of dirt and cans of film filling the void, the building was completed. Some sixty years later this building, grown obsolete and dingy, was marked for demolition and replacement. Bulldozers came and began their digging.

Experiments in thawing and salvaging frozen films took time. Those found near the surface were ruined by water blotches; those excavated at lower levels could be fine. At staff screenings we began to see Dawson City relics: an early Harold Lloyd film not surviving elsewhere; an early Lionel Barrymore appearance—with Lillian Russell; an early (ca. 1915) Universal newsreel. I was fascinated to find that newsreels of that time, seeking to duplicate newspaper attractions, included political cartoons— animated, and biting in their satire. Later newsreels would scarcely have been so venturesome. In all, the Dawson City pay streak added some hundred titles to the collections of the Library of Congress and Canadian Film Archives.

Another ongoing adventure reached still further toward film beginnings. In the 1890s it was not possible to copyright a motion picture; the law did not provide for it. But it did provide for copyrighting *photographs*. In 1894 the Edison Company, wanting to protect films being produced for Edison's Kinetoscope peepshow machines, made a copy of such a film on a long strip of photographic paper (like that used for snapshots) and sent this rolled-up "photograph" to the Copyright Office of the Library of Congress with a check for fifty cents, the applicable copyright fee. It must have puzzled the Copyright Office. But the law did not decree the permissible dimensions of a *photograph*. One could presumably be 35mm wide and fifty feet long. The Copyright Office had no basis for rejecting the application; its acceptance created a precedent welcomed by many producers. From 1894 to 1912, when the law was revised to include motion pictures, several thousand films were copyrighted in this manner, giving birth to the Library's unique "paper print collection." The paper rolls kept getting larger as longer films were made. The paper prints could not be projected: they had no sprocket holes and, besides, were opaque. But they did provide visible evidence that might settle disputes. After the 1912 revision the flood of paper prints subsided. The existing accumulation continued to rest on Library shelves, half forgotten. Most of the films they represented, all made on unstable nitrate film, vanished during the following decades. Nitrate, unless kept at low temperature, can turn to jelly, then to a powder, after which, at temperatures of 106 degrees or higher, spontaneous combustion can take place. Many early nitrate films thus perished in fires; many more were discarded before reaching that stage.* But the paper prints survived. In the 1950s a Hollywood studio detective, Kemp Niver, wondered if new negatives might be made from the paper prints and began experiments. The work was slow. In the absence of sprocket holes, rephotographing had to be done frame by frame, with readjustments for each frame to keep sequences in registry. Successful experiments persuaded Hollywood's Motion Picture Academy to appropriate funds for further work. Its success led to a Congressional appropriation for salvaging three thousand films, all from the earliest years of film history—the *incunabula* of the film medium. A catalogue of these reborn films was published, briefly describing and dating each. Kemp Niver received a special Academy Award for his achievement. As the films were studied, it became clear that much of what had passed as film history, based on reminiscences, was wrong and needed rewriting.

Ironically, thanks to the paper prints, film historians came to be more familiar with films of the 1900s than of the 1910s. Only about 10 percent of the films of the 1910s seem to have survived and some 20 percent of the films of the 1920s. But we know a lot about the earlier years, thanks to the paper prints. They were crucial in my own work on *The Magician and the Cinema.*

On a train ride to Vermont I found myself sitting next to a man who, it turned out, was a choreographer for the Metropolitan Opera. I began to tell him about the paper prints, but he knew all about them. He had just been in Washington studying dance films in the collection, and had made a compilation for his own purposes. Because many early fiction films were made outdoors against existing backgrounds, the paper prints offer telling evidence on developments in architecture, clothing, transportation, parades, recreation. Many public events are documented in the paper prints. The copyrights on all these films had expired, so anybody could order copies, to be made by our MBRS laboratory services section. During my stint at the Library of Congress I had the satisfaction of launching a new catalogue of the three thousand films that had been

---

*Motion picture industries around the world shifted to use of safety film ca. 1950. Duplication of existing nitrate holdings, reflecting decades of social and political history, would remain an ongoing problem into the next century.

rescued from oblivion. The new catalogue incorporated all information gleaned from study of the restored films. Kemp Niver, in failing health, played a leading role in the updating; so did Paul Spehr. The new catalogue is titled *Early Motion Pictures: The Paper Print Collection in the Library of Congress.*

The paper print story hints at pleasures and problems of work in a public archive. The archivist is unlikely to know the range of the collection. Those who come for research may bring unsuspected treasures to the activist's attention. Also, the archivist may never catch up with cataloguing problems. Researchers in quest of "the" truth may be disappointed. The archive is yesterday's testimony, the testimony of many, inevitably ambiguous. It ceaselessly encourages revisionist history. Of course, all history is revisionist. And to the search for yesterday each brings a different today.

In our visits to the evolving Madison facilities we became increasingly interested in a small but unique screening room. Essentially a small theater, it was to have only sixty-odd seats, but its specifications called for a very wide projection booth to serve the room's special functions. The staff had to be able to screen items in any format, any speed, new or obsolete, including wide-screen. The room would serve those purposes during working hours. Its unusual equipment and handsome design raised the question of whether it might not serve some valuable *public* purpose during evening hours.

Soon after the start of our Library of Congress days Dotty and I had been guests of the Boorstins at one of the Juilliard String Quartet concerts in the Library's Coolidge Auditorium. These made use of the Stradivarius instruments owned by the Library, normally on display in a room adjoining the auditorium and used on special occasions. The concerts at the Coolidge Auditorium were free, thanks to an endowment. Boorstin felt that, like lectures and symposiums, such library events should always be free. The Music Division had received, usually by gift, original manuscripts of many classic compositions; these were put on display when performed at a concert. Many celebrated soloists and groups appeared at the concerts. Boorstin wondered whether MBRS might not develop a similar tradition in the gemlike projection room under construction. Its limited seating might be thought a handicap but could turn out to be an advantage. Our public screenings should not seek to compete with cinema showings. They should rather deal with little known treasures from our collections, of little value to commercial exhibitors yet intensely interesting to smaller, specialized audiences. In a small screening room such an audience would not seem "small." Screenings of this sort would offer a parallel to the celebrated Coolidge concerts. Our archival holdings, reflecting a century of film, television, and video, would come to life in such screenings. They would obviously call for a special endowment, like that supporting the concerts. Assuming that someone else would do the fund-raising, I said I would draw up a proposal. Long discussions within MBRS and with Fern, Boorstin, and others, brought the proposal into shape.

I decided, about this time, that I would retire from the Library of Congress in June 1981. The division's move into the Madison building was to begin that summer. Spectacular upheavals would be involved. I felt it was time for a new and younger chief to take over, beginning a new regime. Four years were enough. Vermont called us.

Mary Pickford had died in 1979, aged eighty-six. She had earlier given to the Library of Congress a complete set of her films. She left an immense fortune. The trustees who would deal with allocation of charitable funds were identified in the trade press. One was Charles "Buddy" Rogers, whom she had married in 1937, two years after divorcing Douglas Fairbanks. It occurred to me that I had, on two occasions in the past half-century, briefly crossed the path of Buddy Rogers.

One was in 1929 at Princeton, when Paramount produced *Varsity*, using our campus as background and starring Buddy Rogers in the young hero role. He had previously been seen in *Wings* (1928), the first film to win the Best Picture Oscar, and in *Abie's Irish Rose*. *Varsity's* director decided to engage a few students for bit parts, and that is how I came to be on view in a short sequence, crossing the campus. The film was not a critical success. Buddy Rogers played many subsequent young hero roles, but became a celebrity mainly as the husband of Mary Pickford. My next contact with him came in 1975, when *Tube of Plenty* was published and Oxford University Press arranged a succession of promotional appearances for me, mostly on afternoon talk shows. One television station—I think in Washington, D.C.—scheduled me to follow a Buddy Rogers appearance. I watched and listened to it, awaiting my turn at the edge of the set. I recall the interviewer asking him, with a hint of cheery malice, "How do you *feel* when people address you as 'Mr. Pickford'?" He seemed accustomed to this and answered pleasantly, "I love her so much I don't care what people call me." He added that she was really a marvelous woman to share one's life with. It became the theme of his appearances. Later that day he and I found we were to make the same hop between stations; it seemed convenient to share a cab. I was impressed with how fit he looked. He must have been about seventy but retained some of the boyish look of his *Varsity* days. On the way I mentioned having appeared in *Varsity*. He seemed fascinated by this reminder of an earlier era. We reminisced about it.

Remembering how agreeable he had been, I wrote him a letter early in 1981, addressed to Pickfair, Hollywood. On behalf of the Library of Congress I told what we had in mind about the unusual screening room under construction, and mentioned the hope that it might become the "Mary Pickford Theater in the Library of Congress," site of regular public showings of "pioneer" films—works of the earliest pioneers but also of later ones, men and women of every period who led the way. I mentioned our past meetings in Princeton and Washington and expressed a hope for further discussion. In reply I received an invitation to lunch with him on May 12 at the Brown Derby opposite the Beverly Wilshire Hotel. He explained that a Mr. Edward G. Stotsenberg, financial specialist who was co-executor of the estate, would join us. I gathered he would play a crucial role in fund management.

I had never visualized myself as a fund-raiser. The role rather repelled me—at least, I thought it did. But this was different: I believed in this; I had helped formulate it. It might well be my last executive venture. I wanted to succeed for MBRS and for Dan Boorstin. Winging westward for lunch, I planned my pitch.

At the Brown Derby I was welcomed by Buddy Rogers, looking tanned and as fit as ever. We took our table and awaited Mr. Stotsenberg. Buddy described him as a remarkable person, well along in his seventies but still an ardent runner. He had just come back from running in the New Zealand Marathon, where he had won the senior division. Stotsenberg arrived promptly, a thin ramrod with a springy step. Buddy congratulated him profusely on his victory. Stotsenberg was obviously glowing with pleasure over his achievement. After we ordered, I was asked to explain the proposal. It wasn't easy. I felt that Buddy Rogers was with me but that Mr. Stotsenberg's mind was elsewhere. When I finished he shook his head slightly. "I don't think that's the way we ought to go. I think we should do something for young people." He repeated, "Young people."

Buddy asked a few helpful questions, to emphasize points that interested him. Then he apparently decided to change the subject. He asked Mr. Stotsenberg to explain how he had trained for his race. The question delighted Mr. Stotsenberg. He explained that he had gone to New Zealand at least a month before the race. That was all-important, he said, to get used to the climate, the water, the cooking. It had also given him time to look over the terrain, see what problems there might be. The weeks down there made it possible to be really at peak. He described how it all went. We listened and listened.

Maybe the listening did it. The pitch did not, I am sure. When I bid goodbye, Mr. Stotsenberg was in a fine mood. Back at the Library I reported apparent failure. So I was surprised, some days later, to learn that the Pickford trustees were prepared to provide us with funds. How had this come about? Had Buddy Rogers taken charge? I was not involved in the further fiscal talks. Their upshot was that the public programs of the Mary Pickford Theater would begin in 1983.

By that time Dotty and I were in Vermont, in the peace of the Green Mountains. Various writing projects and the beginnings of an *International Encyclopedia of Communications,* of which I would become editor, were keeping me busy.* But Boorstin invited us back for a scheduled Mary Pickford Theater inaugural festivity, at which he wanted me to preside. I found the small theater looking like a jewel. We showed films and held a symposium. There were reminiscences. Lillian Gish was there, and Douglas Fairbanks Jr., and ninety-year old Blanche Sweet, whose crisp wit was a triumph, and my old friend True Boardman, screen and television writer, who as child actor had performed with both Mary Pickford and Charles Chaplin. The historian Jay Leyda was there too, and film and television critics. A note from Boorstin later described the event as "among the most exciting, enjoyable and memorable ever held here in the library." He added: "Now that the theater is opened and running, I hope that we will see you and Dotty all the more often."

Our Library of Congress years had left us with warm feelings. But they had been a time of looking back, while others—more resoundingly—were proclaiming a future. Their prognostications were a constant reminder

---

* It would appear in 1989 (in four volumes), published by Oxford University Press and the University of Pennsylvania.

Mary Pickford Theater at the Library of Congress, opening festivity, 1983. Blanche Sweet, Douglas Fairbanks, Jr., and the author. (Library of Congress)

that the past was only a prologue, preparing for a tomorrow. Our role had been like that of monastery copyists, tirelessly preserving the testimony of other times. Transferring from ancient documents words of Greek, Roman, Arab, and others, they had made the past available to the present. They had protected the record. In so doing they had apparently set the stage for the social revolution that came with the arrival of paper and the art of printing with movable type. That a new social upheaval, of previously unimagined scope, was now inevitable was the message of the hour. Media that had beguiled the world during our century—telegraph, radio, film, sound recording, television, video, computer, optical fiber, satellite—would merge into a communications superhighway that would change the life of humanity. On this theme euphoria was everywhere. Media annals tell us that each of the individual inventions was similarly welcomed. Each was to give us an informed public and the fulfillment of democracy. The gods of war would cease to plague us. I remembered the predictions that greeted the spectacular arrival of broadcasting in the 1920s. *Radio Broadcast*, a journal created to chronicle the new medium, assured us that

the government will be a living thing to its citizens instead of an abstract and unseen force . . .
it will elicit a new national loyalty and produce a more contented citizenry . . .
elected representatives will not be able to evade their responsibility to those who put them in office . . .
some day in the future the popularity of a political party in office may hinge entirely upon the quality of broadcasting service . . .
at last we may have covenants literally openly arrived at . . .
the people's University of the Air will have a greater student body than all our universities put together . . . *

And an ex-secretary of the navy said on WLAC, North Carolina, on October 16, 1922: "Nobody now fears that a Japanese fleet could deal an unexpected blow on our Pacific possessions. Radio makes surprises impossible."

This record of predictions fosters skepticism. Yet who can resist the new promises, the new euphoria? People of science, people of business, are doing the talking. To our home screens, with the computerized controls at our fingertips, we shall summon not only hundreds of channels but the riches of universities, museums, and archives, the events in sports stadiums, the encounters in political arenas. Our lives will be stretched via teleconferencing, telelearning, teleshopping, telemarketing, telebanking, telemedicine, televoting, teleworship. In all of these, "message movement" will, it is said, replace "people movement," so that the insanities of rush-hour traffic, congested highway, and parking crisis will head toward oblivion. It will all be done from the comfort of one's home. All this is not visionary. The technology is on hand.

But hold on. "All from your own home." That part gives me pause. Is the new world being shaped by people who love gadgets, not people? How else explain these visions in which people are always made to stay home—out of the way—their attention riveted on blessings arranged and displayed for them? Is that what people want or need? Human beings thrive on social relationships, not technical linkages.

The computer, which makes that new world possible and even likely, also prepares for us a world in which all its necessities can be produced

* *Radio Broadcast*, May 1922.

by a fraction of its people. Waves of company lay-offs followed by proclamations of "improved corporate efficiency" (and profits) keep reiterating
that message. What then will be done with the rest of the people?

No doubt many will be kept busy making things that are *not* necessities. This is already a major business focus, backed by an attitude industry that knows how to make the needless—sometimes the harmful—
necessary. No doubt this industry's role will be greatly expanded.

Even so, people for whom no work is available will be numerous, increasingly so in all probability. They will form a vast dependency, perhaps
a danger. They must at all cost be kept busy. And while not needed as
workers, they will be needed as consumers. Here the home screen with
its countless channels and push-buttons will play its most crucial role.
If any of the nonworking multitude cannot afford the equipment, or its
pay-per-view services, will these perhaps have to be given to them—for
the sake of public tranquillity? They *must* be kept busy.

What new-world television software will engage their minds? Will there
be special channels for "approved revolutionary games"?

I write these words at my IBM-compatible computer; later they will
be transferred to a diskette that can hold some five hundred pages of
text for the consideration of publishers. As a media historian, have I any
choice but to swim along with the overwhelming tide? Step by step I find
myself moving willy-nilly toward the proclaimed future. At the same
time, I do keep wondering what sort of society will emerge from that
new-age television. What kinds of humans will it help to shape? A crucial
question, I am sure. As John Leonard has put it, "Television is clearly
more serious than venereal disease."

EPILOGUE

"The past is a foreign country;
they do things differently there."
—L. P. Hartley

Soon after we arrived in the United States, my four-year-old brother Victor came down with scarlet fever. So did my father. The word QUAR-ANTINED appeared on the door of our apartment. The three older children were quickly expelled. Willem, thirteen, went to stay with another Dutch emigrant family. Elsa, twelve, and myself, eleven, were deposited with a Mrs. Calvert, a widow who owned a small brownstone and rented rooms to Columbia students for whom no campus space was available. I got a room whose main decoration was a barber pole. For weeks we had virtually no contact with other family members. We never phoned. For a time we were not allowed to attend school, so we roamed the city. We took five-cent subway rides to the end of the line in Brooklyn, then in the Bronx, and explored. Always we returned unscathed.

Mother nursed the invalids. Father made an early recovery but Victor was ill for months. The scarlet fever rash on his body was joined by another, that of measles. Mother, watching day and night, tried hard to protect her own health. After tending her patients, she would go into the bathroom and dip her fingers into a bowl of Lysol. They grew raw. Just once during that time I made my way to 606 West 115th Street, took the creaky elevator to the seventh floor, rang our doorbell, then ran to the other end of the hall, as far as I could from the QUARANTINED warn-ing. When Mother opened the door a crack, I explained I just wanted to say hello. We talked very briefly across thirty feet of space. I did not try another visit.

Mother later said she constantly prayed, "Lord, send me a sign." In the middle of one night, she went to the bathroom to disinfect her fingers and found a dead rat in the Lysol bowl. She took it as a sign that our troubles would be vanquished. Eventually Victor recovered, but he was left with badly impaired hearing. He became the wit of the family and within a few years was writing a humor column, garnished with jaunty cartoons, for the Horace Mann *Record.*

In due time the family was reunited. A few months later Mother called a "family council." She pointed out that the end of Father's leave of absence from his school in The Hague was imminent. She asked for a vote: Should we go back, or stay in America? I am sure her sense of showmanship called for this democratic exercise. I am also sure that she would not have proposed the vote if she had not been sure of its outcome. The vote, after brief discussion, went 5–1 for staying. Only Willem voted for return to Holland. Yet he was happy to stay.

He changed Willem to Will but remained, in a way, the Dutch member of the family. He moved in Dutch circles, joined the Dutch Club, and continued to speak Dutch impeccably. (My Dutch acquired an American coloration.) During World War II he worked for the Netherlands Purchasing Commission, securing and routing supplies to the Netherlands forces under Eisenhower. Later he became New York agent for the General Netherlands Bank, which earned him "home leave" though he was an American citizen.

Elsa went into early childhood education, teaching for twenty years—before and after World War II—in the nursery school of New York's Riverside Church. During the war she went to England under auspices of the Save the Children Federation to work in wartime residential nurseries in the industrial Midlands and Reading. Later she founded the celebrated Gardens Nursery School serving the international, multi-ethnic, multi-religious families of the Columbia University area.

Victor set out to be a painter, but while painting Indians in the Western states and in Mexico he became more interested in the Indians than in painting them, and turned to anthropology. After studies at Columbia under Margaret Mead and Ruth Benedict he taught at the University of Wisconsin (Milwaukee), while also writing widely used textbooks and occasionally fiction, including stories in *The New Yorker* and *Vogue.*

Will married a Belgian girl. One of his sons married a Swedish girl, the other an Italian. Victor married a Japanese girl. My son Jeff married a German girl (both are professors). Their son's bride-to-be is Chinese (both are lawyers). Thus our family has continued its transnational tradition, always "at our own risk."

When I married Dorothy Beach of Fair Haven, Vermont, she became the first American to join the family. For me it began a long involvement with Vermont. In 1951, at an auction in the village of Benson, I bought for eighty-five dollars an old stone schoolhouse that had stood empty for four decades. Restoring and modernizing it became a family project, and it became our beloved summer home. We gradually unearthed its extraordinary history, which apparently began in 1825, and is told in my book *House with a Past*, published in 1992 by the Vermont Historical Society, dedicated "to Dotty." The place is now owned by our children.

In 1989, two years after her death, I married another Fair Haven girl, Betty Allen, who had been the wife of my Princeton classmate Fred Allen. The four of us had been very close for some thirty years. Dotty and Fred died within a few weeks of each other. When the survivors joined forces two years later, it was a "duet from the old quartet."

Shortly before World War II my father completed his translation of Chaucer's *Canterbury Tales* into Dutch verse in the original meters and sent it off to Holland. Shortly afterwards most communication with Holland ceased. After the war we learned that the work had been published in a deluxe edition and been well received. But all "improper" passages had been deleted, to Father's indignation. Decades later, when he was in his late eighties, a Dutch paperback publisher decided to issue an unexpurgated edition. At ninety, Father had the pleasure of checking its page proofs and sending them off to Holland. A few days later he had a stroke and died.

I hope I may be able to look back at such a fruitful life. Betty asked me recently, on my birthday, "How do you feel?" I considered that for a moment and answered, "Sort of precarious." "Well," she said, resolutely and cheerfully, "It's the Age of Precarious!"

ERIK BARNOUW
CHRONOLOGY

1908	Born in The Hague, Netherlands
1919	Family moved to United States
1919–25	Horace Mann School, New York
1922–23	Catalogued Mulholland magic collection
1925–29	Princeton University
1927	*Open Collars* produced
1928	Publication of *Open Collars*
	University Players, co-founder, actor, director
	Zuider Zee, with collaboration of Joshua Logan
	Became U.S. citizen
1929	Cukor-Kondolf stock company
	Fortune magazine, writer
1929	Palmer Fellowship, for travel
1931–35	Erwin, Wasey & Company
1935–37	Arthur Kudner, Inc.
1937–	Columbia University, lecturer to professor emeritus
1938–48	*Cavalcade of America*, contributor
1939	Married Dorothy M. Beach
1937–40	*Pursuit of Happiness*, series editor, contributor
1939, 1947	*Handbook of Radio Writing*
1940	Birth of son, Jeffrey
1942–44	NBC, script editor
1944–45	Armed Forces Radio Service, supervisor of education unit
1945	Birth of daughter, Susanna
	Radio Drama in Action, editor
1945–46	*Cavalcade of America*, series editor
1946	East and West Association, consultant
1946–61	Theatre Guild, adaptations for radio and television
1947–49	Radio Writers Guild, president
1948	Broadcast of *VD: The Conspiracy of Silence.*

	Ohio State University, Institute for Education by Radio, Outstanding Program of the Year: *VD: The Conspiracy of Silence.*
1948–72	Center for Mass Communication, producer, editor
1949–53	Authors League of America, secretary
1951	Birth of daughter, Karen
	"That Ignorant, Ignorant Cowboy," phonograph record with Tom Glazer
1952	Ohio State University, Institute for Education by Radio, Special Award: "That Ignorant, Ignorant Cowboy."
1956	*Mass Communication: Television, Radio, Film, Press*
1957–59	*Decision: The Constitution in Action,* seven films, producer and writer
1957–59	National Committee, Writers Guild of America, chairman
1959	Gavel Award, American Bar Association, for *Decision*
	Sylvania Award, for *Decision*
1960–68	International Film Seminars, president
1961–62	Fulbright Award, India
1962	*The Television Writer*
1963, 1980	*Indian Film,* written with collaboration of S. Krishnaswamy
1966	*A Tower in Babel,* volume 1 of trilogy "A History of Broadcasting in the United States"
1968	*The Golden Web,* volume 2 of trilogy
1969	Guggenheim Fellowship, for Washington and Hollywood research
1970	*The Image Empire,* volume 3 of trilogy
	Hiroshima-Nagasaki, August 1945, producer
1971	Bancroft Prize, for *The Image Empire*
	Frank Luther Mott Award, for trilogy
	George Polk Award, for trilogy
	Elected to Society of American Historians
	Fable Safe, made with Robert Osborn
1972	JDR III Fund grant, for Asian research
	Silver Dragon Award, Cracow, for *Fable Safe*
1974, 1993	*Documentary: A History of the Non-Fiction Film*
1975, 1992	*Tube of Plenty: The Evolution of American Television*
1976	Woodrow Wilson Fellow, Smithsonian
1977–78	Library of Congress, consultant
1978	*The Sponsor: Notes on a Modern Potentate*
	Indo-American Fellowship, to update *Indian Film*
1978–81	Library of Congress, chief of Motion Picture, Broadcasting and Recorded Sound Division
1981	*The Magician and the Cinema*
	Italian Television Critics book award, for *Il Canale dell'Opulenza (Tube of Plenty)*
1982	Eastman Kodak Gold Medal, Services to film and television

1983–89	*International Encyclopedia of Communications,* 4 volumes, editor-in-chief
1984	Litt. D., Columbia University
1985	Vermont Peace Film Festival, special award for *Hiroshima-Nagasaki, August 1945*
	International Documentary Association, scholarship and preservation award
1987	Death of Dorothy Beach Barnouw
1989	Marriage to Elizabeth Prince Allen
1992	*House with a Past*
1994	International Documentary Festival, Amsterdam, jury chairman
1996	*Media Marathon: A Twentieth-Century Memoir*

INDEX

Library of Congress Cataloging-in-Publication Data
Barnouw, Erik
Media marathon: a twentieth-century memoir / Erik Barnouw.
Includes index.   ISBN 0-8223-1728-1 (cloth: alk. paper).
1. Barnouw, Erik, 1908–   . 2. Mass media specialists—United States
—Biography. I. Title.   P92.5.B37A3 1996   302.23'092—dc20   95-35529 CIP [B]

Erik Barnouw is Professor Emeritus of Dramatic Arts at Columbia University.
He has worked as a director, writer, and producer, and headed the Motion
Picture, Broadcasting and Recorded Sound Division of the Library of Congress.
His many books on the mass media include *Documentary: A History of
the Non-Fiction Film, Tube of Plenty: The Evolution of American
Television,* and *The Magician and the Cinema.*